The Space of
the Transnational

SUNY series, Genders in the Global South
———————
Debra A. Castillo and Shelley Feldman, editors

The Space of the Transnational

Feminisms and *Ummah* in
African and Southeast Asian Writing

Shirin E. Edwin

Published by State University of New York Press, Albany

© 2021 State University of New York

All rights reserved

Printed in the United States of America

No part of this book may be used or reproduced in any manner whatsoever without written permission. No part of this book may be stored in a retrieval system or transmitted in any form or by any means including electronic, electrostatic, magnetic tape, mechanical, photocopying, recording, or otherwise without the prior permission in writing of the publisher.

For information, contact State University of New York Press, Albany, NY
www.sunypress.edu

Library of Congress Cataloging-in-Publication Data

Name: Edwin, Shirin, author.
Title: The space of the transnational : feminisms and ummah in African and Southeast Asian writing / Shirin E. Edwin.
Description: Albany : State University of New York Press, [2021] | Series: SUNY series, genders in the global south | Includes bibliographical references and index.
Identifiers: LCCN 2021040579 (print) | LCCN 2021040580 (ebook) | ISBN 9781438486390 (hardcover : alk. paper) | ISBN 9781438486383 (pbk. : alk. paper) | ISBN 9781438486406 (ebook)
Subjects: LCSH: Feminism—Religious aspects—Islam. | Feminism in literature. | Muslim women authors—Africa. | Ummah (Islam)—Africa. | Muslim women authors—Southeast Asia. | Ummah (Islam)—Southeast Asia.
Classification: LCC HQ1170 .E329 2021 (print) | LCC HQ1170 (ebook) | DDC 305.48/697—dc23
LC record available at https://lccn.loc.gov/2021040579
LC ebook record available at https://lccn.loc.gov/2021040580

10 9 8 7 6 5 4 3 2 1

*With love for my family,
Ayub, Sana, Shuaib and Samreen,
for love received*

Contents

ACKNOWLEDGMENTS ... ix

INTRODUCTION
Mapping Disjunctures and Dissonance:
Transnationalism as Transgeography in *Ummah* ... 1

CHAPTER 1
Ummah and Friendships: Transgeographic Inscriptions of
Transnational Islamic Feminisms ... 55

CHAPTER 2
Windowed Encounters: Gazes, Times, and *Ummah* ... 87

CHAPTER 3
Intimate Bonds: Marriage, Race, and *Ummah* ... 123

CHAPTER 4
The Sterile Womb: Nation Space, Domestic Violence,
Polygamous Relationships, and *Ummah* ... 167

EPILOGUE ... 193

NOTES ... 199

BIBLIOGRAPHY ... 215

INDEX ... 229

Acknowledgments

Like my other professional accomplishments, this book would not have been possible without the love, patience, and encouragement of my husband, Ayub. Each time I think of pausing and entertaining the idea that I've done enough, he recharges my ideas and abilities and inspires me to push on. A growing number of colleagues, well-wishers, and intellectual partners have guided my work, and to them I am eternally indebted. In particular, my dean at New York University Shanghai, Maria Montoya, gave me the space to teach courses that helped me take my research into the classroom. My colleagues Manuel Triano Lopez, Brad Weslake, Christina Jenq, and Xuan Li have provided much support and friendship that made the writing easier and bearable across continents. At NYU Shanghai, Caitlin McKenzie-Mannion was instrumental in locating dozens of materials on Southeast Asian literatures and thus facilitated the research process in many ways. It was in these rare sources that I discovered Coeli Barry's work on Muslims in Southeast Asia. Her support and encouragement have meant much to me while writing this book. Across the institutions I have worked at, I am ever grateful to fellow Africanists, comparatists, and feminists through the years: April Shemak, Alejandro Latinez, Moradewun Adejunmobi, Carli Coetzee, Gaurav Desai, Naminata Diabate, Carmen McCain, and Gabeba Baderoon. They have encouraged my work and enriched my ideas in African and postcolonial studies in innumerable ways. Gabeba, in particular, along with Alicia Decker and Fatima Sadiqi invited me to join a week-long workshop at the International Institute of Languages and Cultures in Fez where I shared preliminary ideas on this project. That experience shaped many points and counterpoints and set the stage for the ideas expressed in this book. Rebecca Colesworthy was instrumental in bringing this project to fruition with her belief in it from the very beginning and her patience in guiding it through. I am thankful for her literary and critical guidance and comments as I honed my argument. I also owe thanks to Ana Jimenez-Moreno who made suggestions to earlier drafts of the book and suggested the title for it. I am also grateful to the two anonymous readers for their helpful comments on earlier drafts of this book, Matthew John Phillips for the index, and Michael Sandlin who patiently copyedited the manuscript with a gimlet eye.

Introduction

Mapping Disjunctures and Dissonance: Transnationalism as Transgeography in *Ummah*

> It is a paradox that a feminism that has insisted on a politics of a historicized self has rendered that self so secularized, that it has paid very little attention to the ways in which spiritual labor and spiritual knowing is primarily a project of self-knowing and transformation that constantly invokes community simply because it requires it.
>
> —M. Jacqui Alexander, *Pedagogies of Crossing*

> When the term *ummah* appears in the Qur'an, it usually refers to human community in a religious sense.
>
> —Frederick Matthewson Denny, "The Meaning of 'Ummah' in the Qur'an"

A recent article in the online edition of *Voice of America News* boldly documents the legality of interfaith marriages in Indonesia, the largest Muslim country in the world. With a population of 220 million, of which roughly 90 percent is Muslim, Indonesia legally permits couples of different faiths to marry.[1] However, as the article reports, the legally backed provision is "culturally discouraged." As a result, private religious groups and organizations such as the International Conference on Religion and Peace, led by Mohammad Monib, help interfaith couples realize their dream of romance and nuptial union. This example is but one instance of the disjuncture between legally permissible but culturally discouraged and disapproved practices. As scholarship on Islam, Muslims, and the Islamic world unremittingly asserts this faith's storied diversity and rich variety to thwart claims of monolithic Muslim uniformity, rarely is the Islamic world's own stance on diversity—its relation to others, including other faiths and cultures within and across it—examined with a sharp eye. Seldom do we ask what Muslims have to say about interactions with other faiths, cultures, and non-Muslims. How do the religion and its practitioners deal with disjunctures in their midst? *The Space of the Transnational* embraces these questions to engage with the dissonance between formally accepted knowledge practices and the unnoticed energies and activisms of informal and aleatory habits and actions. It argues that women's studies in the US academy—as a field of inquiry and knowledge production, as activism in support of women's causes, and as an academic discipline—registers a related disjuncture with respect to transnational feminism. In its conceptualization of transnational feminism, women's studies in the United States aims to forge connections across national borders yet continues to presuppose and reinforce those borders. Although transnationalism nominally enables solidarity in the face of such globally common feminist and socially just causes as gendered subordination, violence, discrimination, poverty, and inequity, the steady accrual of its critical value as a theme in feminist inquiry springs from its impressive ability to span global spaces. Feminists consider uniting across such great gulfs as transnationalism's hard-won reward. But they should know better than to uncritically celebrate such relationships as the nation space itself is fraught with gulfs that multiply inequities and disproportionately affect women and sexual minorities. Such relationships—cross-national coalitions, affiliations, and affinities—are bound to die a death by a thousand disjunctures. Thus, transnationalism's triumphalist claim of breaching national walls remains aspirational at best.

To respond to the discursive disjunctures within women's studies in the North American context, this book spotlights the ability of gendered agencies within marriage, family, and other fundamental social relationships and interfaith interactions to redefine transnationalism (relationships across national boundaries) as transgeography (relationships across geographies of identities). In the creative resistance of mixed marriages, families and communities, aleatory, interreligious dialogues, and encounters, women release unnoticed and, more precisely given my focus on space, *unmapped* energies to fight injustice. Such transgeographic gendered agencies shift the space of (or respatialize) the nation-state and, by extension, the space of the transnational. These agencies trouble the nation-state's presumed status as a monolingual, monoreligious, monoethnic, and heteronormative entity, modifying its internal and external boundaries to make it more inclusive and equitable and remediate gendered citizenship and feminist community. In looking at a selection of fiction and nonfiction by African and Southeast Asian writers, this book considers the literary aesthetics and poetics of the Islamic construct of *ummah* (or community) as a strategy manifestly deployed by Muslim women to solve such widespread gendered problems as domestic and communal violence, polygynous abuse, destitution, and sterility. In literary examples of *ummah*-building strategies, I read a respatialization or shifting of the boundaries of transnational feminist communities from cross-national borders to transgeographic boundaries. Spanning the gulfs between classes, religions, languages, and other such expansive spaces of habits, practices, customs, and rituals within the space of a nation-state is in itself a transnational enterprise. As a claim, it is not self-evident since a number of well-known feminist theorizations that predicate gender and nation on a relationship of subordination, mediated primarily through the patriarchal structures of marriage and family, take the border of the nation-state as the boundary in transnational interactions. In so doing, they concentrate on predominantly monoreligious (monoethnic, monolinguistic, and so on) gendered voices. But transnationalism as simply a coalition of national narratives is insufficiently equitable and inclusive. The untranslated and consequently unmapped agencies present just one such obstacle to transnationalism as cross-nationalism. Thus it is my contention that religiously, linguistically, and ethnically pluralizing the expanding relationships of marital, familial, communal, and national spaces across the geographies of classes, religions, sexualities, ethnicities, and languages even within the boundaries of the nation-state reshapes the space of the national, and consequently the transnational as a more equitable and inclusive sphere of feminist praxis. *Ummah*-building strategies foreground those unmapped agencies—aleatory, informal, and everyday interfaith relationships—that respatialize (modify or shift the space of) the nation as a plural, mixed, equitable, and inclusive space, enabling relationships to unfold transgeographically between classes, religions, languages, ethnicities, and other such "geographies of identities," to borrow Susan Stanford Friedman's term (1998, 35). This enables me to show that national boundaries are not the ones that determine the national and consequently the transnational. The relationships fostered across borders that are not necessarily national is where I suggest we must look to redefine transnationalism equitably and inclusively as transgeography.

At the same time, I read against the assumption of sameness of religious affiliation as homogeneity. I offer examples that delineate the disjunctive bent of the *ummah* as a human community, not unaware of racial, ethnic, linguistic, class-based, and other divisions and disparities. *The Space of the Transnational* thus attempts a retheorization of transnationalism as transgeography via the concept of *ummah* or community.

My literary reading of transnationalism and *ummah* in African and Southeast Asian fiction goes against the assumption that the borders of the nation-state are the only limitations in performing a truly equitable solidarity in feminist causes. Even transnationalism, as feminist theorists have shown (and as I will elaborate), reproduces and extends many of the same "unequal relations of power" and the "inequality of resources around the world" of its predecessors—international and global feminisms (Chowdhury 2011, 1; Nagar and Swarr, 2010, 5; Ferree 2016, 34).[2] The main contention of this book is that transnational feminism in its current and widely accepted definition as cross-national solidarity is fundamentally flawed and in need of urgent revision. Rooted in and disseminated by the North American academy, transnational feminism fails to theorize Muslim women as agents with a particular kind of political self-determination. Moreover, as has been widely stated by Islamic feminist theorists, it focuses its attention on only a fraction of the population of the global Islamic world. Thus when Chandra Mohanty and Linda Carty conceptualize transnational feminism as "ethical and just solidarity across borders based on attentiveness to power and historical specificities and differences," I ask whether these borders are nationally drawn. I then probe further into how a just and ethical solidarity across national borders is conceivable when relationships between national entities are markedly unequal, amplified by numerous differences in access to resources between women in the Global North and Global South. Furthermore, relationships within national borders—across geographies of class, religion, race, ethnicities, and languages—remain fraught with inequities (2015, 9, 10). As a result, certain instantiations of gendered agency, those that are expressed in less dominant and globally circulated philologies, venues, and forms of knowledge production in effect fall through the gaps. They remain unmapped and unknown within a transnational feminist framework because of the conceptualization of transnationalism as cross-nationalism. In failing to account for these creative and unnoticed agencies, transnational feminism also fails to confront solutions to such long-standing gendered problems as discrimination, inequality, and abuse in the form of Islamophobia, domestic and communal violence, and sterility. My study of *ummah* therefore looks at Muslim women's use of Islamic concepts as a way of solving many persistent gendered problems.

This study is organized around the following questions: how can transnational feminist agency work itself out of the impasse of inequalities and exclusions produced by cross-national organizing? What strategies can be crafted to address the direction of the flow of information or "theory" and ideas that maintain unequal relationships between such categories as First World and Third World; Global North and Global South; center and periphery? What kinds of conceptual tools help think through community to disrupt inequalities and reverse the flow of ideas and "theory" from historically dominant centers to the peripheries? Do Muslim women view *ummah* as spaced across other boundaries? What spaces or platforms enable Muslim women to articulate an equitable and inclusive transnational agency? How do Muslim women situate themselves in the national and transnational feminist imaginary as citizens of an *ummah*? What kinds of transnational feminisms or solidarities can be theorized about selves when knowledge about them is enabled only through translation? How can feminists commensurate such experiences that await translation across geographies? If premised on uniting against injustices across or despite national borders, how can constituents representing "national" interests ensure equity and inclusiveness amidst myriad identity lines—languages, ethnicities, religions, and races? In other words, who or what performs the work of transnationalism? Or what can be termed as *national* to claim the right to be in a transnational relationship? Who represents the national culture here? Which class, religion, language, or ethnicity gets to transact cross-nationally? In an age of rising fundamentalism where we are at risk of one racial, religious, or linguistic category becoming dominant, can we content ourselves with transnational to mean *transnational* simply because it defies the limits of national borders? If enabled only through translation, what can Muslim women's solutions to violence, injustice, and discrimination outside of the more popular discursive conceptualizations as subjects of capitalism and patriarchal neoliberalism tell us?[3] More particularly, what will become of such selves in feminist movements that uphold the heterosexual, masculinist, capitalist norm? To reformulate the question: what will become of feminist epistemologies until such feminist praxis is known in other languages?

A number of reasons compel a reimagination of transnationalism as performed by and seen in literary writing. First, the theme of transnationalism is often tangentially critiqued in the works under analysis here.

Even in feted novels such as Mariama Ba's *So Long a Letter*, transnational feminism may not be the preferred topic of critical discussion. Yet Ba remains one of the most prominent voices (as I discuss in chapter 2) to engage the difficulties underlying racial sameness that she optimistically assumed would facilitate unity around common causes, and in particular, cross-national solidarity in Africa in the frenzy of the first years of independence. Most of the fiction studied in the present project consists of short stories, a genre that is also tangential in the literary and critical canon, unable to dislodge the position held by the novel in the literary universe. With the exception of Mariama Ba, Chimamanda Ngozie Adichie and Leila Aboulela, the writers I study in this book—Anna Dao, E. E. Sule, Pearlsha Abubakar, Abidah el-Khalieqy, Abubakar Gimba, and Arifa Macaqua Jamil—remain insufficiently critiqued and mostly unmapped by audiences beyond their linguistic or national regions. Their inclusion refocuses attention on the question of cross-national dissemination of the production of and solidarity with such creative expressions in shaping transnational feminist ideas. Finally, the field of women and gender studies in the American academic context trains the spotlight more heavily on socioscientific disciplines, eclipsing thus literary (nonmeasurable, nonscientific, and nonquantifiable) theorizations of feminist experience.

It is for the above reasons that I choose the literature under consideration in this book: *So Long a Letter* by Mariama Ba; "A Private Experience" by Chimamanda Ngozie Adichie; "Majed" by Leila Aboulela; Anna Dao's "A Perfect Wife"; E. E. Sule's *Sterile Sky*; Abubakar Gimba's *Sacred Apples*; Pearlsha Abubakar's short stories "Ayesha's Pretty Hate Machine," "Maghrib," and her short essay " 'Naunu Na Kaun Yan?" (What's Happening to You?)," Abidah El-Khalieqy's story "Road to Heaven" (translated from Bahasa Indonesia by John H. McGlynn); Arifa Macaqua Jamil's short story "Sakeenah"; and Jemila Abdulai's "#Yennenga." All posit the everyday and assertive politics of a disjunctured relationship of gender to the nation and transnation than has been theorized so far. In tropes of informal, aleatory, and everyday encounters, exchanges and relationships, the writers I have chosen stage Muslim women's rearticulation of the *ummah* as a transgeographic site of relationships with Muslims and non-Muslims, posing fateful challenges to the overinvestment in solidarity as a feminist goal in cross-national relationships that risk excluding or ignoring materially and historically weaker constituents. The literature under consideration in this book thus underscores examples of women who are disconnected from each other in the tenor of their gendered experiences, ranging from sterility to domestic and communal violence. And yet, all recast the relationship of gender to the nation and transnation through an inherently split, mixed, and plural domestic genealogy.

Pertinent to any study on gender is the question posed by Rajeswari Sunder Rajan on women's writing, its location, and on its definition itself. Sunder Rajan asks if "women's writing [is] to be located within the work/the act of writing or in the critical reading that disengages it for us?" (1993, 4). I would say it is lodged in both. The writers I examine and their writing function as counterpublics—a subordinate category of religious, sexual, and gendered minorities who destabilize the epistemic authority of revered knowledge practices and heteronormative sexualities. However, my choice in selecting the case studies under analysis here has more to do with my investment in tracking an unmistakable shift in the way the writers under analysis illustrate the space of relationships in their writing to place on the map of feminist knowledge production and practices a reimagination of transnationalism. As I discuss in later chapters, the motivations for writing vary from one writer to another. At best, we can assess a writer's motives based on their own accounts—interviews and firsthand reports of their writing experience or through interpretive techniques. By citing Coeli Barry, in chapter 3 I will point out that Southeast Asian writers—Muslim Filipino writers in particular—write in diverse venues, forms, and genres, making it nearly impossible to compile their work, let alone guess the motives behind their craft. Precisely then, it is in this difficulty of collecting, comprehending, and evaluating feminist expression, the transnational unmappability of feminist expression, that I locate the impetus to question the current dispensation of transnational feminist theories that seem confident of the sites of knowledge production and sources of feminist knowledge and lay claim to transnational feminist activity. In the rest of this introduction, I elaborate on the main definitional and theoretical excursions underpinning the conception of transgeographic feminisms. I begin with unmappability.

Disjunctures and Dissonance

Unmappability, as in the case of interfaith marriages in Indonesia (in the opening example), indexes the discouragement, deterrence, and tacit social disapproval of a legally permissible practice—unnoticed and unexpressed attitudes, avid habits, and practices that may not readily map onto legal, formal, or official records and observations of communal relationships. Likewise, for practices and methodologies of feminist knowledge production, unmappability instantiates the inaccessibility or inscrutability of feminist agencies in at least two ways. First, unmappability raises questions about informal acts of community. Second, unmappability raises questions about the expression of knowledge in philologies other than the globally dominant and imperially resonant mediums of English and French. Despite being assertive sites of anti-imperial and decolonial knowledge production and practices, literature and literary expression face progressive marginalization and obscurity in the interdisciplinary field of women's studies in the United States. The privileging of certain methodologies over others is primarily responsible for the marginalization of literature as a site of feminist knowledge production. With the bulk of the field resolutely moving toward and insisting on "factual," tangible, and verifiable data as pursued by the methodologies of a few select disciplines—anthropology, political science, sociology, and even history—women's studies in North American institutions of higher education undervalue literary knowledge production as mostly "fictional," with little or no bearing on policy changes and legal reforms for gender-related causes.[4] This preference for quantifiable proof in academic disciplines echoes the broader debate in higher education on employment-driven diplomas or degrees. Humanities subjects broadly (and literary studies within these), as is well-known in academia, are perceived to be poorly correlated with job acquisition in higher education. Nor are they considered as critical to the future as STEM fields. Literature itself reveals disjunctures in transnationalization or cross-national relationships in the unmappability of knowledge practices in modes other than the dominant philologies of English or French. Thus, on every level of construction of self and identity, particularly with regard to gendered citizenship, the mappability of feminist experiences in unofficial expressions—in unnoticed sites of knowledge production such as literary expression, particularly in languages other than the dominant philologies—remains hindered, disjunctured, by hierarchies of relationships between geographies. It is precisely such disjunctures, between the epistemic authority of academic disciplines, methodologies, venues of knowledge production, experiences, and practices outside formal and official categories, as I will argue throughout this book, that chafe at the most widely held iteration of transnational feminism.

Thus, the first disjuncture appears in the current and widely accepted definition and understanding of transnational feminism as cross-national feminism, revealing the ignorance of conceptual tools emanating from the materially and historically weaker constituents in transnational relationships: Global South diasporas. Chandra Mohanty and M. Jacqui Alexander qualify this inequality in the persistence of "hierarchical relationships" among "geographies" that complicate not just constructions of self and identity but concomitantly women's relationship to transnationalization (1996, xvii). The second disjuncture emerges in methodologies and sites of feminist knowledge production. Women's studies focuses increasingly on the social justice methodologies of such sites of activism and knowledge production that redound to policy-driven and legally tangible benefits. They omit thus the unnoticed energies of informal and aleatory activisms that may not directly lead to legal and politically actionable gains and policy benefits. As a result, when expressed as cross-national feminism, feminist expressions fail to be mapped because of hierarchies and inequalities that persist within nation-state borders, impeding thus the equitable mapping of expressions and activisms across national boundaries onto a transnational landscape. Thus, Richa Nagar and Amanda Swarr underline the imperative in transnational feminism to "a continuous commitment to produce self-reflexive and dialogic critiques of its [transnational feminism's] own practices rather than a search for resolutions or closures" so it may remain alert "to overlapping hegemonic power structures at multiple temporal and geographic scales" (2010, 9). As such, disjuncture or dissonance between the methodologies of legally tangible spaces and those of informal knowledge practices in unnoticed and aleatory sites of knowledge production become particularly discernible in the case of gendered citizenship. In such structures of gendered relationships as family, community, and nation-state, women's citizenship is mediated by their gendered identities of wife, mother, or daughter—as wards of a patriarchal order. National genealogies are domestic genealogies, argues Anne McClintock, to underscore gendered membership in society as hierarchical and mediated by subordination to male privilege. "Nations are symbolically figured as domestic genealogies" and "masculine family drama," writes McClintock (1997, 91). Using both these disjunctures—definitional and methodological—this book suggests that the subordination of gendered citizenship, as a site of knowledge production and practices, redefines and reshapes the space of the nation-state and consequently the space of the transnational. Unmapped agencies in everyday relationships—interfaith dialogues, conversations, marriages, family structures, and aleatory exchanges—actively contest the space of the nation as monocultural, and by extension they question the formation and site of the transnational.

Ummah as Transgeography

I find the literary aesthetic of *ummah* or community pointedly useful in disrupting transnationalism as cross-nationalism because the Islamic construct of community is neither wholly cross-national—bonding fundamentally over faith, or "faith community" as Lamin Sanneh terms it—across a variety of such geographies as races, classes, ethnicities, and most important, as intended here, across religions (2016, 11). Nor is it locally rooted as its most central connotation—community—is premised on relationships, connections, and networks. Indeed, to be a Muslim, as Sylviane Diouf succinctly states, entails an observance of a panoply of rules concerning habits and behavior, including interacting appropriately with coreligionists and non-Muslims (2013, 99). It is in this feature of the *ummah* as a framework of the everyday and assertive politics of interactions, aleatory exchanges, dialogues, and relationships that I locate an alternative energy and agency to transnational feminism, conceived perforce as cross-national feminism, sited mostly in formal and policy-oriented activisms. The ethics and centrality of *ummah* for Muslim women occasion a redefinition of transnational feminism as community to serve as a fundamental space of daily interactions from the smallest of social spaces (family units) to the broadest (transnational socioscapes). More recently, the *ummah* has come under increased academic scrutiny because of the global stereotypes attached to Muslims, namely as a transnational breeding ground for global terrorism.[5] Overemphasis of its meaning as *global* community has meant that its fundamental sense of community—even between two people—is woefully overlooked. Even "inter-Islamic" and "trans-communal" relationships that Margot Badran identifies in the "co-mingling of Muslims and those of other religious backgrounds, and . . . [where] family space (marriages between Muslims and non-Muslims are continually increasing)," tend to be understudied about the *ummah* (2010, xvi).[6]

One idea about the *ummah* poses more frequent critical challenges than any other to the variety of its meanings: implying homogeneity as Muslims bond over a common faith. Can there be an *ummah* despite such diversity? I argue that these common critical debates stem from an overemphasis on sameness about *ummah* as Muslim community. In her pragmatic rumination on the *ummah* and its cross-national possibilities, noted African American Islamic scholar Jamillah Karim uses a much-cited *hadith* (Muhammad's teachings on ideal speech and behavior) that unequivocally underlines the bonds of religious brotherhood: "A Muslim is the brother of a Muslim. He neither oppresses him nor humiliates him nor looks down upon him" (2008, 7). Just treatment that Karim evokes as a basis for community in the cited *hadith*, and as I discuss in greater detail later in this introduction and in chapter 1, is directed not only toward other Muslims but in general toward all humans. Nevertheless, Karim's focus rests on just treatment in the Muslim *ummah* in America today: "As challenged by racial injustice, negotiating Islamic sisterhood and brotherhood thus means negotiating race and class inequalities" (7). If the *ummah* is impaired by such divisions as race, ethnicity, and other identity lines, it is also repaired by a recuperation of *ummah*-building relationships, underemphasized in knowledge and practices. Mixed marriages, interfaith connections, dialogues, and encounters are some such ways of re-membering the *ummah*. As I discuss in chapter 2, Mariama Ba's treatment of the *ummah* in the interfaith relationship of her minor Christian character Jacqueline from the Ivory Coast raises the crucial question on the unity of the *ummah* that remains disjunctured, if not by race (as Karim focuses on this particular category of identity) but by class, ethnicity, and even language within the same nation-state. Ba then asks whether as a black woman Jacqueline's interfaith marriage to a black Senegalese Muslim would not be as anomalous as her own failed and tumultous marriage to a Black Senegalese Muslim. To reiterate the premise of this study, *ummah* then is not just a transnationally articulated relationship. It is also and equally a transgeographically sustained effort toward community.

Reemphasizing *ummah* as a transgeographic community shifts the boundaries of transnationalism to borders other than national ones. It also shifts the boundaries of the *ummah* as more than simply a community of Muslims. In the literature I analyze, this shifting or respatializing of the *ummah* is visible in Muslim women's redefinitions of gender relations to the nation-state. As a result, the nation, too, is redefined through a shifting of its borders. These borders, I show, are transgeographic—located across classes, genders, religions, ethnicities, races, and other geographic spaces within the nation-state. Notwithstanding much debate around inclusions and exclusions, the *ummah* remained cognizant and accepting of other faiths and systems of belief. As Abdullah al-Ahsan (2007) posits, even in its narrowest sense, as the "*ummah* of Muhammad" consolidated under Muhammad during the Medinan period with the promulgation of the "Constitution of Madinah," the *ummah* retained a topological quality.[7] The *Oxford Dictionary of Islam* defines *ummah* as

> Muslim community. A fundamental concept in Islam, expressing the essential unity and theoretical equality of Muslims from diverse cultural and geographical settings. In the Quran, *ummah* designates people to whom God has sent a prophet or people who are objects of a divine plan of salvation.

It is not my intention here to present the *ummah* as a homogenous, unified collective. Even a casual glance at the Qur'an affirms the variety of connotations of the word *ummah* across verses from the Meccan and Medinan periods, from its narrowest meaning as an individual embodying virtues of a community to its broadest implications as a community of species interspersed with a range of adjunct meanings.[8] I aim to show that literary attempts at defamiliarizing this range of adjunct meanings of *ummah* in its sixty-four occurrences in the Qur'an have since long functionalized the concept of *ummah* to recast women's relationships to family, community, nation, and transnation.[9] Thus, I am interested in extracting how Muslim women defamiliarize community or *ummah* in everyday and informal interactions as such everyday activist agencies may not always be plotted onto the more formalized canvas of feminist activity or religious meanings.

Transnationalism and Transgeography

Inevitably, transnationalism evinces interest in an entire critical and theoretical corpus of concepts that explains global relationships today. Arjun Appadurai's well-known model of the global cultural economy immediately comes to mind. Deterritorialization, as Appadurai terms it, reenvisions the world on differing scales, of "alternative fears," and "disjunctures" rather than on the tradition of bipolarity, center-periphery models, or the linear movement of globalization as a homogenizing force (1996, 39).[10] Similar such concepts, "translocality," rootedness, and rootlessness, local or universal, are predicated on geography as place or physical territory, scaled as local, national, or international.[11] Translocalism then pertains to the traversal of distinct places or territories. When rejecting the idea of rootedness and rootlessness to broaden the imaginary of the local and the universal, theorists are also relying on the geography of place or territory. Appadurai also bases his model of global cultural flow or deterritorialization on the predictable distinction between national and transnational using the boundaries of the nation-state to determine transnational scales. The transnational in this case is located manifestly beyond the borders of the nation-state, distancing but never quite canceling the cognizance of the dominant center, priding itself thus for being unfettered by the national boundary.

Similarly, Peter Mandaville's study on transnational Islamic politics suggests translocal Islam. Mandaville highlights "the Muslim world's experiences with globalization," where translocal politics appends experiences of Muslims within the boundaries of the nation-states to Muslims in the broader world in an effort to capture the changing patterns of lived experiences of Muslims (2002, 2). Translocalism, as Mandaville uses the term, is interested in globalized patterns of change produced by such processes as diasporas and migrations across national borders that influence lived experiences. As I will elaborate in the section on definitions of transnationalism later in the introduction, the various conceptualizations of transnationalism—translocalism, transterritorialism—all spring from an avowed engagement with the borders of the nation-state. The kind of respatialization I am proposing differs also from the transnationalism that Paul Gilroy conjures as planetary consciousness with political and moral dimensions in anticolonial struggles and that ended the French and British empires (2005, 290). "[T]hink, for example, of Nelson Mandela's travel to Algeria for military training. What network of solidarity and cross-cultural connectedness made that association possible?" urges Gilroy as a cross-national (South Africa and Algeria) stimulus for "multi-culture and a support for anti-racist solidarity" (290). But anticolonial struggles also registered across many diverse forms—methods, actors, and means—and geographies (rural, urban, linguistic, ethnic, gendered, religious). They resulted in, as Gilroy reminds us, an unequal world: "That world became not a limitless globe, but a small, fragile, and finite place, one planet among others with strictly limited resources that are unequally allocated" (290). Edouard Glissant (1989) among numerous other cultural theorists, has written much in the context of decolonization in Africa and particularly on asymmetries between "lived experience" and the imposition of a "single History or an *official* way of thinking through which it passively consents in the ideology "represented" by its elite (93, emphasis added). Cross-fertilizations of histories, Glissant reminds us, is one such strategy of repossessing both "a true sense of one's time and identity" to re-evaluate asymmetrical and imposed power (93).[12] Respatializing transnational relationships as transgeographic connections aims to address these exclusions, inequalities, and asymmetries that emerge when connecting the world only across national borders that miss genealogies of identities that can be repossessed by shifting the boundaries of transnationalism.

The literature I examine in this book supports my contention of shifting the space or respatializing transnationalism as transgeography, as more than a cross-national accomplishment. In my reading, I modify the idea of local or universal as a physical, geographic space—a place inside or beyond a physical territorial boundary. I treat geography as a human category of identities, quite simply to observe the gulfs between two or more races, religions, ethnicities, genders, or languages even within the same nation space. In their definition of transnationalism, Laura Briggs, Gladys McCormick, and J. T. Way question its reliance on the framework of the nation "in place of a long and deeply embedded modernist tradition of taking the nation as the framework within which one can study things (literatures, histories and so forth), the nation itself has to be a question" (2008, 628). I envisage transgeography and consequently the transnational as relationships across boundaries of class, religion, sexuality, language, ethnicity, and other spaces of identity formations, and not perforce as relationships within or across the boundaries of the nation-state. In one sense, crossing the geographic divide between rural and urban landscapes within a nation-state can be termed "transnational." The most recognizable example of such an idea is undoubtedly subalterneity, which deconstructs the fraught relationships of marginalized communities to the center or the nation-state. However, by delving deeper, subalterneity revealed that the painful struggles for social justice by lower-caste peasant groups and laborers were yet further disjunctured by the discrepant hierarchies of genders, languages, castes, and religions to problematize the definition of the transnational as simply cross-national. I argue, then, that "geographies of identities," as defined by Susan Stanford Friedman—as a broad analytical panorama of gynocriticism and gynesis—connotes more suitably the relationship I aim to uncover in my redefinition of transnationalism, where two or more such geographies of identity as religions, classes, ethnicities, sexualities, languages even within the same nation-state can lay claim to transnationalism (1998, 35).

Transgeography refocuses attention on the concept of *ummah* as more than a global connection of similar religious beliefs, thus enabling a redefinition of the relationships of gender to the nation through the idea of *ummah*. It also corrects three of the most salient problems within transnational feminist theorizations (see Nagar and Swarr, 2010).[13] First, transgeographic feminism tackles the persistence of exclusions and nonrecognitions between historically and materially unequal sites both nationally and transnationally by capturing relationships engaged in common feminist causes that have come to animate the anti-imperial and decolonial spirit of transnational feminist activity "around a common agenda such as women's human rights, reproductive health and rights, violence against women, peace and antimilitarism, or feminist economies," as Valentine Moghadam deftly lists the most prominent causes that animate transnational feminist activity (2005, 4). Secondly, a transgeographic feminism rethinks the overinvestment in solidarity as a goal of transnational feminist politics that Third World feminists have identified as characteristic of misrecognitions and exclusions of their agendas in such transnational frameworks as global and international feminisms that tended to privilege the agendas of women in the Global North (Boehmer 2005, 187).[14] And third, transgeographic feminisms address the long-standing problem of the flow of influences, ideas, and "theory" from dominant centers to historically and materially less powerful sites by rendering the former what I would term a "distant presence," where issues are worked out without basing their authority in dominant centers of the Global North (Grewal and Kaplan 1994, 2).

Unmappable Translations: Literary Transnationalisms

Literary expression as a site of feminist knowledge production enables the reimagination that I foreground in this book. Thus I connect literary expression as a site of knowledge production with the discipline of women's studies in the American academic context, primarily positioned in the social sciences, to map the parallels between these two theoretical and academic orientations on feminist knowledge production. One elliptical example for now should sufficiently accentuate my aim in what sociologist Elora Chowdhury calls the "dependency chain," which requires local feminist organizations to learn English, and what Aamir Mufti and other literary theorists have identified as a subsumption of "writing traditions of the world into the European cultural system" in postcolonial literatures in their continued efforts to decode and recode such terms as "world literatures," "Global English," "world library," or "universal libraries" as signs of the unremitting dominance of English and other European colonial systems (2011, 5; 2016, 149, 156).[15] The parallelism in these challenges posed by dependency and subsumption signpost for me the need to work out a theorization of the transnational that addresses issues of commonly recognized discrepant power structures more equitably and inclusively as literary expression remains poorly analyzed in current theorizations of transnational feminisms. More particularly, this book is concerned with the field of women's studies in the North American context that has largely focused on such methodologies as ethnographic inquiries to legitimize women's experiences. It is thus useful to remind ourselves of the dangers of what Mufti and James Clifford term "ethnographic authority" and "ethnographic philanthropy," a cultural mode drawing heavily from methodologies that came in the wake of postcolonial transitions as a "reaggregation" of "imperial power," to evoke Mufti again, foregrounding the paradox of "global solidarity" out of empathy for victims of racial and imperial violence while producing a telos of political desires aimed at circling the wagons of common feminist causes (2013, 14, 16).[16]

Or perhaps these discrepancies pertain more to material truths. The United States and Great Britain account for the largest number of institutions of higher education and the most prestigious centers of learning in the world. Arguably, some of the most influential schools of contemporary thought and cultural studies, especially postcolonial studies, had their origins here. As B. Venkat Mani points out in his study of the rather felicitous migration of books or "bibliomigrancy," as he terms it, "55 to 60 per cent of translated works are originally written in English. However, only 2 to 4 per cent of books published in the United States and United Kingdom are translated from other languages" (2017, 6). How truly transnational, equitable, and representative is the scholarship on world literature in the United States and United Kingdom when only a fraction of these works are translations from other languages? Like Mani, Aarthi Vadde spotlights a chimeric pattern in aesthetic tools and methods in the quest for a communicative internationalism through such strategies as autotranslations to mediate and negotiate "uncommonness" and "illegibility" while showing awareness of the rootedness of literary and artistic expressions in cultural conventions. To this end, Vadde (2016) reads Rabindranath Tagore's Nobel Prize–winning *Gitanjali* as a chimeric model of literary and cultural conjunctures "to disclose the entanglement of translatability and illegibility in cross-cultural discourse and to affirm the particularity of national languages and literatures while challenging the myth of their purity and self-sufficiency" (40–41).

Despite such robust phenomena as bibliomigrancy, recoding, and aesthetic shifting, which facilitate the travel of literary expressions, I want to question how writers such as the ones I study in the present project—Abidah el-Khalieqy, Pearlsha Abubakar, and Balaraba Ramat Yakubu—are all widely read within their immediate regional domains and even translated into English but remain relatively unknown in the United States and United Kingdom. What implications then do such illegibility and unknowability have for transnational feminism? As I discuss in a later section, not all women take the nation-state, capitalism (class-based), or globalization as overarching and universalizing frameworks for organizing their lives despite the fact that these forces ineluctably regulate gender. Compounding this disengagement is the persistent problem of translation or communication in transnational feminist organizing. However, the problem of translation, commonly identified as a setback in the circulation and transaction of literary expressions in languages other than English, forces questions on the knowledge and mapping of experiences on transnational feminist landscapes. These chasms, as I discuss throughout this book, trouble the imperative of solidarity that underpins transnational feminist organizing. In the remaining part of this introduction, I elaborate on literature as a site of knowledge production that enables the redefinition I undertake in this book. I also explain the theoretical terms and concepts—"contact zones," "Muslim cosmopolitanism," and "dissident relationality"—that clarify the topologies of the theorization of community that I propose in this study. In the introduction, I also address my choice of Africa and Southeast Asia—two predominantly Muslim but geographically distant regions—as totemic sites of transgeographic communities.

Feminist Bonds of Faith: African and Southeast Asian Islams

I focus on Islam in Africa and Southeast Asia because it is the most widely practiced religion in these regions. While South Asia is home to the largest number of Muslims; Southeast Asia is metonymically called the "Muslim archipelago," accounting for the world's three hundred million Muslims, and Africa constitutes the second-largest agglomeration of Muslims in the world, ranging between four hundred to five hundred million. With Sunni majority communities, Islam is also practiced by sections of society that make up Shia, Ahmadi, and other sects. In sub-Saharan Africa, Islam is distributed among Sunni, Shia, Ahmadi, Tijane, Mouride, and numerous other denominations. This fact alone, that Muslims are called to bond over faith but remain disjunctured in their approaches to the faith, evokes Mohanty and Alexander's question, "How do we understand the production and reception of diverse feminisms within a framework of transnational . . . movements?" (1994, 2–3). Thus I probe the ways in which writers in the two largest and most diverse pockets of Muslim societies in the world engage with such concepts as community, solidarity, and citizenship and map more broadly the production and reception of such connections transnationally. In the literature that I analyze from these diverse and distant regions, numerous overlapping themes of gendered struggle and injustice emerge. Despite incommensurate disparities in the practices and forms of Islam across the globe, the treatment and perceptions of gender register remarkable parallels across diverse geographies. First, I will address the treatment of gender. In both Southeast Asia and Africa, broadly considered, the practice of dowry (or bride price), euphemistically termed "gift giving" in Nigeria, disproportionately burdens women in society. As my comparative studies make explicit, expectations of fulfilling biological roles—motherhood—determine women's value in society. Sterility is thus a ponderous burden for women in Africa and Southeast Asia to bear in self-definitions. Women also suffer domestic violence, negligence, and destitution. These topoi—male guardianship (*wali*), dowry (*mahr*), sterility, denial of marriage, maintainence (*nafaqah*), lack of reproductive rights, and destitution—are studied through the lens of multireligious relationships in the literature analyzed here from these two regions.[17] Poverty in both Africa and Southeast Asia particularly exacerbates Muslim women's conditions as they face more acutely the side effects of religious discrimination, as well as the minoritization and phobic treatment of Muslims. The wide gulfs in religious differences on account of class differences (or producing class differences) and concomitant linguistic gaps between communities, as I will discuss in the literature from Africa and Southeast Asia, create a relationship that spans divides no less deep than national boundaries.

More important to my study of transgeographic feminisms is the changing nature of the meaning and character of *ummah* as seen in Muslim interactions with peoples of other faiths and systems of belief in the region than the density of Muslim populations in Africa. Thus, as the statistics below explain, topologies shape identities more significantly than the presence of the religions in predominantly homogenous societies. Africa is the region where both Christianity and Islam will proliferate and spread at steady rates, owing to internal migrations, higher birth rates, and overall population growth. Robert Dowd notes, "Christians and Muslims are coming into contact with each other in sub-Saharan Africa like in few other regions of the world" (2015, 16). Dowd statistically maps the percentages of Muslim and Christian Africans to state that even though the number of Christian-majority countries in Africa is double that of Muslim-majority countries (seventeen Christian majority countries to eight Muslim majority countries), "the number of Muslims, even in many predominantly Christian countries of the region, is considerable" (16). Despite the predominance of these two religions in the African region, the largest Muslim country in Africa, Nigeria, is also considered one of the most "religiously diverse and vibrant societies in the world" (17). Such figures and observations are therefore immediately put to the test in Dowd's considered statement on the diversity of even a Muslim-majority country. The idea of *ummah* and definitions of transnational, then, are also called into question in light of such disjunctures.

But it is certainly not only Islam's density in the region that makes it unique. Islam accounts for the region's ability to serve as a "contact zone"—a social space—according to Pratt (1991), "where cultures meet, clash, and grapple with each other, often in contexts of highly asymmetrical power" (34). In Malaysia, Malay identity is of a piece with Islam: "To be Malay *is* to be Muslim," declares Andrew Hock Soon Ng (2009, 129). Islam dates back to the ninth century in Southeast Asia to the presence of trade networks with the Middle East, China, and South Asia. Maritime transmission of the religion meant that it also settled in these parts of Southeast Asia most extensively but retained its cosmopolitan character owing to the fluidity of trade routes. But the religion began to spread steadily among the inhabitants of Southeast Asia in the twelfth and thirteenth centuries with the establishment of kingdoms and sultanates along these maritime trading routes by local leaders and princes who commonly converted to Islam. Islam reached the Philippines as early as the fourteenth century. As reported in *Global Security*:

Other important sultanates in Southeast Asia around the time of Melaka's ascendancy included Aceh in northern Sumatra; Johor on the Malay peninsula; the port cities of Demak and Banten on the north coast of Java; Ternate and Tidore in what is now Maluku: and the kingdom of Mataram . . . a trading kingdom in central Java.[18]

On religion in the Philippines, Jack Miller notes, "beginning in 1350, Islam had been spreading northward from Indonesia into the Philippine archipelago. By the time the Spanish arrived in the 16th century, Islam was firmly established on Mindanao and Sulu and had outposts on Cebu and Luzon." Islam's ability to coexist and interact with other faiths is the product of tropes of contacts—dialogues, encounters, interreligious marriages, immigration, exchanges, and interactions—within more immediate boundaries rather than broader national ones that stage cross-national engagements. Such interactions, as analyzed in this book, redefine transnationalism by shifting its space from cross-national exchanges to transgeographic ones. Such a respatialization can therefore prompt us to rethink and reimagine transnational feminisms.

Reconstellating Spaces:
Local, National, Transnational, International, Global

Yet somehow, it would seem impossible, contradictory, and semantically illogical to imagine the transnational as something not *across the national*, as the term suggests, but transgeographically even within national borders. What would such transnational feminism look like in light of some of the most salient definitions of the transnational that place it de rigueur beyond the national level? In such disciplines as women's studies in the American academic context, for instance, "cross-border feminist praxis" (as Elora Chowdhury terms it), it seems, has the valence of "cross-national" (2011, 7). Notably, Chandra Mohanty and Jacqui Alexander argue for the need to "understand the local in relation to larger cross-national processes" (1996, xix).[19] Similarly, Valentine Moghadam defines the transnational as a cross-national network beyond two or more nation-states "organized above the national level that unite women from three or more countries . . . in a 'transnational public sphere' " (2005, 4). Recent formulations of transnationalism as cross-nationalism have not changed much. Notably,

Lorgia Garcia Peña extends several such conceptual configurations of the "discomfort of liminalities," as expressed by such notable theorists of race, gender, and national identity as Gloria Anzaldúa ("living on barbwire"); Luis Rafael Sanchez (Puerto Rico as "flying bus"); and Gustavo Perez Firmat (Cuban American transnationalism as "living on the hyphen"), to compellingly frontline transnationalism as "subjectivities across national spaces" or as lying between nation-states (2016, 3). Both the physical and embodied border space, argues Garcia Peña, empowers the "border-immigrant-transnational" to claim and contest the unnatural boundaries between two national territories as the body of the black Dominican enacts disruptions outside its nationally defined space in the neighboring United States through language, race, ethnicity, and nationality. In the United States, when the Dominican native or the border-immigrant transnational birthed from the border spaces between nation-states (or transnationally) speaks, her diction of Spanish distinguishes/contra-dicts, to use Garcia Peña's inventive concept of language and stories bucking official histories, narratives, and archives of personhood in the border spaces of the United States, Dominican Republic, and Haiti. To repeat the central question that this project explores, what if the transnational border space were elsewhere—between classes, races, religions, or dialects—even within the same nation-state? Can such relationships be termed transnational? In literary studies, to be transnational, a study would need to compare two or more writers from different national affiliations: say, for instance, the Zimbabwean Tsitsi Dangarembga and the Indian Arundathi Roy, or another such trans-nationally comparative study of the African American writer W. E. B. DuBois and the African Leopold Sedar Senghor (the continent standing in for a country to match the definition of transnational) (see Boehmer 2005, 187).[20] I would say that even a comparison between Zimbabweans Yvonne Vera and Dangarembga or between Mariama Ba and Ken Bugul, both Senegalese, would qualify as transnational.

Yet more distinctions drive the definitions of transnationalism on the basis of "national borders" and "discrete national borders" (Chowdhury, 2011, 2). But unlike internationalism, insists Elora Chowdhury, at least transnationalism does not prioritize them as "discrete," meaning that national borders, discrete or otherwise, determine how we imagine and talk about transnational organizing. Demarcating it also from such other spaces as the local, Chowdhury says, "I am interested in how and whether *transnational* praxis of gender violence advocacy articulates with *local* feminist responses" (emphasis added, 2). Jacqui Alexander differentiates between national and transnational when she states that in the category of the transnational "*national* and *transnational* processes are mutually, although unequally, imbricated (emphasis added, 183). In so doing, Alexander also demarcates the national from the transnational and sets them up as two entities. I suspect that this triptych of terms—local, national, and international—is not only a precondition in feminist theorizations of transnationalism but also that transnationalism is largely delimited and constructed in relation to the borders of the nation-state, with the local sited within and the transnational outside national borders. Such a spatialization does not effectively address inequalities and exclusions despite overcoming the limits of national boundaries as it surmounts only one kind of obstacle, namely nationally bound constraints to uniting around feminist causes. Aamir Mufti uncovers the paradoxical problem of the transnational not as one simply "within the confines of a single and discrete national culture or even by means of a comparison of such discrete entities," but in the affinity for national affiliation (2007, 10). He thus recommends, if only "partially and momentarily," "standing outside national identification" to counter the dominance of the framework of the geographical boundary of the nation-state in transnational analyses of literature, culture, and theory (10). Echoing the conceptual tenor of the idea of *ummah*—affinity over faith but not over nationality—though not explicitly naming the term itself, Mufti suggests suspending, if momentarily, national identification. Quoting Hannah Arendt, Mufti laments, in the context of the minoritization of Muslims in India during the upsurge of nationalism in the late nineteenth and early twentieth centuries, the process by which "every person should be left citizen of one state, and of one only" (138). But in so doing, Mufti recognizes the near impossibility of such a project that can only, by his own admission, be imagined through a partial and momentary suspension of national identification.

Transgeography as Incomplete, Open-Ended Nation Spaces

Crucially, for Mufti (and I agree), without consideration of the minority question, the project of the nation "is always open-ended, incomplete, and impossible to achieve" (2007, 12). Nationalism always unsettles rather than settles people, argues Mufti. This unsettlement, I believe, lies in the "extraterritorial" character of Muslims in particular but not because of, as Mufti suggests, their "cultural lineages" and search for "national roots" outside a particular nation-state (136). Rather, Muslims imagine forms of community that are not premised on the borders of the nation-state. In place of the framework of the nation, the *ummah* as an extraterritorial structure functions as an unsettling framework for analyzing exclusions and marginalizations to the modern nation-state. Suspending national identification, however partially and momentarily, may not be the solution for rebalancing inequitable power relations. The project of the nation, and from it the transnational, must be recast by unsettling boundaries of relationships, for if the project of the nation is contingent for its completeness on its minorities, then it follows that the texture of any kind of transnational space is also deeply unsettled and open ended. For this, the uncritical conception and assumption of the transnational as cross-national must be problematized. I refer to national boundaries not because they are crucial for imagining transnationalism. I focus on them to locate and, more importantly, shift the transnational, delimited thus far as a sphere beyond two or more national sites, or to borrow Mufti's words, "within the confines of a single and discrete national culture" (10).[21] The space of a single national culture, as I show in the literature under analysis here, is actively contested by the aleatory and everyday activisms of gendered agencies. An extremely useful model of "transnational subjectivities" is therefore proffered by Pninia Werbner, who understands the transnational as a delicate balance between *class*—to use just one example of geographies—rather than as national divisions of northern elites (high-status professionals in Europe) and working-class migrants (menial and socially lower employment). Werbner's understanding inclusively instantiates the transnational hybrid of a "working-class cosmopolitan" who constructs an enclosed and *class*-encapsulated world around her but also gains knowledge and familiarity of other *class* cultures (1999, 17,18).[22]

Nor is it critically satisfying to claim the model of the expanded nation or transterritorial nation-state as transnationalism. One well-known manifestation of the attempt to make sense of ineluctable inequalities and exclusions in the current global context is that the local and the global are irrevocably twined. The idea that minorities and marginal groups (especially women) redefine the nation-state with counternarratives is also not new. Most notably, Homi Bhabha's theorizations on languages, accents, and the vernacular disrupting the hegemony of the imperial philology imagine the space of minorities contesting authority. It also recalls Grewal and Kaplan's delineation of a similar postmodern condition of multiple hegemonies in their milestone collection, *Scattered Hegemonies*, which rearticulates "histories of how people in different locations and circumstances are linked by the spread of and resistance to modern capitalist social formations even as their experiences of these phenomena are not at all the same or equal" (1994, 5). Simply put, the local cannot be taken as the neat obverse of the global. For feminist transnationalisms, to use but one open-ended disjuncture, Yajaira Padilla's study on the Salvadoran transnation is apposite here. Padilla uses the framework of the expanding nation-state as her model for the open-ended transnational. This includes not only Salvadoran literature within the country but also outside it, particularly in the United States, as one seamless connected community that shapes transnationalism as a "transterritorial nation" (2012, 6). Recalling Appadurai's deterritorial flow of capital, goods, peoples, ideas, and tastes that flattens borders, Padilla identifies transnationalism or the expanded nation-state as an emergent community where "identities defined within and across national and ethnic lines as both Salvadorian and Salvadorian-American are taking shape within this emergent community" (7). Padilla claims that such processes outside the nation-state, as its burgeoning foreign diaspora and their connections with constituents within the nation-state through remittances, fashion, travel, and other transterritorial connections, transform the nation-state into a "transnation" (6). The model of transnationalism, "trans-Salvadoran," in Padilla's study is beholden to both external (US-Salvadoran) and internal (Salvadoran) movements that disrupt the homogenizing nationalist and internationalist narratives of race, class, and gender differences (7). The global and local, in other words, remain centrally twined.

A corollary of transnationalism as a transterritorial open-ended or expanded nation-space model is to solve unequal distributions of power and resources that result in exclusions and oversights of alternate epistemes. Arif Dirlik (1997) elucidates the current global conjuncture by highlighting the decentering of capitalism or an "unprecedented fragmentation" concomitant with the "disappearance of a center to capitalism and, locally, in the fragmentation of the production process into subnational regions and localities" (518). But Dirlik warns that this fragmentation or "disappearance of a center to capitalism" cannot be taken to exemplify a weakening of the Global North (Europe or America). A decentering simply means, as Dirlik specifies, that capitalism or analogous hegemonies now have more than one center. He states that

> there is a decentering of capitalism nationally. In other words, it is increasingly difficult to point to any one nation or region as the center of global capitalism . . . a network of urban formations, without a clearly definable center. (517)

Similarly, as Chowdhury explains, transnationalism and its concomitant goal of solidarity run the risk of reifying unequal material relations and power, not to mention the risk that it is formulated as a counterresponse, in the first place, to the homogenization of the world by global capital as part of what Briggs, McCormick, and Way term as "a single imperial system" (2008, 627).[23] Maitrayee Mukhopadhyay (2015) most aptly describes transnational feminism as the codification of knowledge about Third World women and the erasure of differences between them by both Western and Third World elites:

> the nonrecognition of . . . differences is a political act and leads to domination by those who are in a position to appropriate and codify scholarship and "knowledge" about women in the third world by using particular analytical categories that take as their primary point of reference feminist interests as they have been articulated in the United States and Western Europe (or indeed the interests of the intellectual middle-class elites in the Third World who take their lives as the reference point in describing the Other in their societies—the poor, rural women.[24] (609)

James Ferguson has similarly expressed skepticism about the idea of a "globally connected" world by pointing out that even global links connect in "selective, discontinuous, and point-to-point fashion" (2006, 14). They may "span the globe," asserts Ferguson, but "they do not cover it," to illuminate exclusions and inequities in global relations (14).

Therefore to specifically address this predicament of multiple hegemonic centers or discrepant hierarchies, redefining relationships between familiar terms—local, global, national, transnational, and international—acquires immediacy. Thus, in a bold attempt to take on structural and historical inequities, originary points of reference, and "the direction of flows of information, "theory," and influences (as termed by Grewal and Kaplan, Elora Chowdhury, following Alvarez and Friedman) "reverse" transnationalism (Grewal and Kaplan 1994, 2). Reversing transnationalism meant, as Mukhopadhyay asserts, "reversing the basic tenets" with the heightened awareness that transnationalism's initial impulse to account for differences reproduced the homogenization it sought to defeat (2015, 611). This inequality, exclusion, and widespread disconjunction in power relations is particularly pertinent to Muslim societies in many nation-states in Africa and Southeast Asia. This is because the concept of *ummah* or community is not, as I will demonstrate in my comparative case studies of Muslim women's disparate encounters, exchanges, and interreligious relationships, produced from one group, religion, or world. More importantly, "modern capitalist and social formations" cannot be considered as an overarching umbrella within which to explore new sites of knowledge production (Grewal and Kaplan 1994, 5). I would argue that capitalist formations and even Marxist critiques have failed to recognize a range of sites and strategies that thrive outside the purview of capitalist hegemonies. The most glaring oversight is of course the unconsidered epistemes of non-Western and European peoples. The understudied significance and productive connections of such constructs as *ummah*, the constitution of Medina, or even Muhammad's political leadership (to mention only a fraction of undervalued epistemes), as models of governance, social justice, and reform, all point to the epistemic disjunctures in transnational theorizations of feminist praxis and solidarity. Focusing then on transnationalism outside of its formulation as a space determined, mediated by or contingent on national borders, on transgeographic sites of power relations, shifts the attention from overarching frameworks and what such frameworks have underestimated.[25] More important, shifting the spaces of transnational feminist expression and activity keeps in check the danger of normativizing even anticolonial discourses (Nagar and Swarr, 2010, 3). The scale of diversity among Muslims that I posit is effectively captured by women's community-building gestures or fostering the *ummah* that are integral to strategizing solutions for gendered issues. These gestures enable a rearticulation of the transnational as more than a space across national boundaries that risk reproducing unequal power relations and exclusions. In the next section, I elaborate on the ways in which codifying certain sites of knowledge production in the theorization of transnational feminism reproduces exclusions and inequalities.

Democratizing Knowledge Production: Transgeography and the Discipline of Women's and Gender Studies in the United States

Although in the present project, I use "respatialization" to mean a shifting of spaces within which to formulate relationships, the term generally refers to extricating underarticulated spaces of knowledge production that reveal radical feminist practice in addition to the more recognizable sites of knowledge production. Such an endeavor, argue feminist theorists, inherently and simultaneously addresses multiple power differentials between knowledge producers and disseminators, typically placed in fabulously privileged (academic and wealthy) centers in the Global North, metaphorically also modeling broader discrepancies in wealth and power. Respatializing transnationalism as transgeography involves, to paraphrase Elleke Boehmer, "cutting out the western metropolis as a venue of exchange" (2005, 188). In particular, I focus on strategies that rebalance relations to render the Global North as a "distant presence," a presence that finds referents and measures in sites other than the West (Friedman, 2015, 4). One such strategy entails bridging dichotomies between such sites as artistic, scholarly, and activist in the creation of "new spaces, political and intellectual initiatives beyond disciplinary borders, academic/artistic/activist divides, and North/South dichotomies," and turn to "new sites for action at the local, national and transnational levels in which to enact new political, economic and cultural practices" (Nagar and Swarr 2010, 6; Desai, 16). Heeding this call to democratize knowledge production and practices, Mohanty and Alexander (1996) urge an examination of the multiple genealogies of knowledge production in their pivotal text *Feminist Genealogies*:

> to understand the relationship between . . . the politics of knowledge production by examining the academy as one site in which transnational feminist knowledge is produced, while examining those knowledges that derive from political mobilizations that push up, in, and against the academy ultimately foregrounding the existence of multiple genealogies of radical feminist practice. (26)

An obvious corollary of this critical endeavor to address power differentials is that knowledge production falls in the remit of only certain kinds of activist and community-based labor, leading Mohanty and Alexander to insist on "recognition that knowledge is produced by activist and community-based political work, that some knowledges *can only* emerge within these contexts and locations" (27) (emphasis added). Specifically, the "transnational public sphere," as Moghadam (2015) denominates the space of transnational feminism, is composed of a slew of networks, including DAWN, Code Pink, Marche Mondiale, MADRE, WIDE, WLP, and WLUML, among others, involved in coalition building and solidarity across national borders (13, 62).[26] Transnational feminism, suggests Moghadam, is most easily identified in a variety of strategies, including "protests, petitions, conferences, coalition building and mobilizes women from three or more countries" (2).

Insisting that some epistemologies can emerge *only* through community-based and particular kinds of activist work weakens the commitment of radical feminist praxis to diverse genealogies and differences. It expediently broadens the site of knowledge production and knowledge practices to allow only consensually prioritized types of feminist activity—community-based and organized actions such as in formally organized movements and platforms. The democratic gesture that enables us to broaden feminist praxis to other sites of knowledge production as a nonhegemonic imperative ironically exercises normative control over its means (political mobilization) and ends (solidarity). It reproduces the hegemony it seeks to dispel, failing to resist, as Nagar and Swarr put it, "a priori predictions and injunctions of what might constitute feminist politics at a given time and place" (2010, 5). How then would one explain transnational feminism today to a student of feminist literatures when the theoretical framework remains grounded in socioscientific methodologies—policies, interviews, fieldwork, and ethnographies of participants or "factual" evidence from only certain types of activist and movement-building subjects?

If feminisms are located solely in organizations and in movement-based activisms, how realistically and meaningfully aspirational is literary or poetic activism toward feminist goals? In a rare but brief gesture, Amrita Basu identifies the role of "magazines, bookstores, publishers, novels, poetry, plays, and performances" that have, in fact, preceded the emergence of women's movements to gesture to nonmovement sites of mobilization (1995, 5). Susan Koshy, likewise, alludes to such sites of knowledge production as "films, stories, theatrical and quotidian performances, and new media" that precede the accrual of social density for empirical analysis in socio-scientific disciplines (1995, 1548). Crucially, Basu's recognition of literature in creating feminist politics accentuates the difficult mapping of feminist experience that state or policy changes simply cannot index. She rightly observes that feminist changes have a "greater impact on individuals than on groups, on family relations than on state policy, and on the art than on politics" to foreground the oversight of a multiplicity of foundations of knowledge production in feminist mobilizations geared toward state policy, politics, and groups (1995, 5). Nagar and Swarr also argue for the urgent need to dismantle dichotomies in feminist theory and praxis, especially the vigorously upheld division between "academia/activism" (2010, 2). They thus retheorize transnational feminism "as inherently unstable" and "whose survival and evolution hinge on a continuous commitment to produce self-reflexive and dialogic critiques of its own practices rather than a search for resolutions or closures" (9).

A concern threading this book is the applicability of chiefly socio-scientific theories of transnational feminisms in the context of women's studies in the American academy to such sites of knowledge production and practices—literature, for instance—that remain discrete and maintain "quite different disciplinary affiliations even when their historical and geopolitical points of reference have converged," as Revathi Krishnaswamy puts it (2008, 2). Thus, "postcolonialism evolved mainly in the humanities, whereas globalization theory evolved mainly in the social sciences," writes Krishnaswamy (2). Indeed, Krishnaswamy and more recently Peter Morey have explored the key disciplinary and theoretical routes for studying such paradigms as postcolonialism, globalization, world literatures, and world systems. They note a remarkable similarity between the vocabularies of these paradigms. And yet Krishnaswamy observes an absence of "explicit cross-referencing and acknowledgements" that deepens the confused relationship between postcolonialism and the global (2, 3). What Koshy has compellingly argued about race studies is therefore also relevant to literary studies, as it underlines the basic differences in the sites of knowledge production between the social sciences or sociological inquiry, in particular, and the humanities. Koshy questions the purported "epistemological authority" and "disciplinary priority" of the social sciences owing to their cathexis with what is deemed as "real," leading to the unquestioned belief of being better equipped to deal with recent ambiguous and inscrutable developments in race studies (1995, 1545). Koshy ponders the tools for analyzing memories, anxieties, and desires beneath rational consciousness:

> Sociological studies may point to the permeation of psychic life and everyday experience by racial meanings, but their analytic tools restrict them from analyzing desires, anxieties, memories, and dispositions that lie beneath the threshold of rational consciousness . . . the politics of race that emerges from the politics of race as it is represented in the texts that provide the primary sources of sociological analysis, like surveys, census categories, legal documents or interviews. (1545)

From this, how can we apply current theorizations of transnational feminism to feminist expressions not articulated in surveys, petitions, interviews, calculable, and quantifiable strategies most commonly listed to recognize transnational feminism? How can we articulate the transnational when feminist experiences, to adapt Lila Abu Lughod's expression, come to personhood literally in another language? In her illuminating ruminations on living a feminist life, Sara Ahmed (2017) democratizes the definition of feminist movements by recognizing that "a feminist movement might happen in the growing connections between those who recognize something—power relations, gender violence, gender as violence—as being what they are up against" (3). And Ahmed goes on to inspiringly claim that "feminism needs to be everywhere" (4). Whether in "domestic arrangements," "at home," "in parliament," or "at the university," "the personal is political," writes Ahmed, reminding us of the motto of the second-wave feminists (3–4). To repose Mohanty and Alexander's question on how we could *produce* and *receive* such diverse but similar feminisms (even if produced in different words, as Ahmed proposes), in a transnational feminist framework, one must recognize two parts of the problem of transnationalism: 1) of unmapped agencies such as the ones Ahmed astutely spots and 2) of the possibilities and limits of connecting the unnoticed energies of everyday activisms and movements to broader landscapes. Though nearly all the literature under consideration in this book is in English, and by women (with the exception of *Sterile Sky* and *Sacred Apples*), the critical responses to them, if in languages other than English—say Tagalog, Bahasa Indonesia, Hausa, or Malay—would remain inaccessible for critical engagement in this study. Aware of its own limitations as it engages literature that belongs to a broader apparatus of literary production and circulation originally in languages other than English, this book self-consciously probes its own boundaries, which are available only if circulated in more dominant philologies.

Transgeographic Genealogies:
Gender, Family, Community, Nation, and Transnation

As I detail in this section, both these facets of transnational feminism—its articulation in cross-national sites and solely in such given sites of knowledge production and practices as official reports, petitions, marches, and protests—can be traced to the relationship of gender to the nation chiefly as a discrete space, where the nation itself is conceived as inclusive in its vision of various identities despite its mistrust of minorities, including women. Furthermore, gendered identity within such a unitary nation space is also conceived as heteronormative. Elleke Boehmer has famously commented on women's subordinate status in marriage and family as extending to their feeling of alienation in the community and nation and to their citizenship as mediated through their male counterparts, "where male nationalists have claimed, won and ruled the 'motherland,' this same motherland may not signify 'home' and 'source' to women" (2005, 90).[27] Boehmer recognizes the family as a "formative structure" of nationalism to emphasize the point that nationalisms are not "sui generis" but grow "in conjunction with the hierarchical structure in the formations of the bourgeois family" (31). Boehmer claims that with the male at the head of the family structure (while also occupying the public sphere), coupled with the public-private divide where the domestic space is coded as private and feminine, narratives of nationalism naturalize the sexual division of labor (31). Although she panoramically details gendered subordination within marriage, family, and society (and its emotional consequences on her protagonist Ramatoulaye), as I discuss in detail in chapter 2, in her novel, *So Long a Letter*, Mariama Ba is not far off from the metaphorization of family and nation when stating that "the nation is made up of all the families, rich or poor, united or separated, aware or unaware. The success of the nation therefore depends inevitably on the family" (1979, 89). As briefly noted earlier, Anne McClintock (1997, 91) similarly reads gender, marriage, and family as conjunctural and as expanding metaphors of women's subordinate status in the nation to declare that "nations are symbolically figured as domestic genealogies"—"masculine family drama" or as a "unitary and hierarchical structure of the patriarchal family," as Boehmer borrows from Freud (Boehmer 2005, 28, 32). All three, Boehmer, Ba, and McClintock, glimpse in the modern nation-state's anchoring of nationalism unmistakable specters of former feudal and religious authorities for legitimation, operating on "gender-domination" (Boehmer 2005, 32). Feminist epistemologies under threat from nationalist patriarchal decrees, unabated imperialism, and racial politics within feminisms are redeemed through their transnational usefulness. McClintock argues thus:

> Denouncing all feminisms as imperialist, however, erases from memory the long histories of women's resistance to local and imperialist patriarchies. As Kumari Jayawardena notes . . . many

women's mutinies around the world predated Western feminism, or occurred without any contact with Western feminists. Moreover, if all feminisms are derided as a pathology of the West, there is a very real danger that Western, white feminists will remain hegemonic, for the simple reason that such women have comparatively privileged access to publishing, the international media, education and money. A good deal of this feminism may well be inappropriate to women living under very different situations. . . . The singular contribution of nationalist feminism has been its insistence on relating feminist struggles to other liberation movements. (1993, 77)

McClintock thus advocates for the need to sustain a feminist epistemology even at the risk of the erasure it may face on account of being seen as too Westernized; the possibility of being drowned out by white feminist agendas, as previously noted; and threats from local patriarchies. She concludes the foregoing long passage with a transnational twist—by rescuing nationalist feminism for insisting on resonating with (bolstering perhaps) other liberation struggles.

I find it problematic that women's nationalist struggles are the platform on which to build transnational movements of liberation, for such efforts, like the patriarchal and imperial visions of the nation space remain oblivious to women's plural, mixed, and transgeographic genealogies of self, marriage, family, community, nation, and transnation. Nationalist narratives, in other words, presuppose the membership of gender to communities and gendered identities as a given and what is assumed as given is the unitary nationalist narrative. Mixed marriages are one such trope for reconstellating the site of self, marriage, family, community, and nation that disrupt the single nationalist narrative. Even though Sangeeta Ray alludes to the analogous extension of domestic symbols of women's purity and other virtues that cultivate national narratives, disproportionately burdening perceptions of women, in her succinct observation, "the purity of the family mirrors the purity of the nation." She warns that this purity was of a very particular kind in that it was conceived using not just any Hindu woman but an upper-caste one (2000, 136). Even for literary stalwarts such as Rabindranath Tagore and Bankim Chandra Chatterjee, clarifies Ray, the vision of India until the early years of the twentieth century was based on Hindu revivalism, of the woman as an upper-caste Hindu woman and of the vision of India as coded: where the "upper-class Hindu woman becomes the pivotal site through which Indian nationalism consolidates its identification with Hinduism," writes Ray (7, 136).[28] Put differently, it was a site—an upper-caste Hindu one—that served as the terrain for the nation, oblivious to its caste, class, and religious minorities. Ray quotes Sumit Sarkar's appraisal of Tagore's *Swadesh Samaj* address of 1904 to underscore the Nobel Laureate's vision of the nation as a monoreligious one:

> It is obvious that Tagore's political views in 1904 had failed to take into account the problem of integrating the Muslims and the low-caste Hindus-always outside the pale of the traditional *samaj* into the national movement. (94)

It was only much later, notes Ray, that Tagore began to write songs that would "enable both Muslims and Hindus to celebrate their common relationship to the land" (96).

Like Ray, Lata Mani scrutinizes the national symbolism of women by focusing on the infamous practice of *sati*—widow burning—in colonial India. This is done not only to point out the muted and marginalized voice of the widow, "neither subjects nor objects of concerns in the debate on its prohibition," in the discussion and debate over her life and death but, more importantly (and as I will argue throughout this book), to underscore the nuance of how an "exceptional and caste-specific practice" in Hinduism came to signify "the oppression of all Indian women." This led to important questions on how transnational debates on Indian gender and women can take place on the basis of a well-known custom and practice that was after all, in itself "internally differentiated" on religious, caste, and class lines (1998, 2, 4). Kumkum Sangari and Sudesh Vaid posit an equally necessary distinction and "serious limitation" of an approach to gender and nationalism in their influential anthology on the feminist historiography of colonial India. Sangari and Vaid note that the essays in their collection pertain to the "dominant Hindu community, largely in the north of India, and deal mainly with the middle class" (1990, 4). Powerfully then, they recognize that "it is not possible to understand a dominant class or religious community without locating its relationship to other strata and religious groups" (4). This is not to say that women in minority groups do not face the challenge of patriarchal dominance. Quite the contrary, their strategies of dealing with patriarchal dominance in national and transnational narratives, as per the focus of this book, suggest previously uncharted ways of imagining feminist responses to gendered problems. In a similar vein, Nira Yuval Davis and Floya Anthias sharply question the givenness of women's memberships to ethnic and national groups. They observe, "as a rule, ethnic groups often specify membership as a 'natural' right of being born into them, although there may be other ways of joining" (1989, 2). The optic of degrees of oppression, however, especially about Third World women, is generalized as a given.

To put forth a feminist utopian alternative, a fitting rejoinder and counterpoint to the more prevalent expressions of gender and nation as exclusively upper-caste Hindu by elitist male writers (Tagore, Chatterjee, and others), Ray briefly analyzes the Bangladeshi writer Rokhaya Sakhwat Hussain's prescient novella *Sultana's Dream*. Similarly, my book intervenes to expose domestic genealogies or "masculine family drama" by African and Southeast Asian writers as essentially multireligious, plural, and mixed (McClintock, 1993, 91). The "nation as fiction" that Boehmer recognizes women and minorities as reclaiming by fighting their marginalization by male nationalist discourses, I contend, is not simply to seek access to a male-dominant space by a unique and "unplaced" gendered ideology of male versus female (Boehmer, 2005, 36). Rather, as I show in my reading, women strategize to pluralize the national narrative by interweaving it with other voices to oppose gendered problems of domestic and communal violence, sterility, polygynous abuse, and destitution. In aleatory exchanges, encounters, relationships, and dialogues emerge also new imaginaries of the transnational. Simply put, these mixed agencies recast the source of the self, marriage, family, and community as incontrovertibly plural. They redesign the nation as plural, setting up in turn a transnational space that is more equitable and inclusive than a unitary domestic genealogy or source of gendered subordination.

Untranslatable Transnational Solidarities and Feminist Praxis: African and Southeast Asian Vernaculars

Variously termed and defined as "common collective identity," "coalitions," "alliances," "linkages," and "collaboration and complicity," solidarity is increasingly seen as a "political necessity" despite gender differences and "differential oppressions" (Basu 2010, 5; Chowdhury and Philipose, 2016, 5; Chowdhury 2011, 165). Feminists insist on it as the last straw in the face of debilitating capitalism even for "people who seldom see one another and who lack embedded relations" (Basu 2010, 6). Solidarity is also seen as a vehicle for "personal and collective transformation because of its grounding in a feeling of interdependence" (Basu 2010, 5). In this regard, I find useful Maitrayee Mukhopadhyay's description of the situation in women's studies in the American academic context as, "the construction of the implicitly consensual priority issues around which all women are apparently expected to organize. Nowhere is this more evident than in the field of women's rights and citizenship" (2015, 611–612). Against this theoretical overinvestment in solidarity, literary examples tangibly thwart solidarity as a viable goal of transnational feminist practice. Published in 1990, the Hausa novelist Balaraba Ramat Yakubu's novel, *Alhaki Kuykeyo Ne . . .* , translated only in 2012 into English, underscores with immediacy the limits of transnational feminism as a cross-national solidarity project[29] (2012, 2, 5). As the face of *soyayya* fiction, Ramat Yakubu's name alone is enough to sell thousands of copies of a *soyayya* novel. Yet she remains unknown outside of Nigeria. If not translated, then knowledge of this important *soyayya* feminist literary movement in the vernacular, pioneered by Muslim women, would have never reached beyond Hausa-speaking audiences. This would have left many feminist experiences of Muslim women unmapped, unconsidered, and ignored on transnational or even subnational levels.[30]

Internal differentiations are therefore more challenging in the mappability on a transnational feminist landscape. In Southeast Asian writing, and in Malaysian society in particular, Andrew Hock Soon Ng studies the splicing of religion, race, and ethnicity with the linguistic choices of writers. Malay (race, ethnicity, and languages) is synonymous with Islam (religious identity), explains Ng, and thus writing in English can be construed as a betrayal of one's national identity:

> to write in a language other than the national language is tantamount to a compromise of his or her own ethnic identity. And since another signifier of Malayness is religion, the three categories (language, race, religion) become fused into a single identity. It is therefore unsurprising that there are very few Malay Anglophone writers. (2011, 195)

Ousseina Alidou has made a similar observation about the interchangeability of Hausa culture (ethnicity and language) with Islam to the point that even the small populations of Christians and Animists living among dominant populations of Hausa people "tend to be Islamic in cultural practices" and are often mistaken for Muslims (132). Bolstering the active claim to a racial, ethnoreligious identity and pride through language is also a contestation of the psychology of superiority tied to colonial philologies (in these cases, English). When conflated with Jamillah Karim's concern that race undercuts *ummatic* solidarity and the ontology of the *ummah*, the examples of Hausa and Malay (fused as languages, interchangeable with religion and ethnicities) instantiate a facet of *ummah* that is less undermining than illustrative of its imagination among Muslims.

The history of education in the vernacular in former colonies further reveals the internally differentiated psychology of a superior station that knowledge of European languages conferred on the colonized peoples. A well-known symptom of this psychopolitical phenomenon, explains Moredwun Adejunmobi, was that the intended beneficiaries of literature in the vernacular found the language of this literature unattractive (2008, 182). In turn, this unattractiveness of the vernacular permeated and widened class, economic, and religious differences, emerging as the stumbling block in the circulation of literatures across boundaries. Chimamanda Ngozie Adichie's short story, "A Private Experience," along with Mariama Ba's novel *So Long a Letter* and Abubakar Gimba's novel *Sacred Apples* (in chapter 2), shed light on this transhistorical and transspatial condition of social adjustments in postcolonial African societies where language proficiencies are directly related to social and religious stratification and, by extension, benefits and privileges across religious communities. Adding to these internal differentiations of the production and reception of the vernacular is Dahlia Martin's insightful study on the use of popular culture in Malaysia by Muslim women who actively contest both colonial constructs of the Malay as the "lazy native" and the heavily nationalist propaganda of Malay identity or the ethnic superiority of Malay peoples (2014, 419). As a counterpoint to Ng's study that illustrates the indivisibility of ethnicity and religious identities—Malay and Islam—Martin reveals Muslim women's aspirations for a modernity grounded in *ummah* or global community that rejects both the Western deprecatory construct of the Malay as a "lazy native" and the ethnic ideal of Malay identity as a matter of inordinate pride for Malaysians. Instead, Martin documents Muslim women's conscious splitting of religious identity and ethnicity to privilege Islam or religious identity by rerouting it through the idea of a global community or *ummah*, something greater and much wider than the provincial and racist scope of both ethnic and Western ideals. Thus in her examination of popular culture, encompassing films and popular TV serials—*Sepet, Nur Kasih, Ombak Rindu*—Martin exposes popular culture as a site of knowledge production and practices where Muslim women craft their subjectivities as "religious and gendered agents" by claiming affiliation with a global community or *ummah* through travel, tourism, and pilgrimages to Mecca (or *hajj* and *umra*), bonding thus with a broader imaginary of Islam that eschews both the provincial pride proffered by Malay identity and the racist arrogance of the Western ideal that demeans Malayness (408). Nevertheless, such sites of knowledge production (or "tactics" as Martin terms them) like *soyayya* fiction or popular TV serials in the vernacular remain untranslated and therefore unmapped, for most part, posing obstacles to conceptualizing the transnational connectivity of feminist knowledge production and practices and receiving women's active contestation of ethnic and imperial identities through such constructs as a globalized ideal of community or *ummah* (408).

Along these lines, Noritah Omar's pointed critique of the construction of a "national Malay identity" or a "national ideal" raises the question of the inclusive and fair representation of what can truly be termed "national concerns" (2014, 132). Omar thus exposes the pitfalls in the pursuit of a unified national Malay culture underwritten by one religion (Islam) and one language and ethnicity (Malay) that was modeled on, argues Omar, the monolithic and monocultural "universalist European idealism . . . as the measure of the European nations' intellectual progress" (133, 134). However, the increased preference for Malaysian literature in English emerged precisely to oppose Malay literature being anointed as the national literature of Malaysia and to navigate the internally refracted ethno-religious-linguistic and racial landscapes of a plural society. Ironically thus, writing in the colonial medium—English—appeared to be a more inclusive, equitable, and less racist option for a number of non-Malay (and therefore non-Muslim) writers precisely because it defused tensions between various groups *within* Malaysia on account of ethnic, racial, religious, and linguistic differences (132). Unsurprisingly, both Malay literature and non-Malay literature (literature by Malaysians consciously opting to write in English), concludes Omar, emerge as reflections of an imperial master narrative than genuine iterations of decolonial literature (133). Despite its minority voices, if the nation continues the trajectory of an imperial master discourse, what implications can it produce for transnational relations?

On the one hand, translation enables not only "new positional, locational, spatial—that is, geographical—concepts of identity," as Susan

Stanford Friedman terms "locational feminisms" but also, to reprise Lila Abu Lughod's phrase that women's experiences "come to personhood in another language" (Friedman, 1998, 17, 18; Abu Lughod 2002, 789). Friedman advocates for an acceptance of contradictions and constant negotiations for locational feminisms to succeed (1998, 34). Locational feminisms actively interrogate the work performed by transnational aspirations. For instance, the trope of travel in the performance of the pilgrimage to Mecca or the *hajj* functions as a global unifier for Muslims that all Muslims assemble in one place to perform it. More than any of the other articles of faith in Islam, *hajj* is the true instantiation of transnational solidarity and fosters the spirit of community or *ummah* as the entire Muslim *ummah* gathers at the holiest site of Islam in Mecca. However, the *hajj* does not constitute transnationalism beyond the presence of disparate Muslims in one place. It serves as the spiritual imaginary of unity as millions of believers congregate at a site but do not go beyond that moment of common physical presence. As I discuss in detail in chapter 4, Abidah el-Khalieqy's novel *Geni Jora* also illustrates a transnational journey where the novel's main protagonist Jora feels empowered by her travel to Islam's holiest sites in Mecca, Syria, Jordan, and Morocco. Yet, this empowerment and liberation are meaningful only insofar as the eponymous heroine, Jora, respatializes them to break from her stifling education in a *pesantren* (rural) society, to expose gaping disjunctures between pesantren and urban cultures where Jordan, Syria, or other such international spaces do little to narrow the transgeographic chasms (rural and urban divides corresponding to conservative and modernized iterations of Islam within Indonesia). Thus the transnational journey between various nation-states outside Indonesia does not augur any cross-national solidarity or purpose to el-Khalieqy's heroine. To be sure, Martin's analysis, cited above, asserts the transgeography of class divides in the respatialization of transnationalist practices where transnationalism signifies the construction of subjectivities by women as religious and gendered agents in Malaysian society, centered on the tactics of tackling the disparities between *middle-class* Malay-Malaysian women and the nationalist political *elite* (2014, 418).

Locational feminisms also explain the solicitous subscription to "gift giving," a patently mercenary and exploitative capitalistic practice in Hausa society by the main protagonist in Yakubu's novel, Rabi, who is abandoned by her husband for another woman. That is, Rabi is able to survive only by aspiring to her daughter's marriage to an affluent man and securing for her daughter enough material security. She creatively purposes both the multidimensional practice of bridewealth or bridal compensation along with Islamic rituals and rites of bestowing goodwill and blessings to a bride that will, in fact, financially (and spiritually) protect her from the destitution that ruined Rabi.[31] On the other hand, the novel's translation into English by an Indian publisher in Chennai makes it only ostensibly transnational or cross-national as material and editorial constraints slow the process of transnational travel. The publisher of *Sin Is a Puppy That Follows You Home*, Rakesh, notes the four-way process of finding an appropriate title, a suitable translator, editor, and publisher to underscore the skepticism surrounding the possibility of bringing a similarly popular novel across cross-national boundaries closer to transnational audiences.[32] It remains to be seen if the novel was also translated into Yoruba, Igbo, and other African languages. As Mukoma wa Ngugi (2018) notes, Chinua Achebe's *Things Fall Apart* figures as the most widely translated African novel in no less than fifty languages but remains yet to be translated into Igbo, Achebe's mother tongue. Ngugi writes:

> To be sure, it has been translated into 10 or so African languages, but considering there are over 2,000 African languages in Africa, that is still an infinitesimal number . . . Translating African novels into African languages is the exception, rather than the norm. (1–2)

Global South–South dialogues or "minor transnationalisms" then, as these connections are popularly called, must also consider translations (conversations) within national boundaries. They must celebrate translation as it fosters communication across cultures, languages, and periods, not perforce cross-national.

Although Emily Apter and others recognize the value of translation, they caution (and I would include cross-national conversations in this) that translation also fails (2003, 7).[33] I am skeptical therefore of what the consequences of untranslatability signify for transnational solidarity and not of untranslatability itself as Apter has famously theorized the concept to argue against "the world literary purview as a given, integral to oppositional theoretical paradigms," and resist the "entrepreneurial" drive at anthologizing and curricularizing world literature, redistributed as a deprovincialized counterforce to the European canon (2003, 5, 6). In other words, Apter resists the impulse to manage world literary endeavors and to cover ground in an attempt to pause on the incommensurability or "speed bumps" of literary expressions (2003, 3). In a recent essay on her well-known study, Apter clarifies its aim: "I wanted a cosmology that recognized the universe as more dark space than connective constellation, a cartography that added voids and subtracted from solids" (2019, 196). These "voids" and "dark spaces" gesture to recognizing the transnational as transgeographic, not least because they broaden the possibilities of inclusive and equitable relationships. But they expose unmappability, interrogating solidarity as an aspired aim of cross-national feminisms. To Mohanty and Alexander's observation of the global conjuncture marked by the "imbrication of contemporary practices of postcolonial and advanced colonial states with capitalist processes of recolonization" and the resultant fluidity of capital, ideas, and humans that traverses national boundaries from advanced capitalist states into postcolonial nation-states to "produce an exploited feminized workforce," Ramat Yakubu responds by offering Hausa Muslim women's conjunctural defiance of Western understandings of identity construction (1996, xxiv, xxi).[34] Yakubu voluntarily subscribes to the heterosexual, hegemonic, masculinist, and capitalist framework for no other benefit than financial security. She claims the oppressive practice of dowry, euphemistically termed "gift giving" in Hausa society and somewhat ironically protecting her family from financial destitution. Debarati Sen similarly observes women's skepticism of transnational movements of fair-trade practices *while using the same platforms* to "give voice to their situated desires for economic and social justice" (2017, 4). Essentially, in her study of "women's justice imaginaries," Sen urges a reconsideration of their "perceptions of social justice" (5). And finally, Achille Mbembe has expressed a similar idea in his deep skepticism of the Marxist dictum that "the working class is the only practical agency that can engage in universal emancipatory activity," for a claim to such universalism disavows "any possible multiplicity of foundations for the exercise of social power" (2002, 244). It is therefore impractical to imagine solidarity and the goals to end discriminatory injustice as consensually shared by all constituents. It is also unrealistic to claim solidarity as a goal of relationships that are inherently unequal. The question about the possibilities and limits of connecting gendered expressions as similar and as diverse as Hausa literature and Malay popular TV serials and films must be reposed. While a respatialized transnationalism resists deference to the sovereignty of nation-states, it does not uncritically embrace solidarity that risks reproducing a deference to a consensually imagined transnationalism, conceived to refute inequalities and exclusions (see Gilroy 2005). To consider potential solutions, I make explicit below the texture of the *ummah* as a transgeographic space that unfurls in four theoretical constructs.

Conjunctures of Contacts, Friendships, Dissidence, and Minor Transnationalisms

Respatializing transnational spaces as transgeography pivots on a cluster of interrelated theoretical strategies. In this section, I focus on four concepts that I take up again more elaborately in chapter 1. These are "minor transnationalisms," "dissident relationality," "contact zones," and "Muslim cosmopolitanism" to read the tropes of contacts, exchanges, and relationships as *ummah*-building strategies that women deploy in their solutions to gendered problems. I begin with Françoise Lionnet and Shu Mei Shih's idea of "minor transnationalism" that interacts laterally or transversally (between the margins) rather than vertically (between the center and margins, the center and the periphery, or locally and globally in relations of opposition or assimilation) (2,7).[35] Just as respatialization connotes (to evoke Boehmer again) cutting out the West as a venue of exchange, Shih and Lionnet explain how minor transnationalisms instantiate not postnationalist or "nomadic identities" unmoored from the control of the state but "a space of exchange and participation," "where it is still possible for cultures to be produced and performed *without necessary mediation by the center*" (5, emphasis added). As such, the transnational can be found across different and "multiple spatialities and temporalities" and works both "within and beyond nation-states," suggest Lionnet and Shih (6, 9). The idea of distancing the west as a center of mediation, as the preferred venue of exchange, is expressed variously across cultural, gender, and literary studies. Simon Gikandi traces the ascent of comparative literature in the disciplinary decentering of Europe, where, as a constant source of critical engagement, the "gaze" of the West or center is taken to be the organizing principle for thought and literary expression. Postcolonial criticism, suggests Gikandi, "will not reject Europe completely, but it will not base its authority on its texts and traditions" (2011, 256). Susan Stanford Friedman terms this relationship as structuring the sign to formulate a solution, something more encompassing that can crack "open the door of the West's exclusivity" and develop planetary modernisms that geohistorically resist using the "West as the measure by which all other modernities are understood" (2015, 4). In a similar vein, Sadia Abbas asks whether topics that Muslims discuss among themselves can be unhinged from the orbit of the West as interlocutor. Is it unimaginable, asks Abbas, that Muslims disagree among themselves and have a rhythm of their own outside their existence that seems to be there only to respond to the West and explain their religion (2014, 55)? More recently, Mukoma wa Ngugi has expounded the idea of a "rooted transnationalism" or "globalectics" over the dialectical tensions that trap formerly colonized constituents in the gaze of the West (164–166). If dismissed merely as "racist," argues Ngugi, then the internal contradictions of the West vis-à-vis slavery, racism, imperialism, and even Enlightenment would remain unexposed (166).

The emphasis on relationships across national boundaries—between margins laterally and transversally—insufficiently pressurizes the transnational conceived in relation to the nation-state. For instance, South–South relationships are also conceptualized as extending across the borders of the respective nation-states. They may obviate the power of the center (Europe, Global North), but they may not be inclusively and equitably representative as national voices partaking in a cross-national exercise of common feminist causes. Furthermore, Lionnet and Shih bracingly critique the binary model of transnationalism as bounded by the hierarchical relationship of established binaries—the local and global, the major and minor—to propose minor transnationalisms that blunt the center's power in transnationalism. Inequalities then, in a model where a minor transnationalism is conceived, are taken to exist essentially across and *between* such established spaces as major and minor, local and global, Global North and Global South, and minor–minor (South–South) relationships that obviate mediation by the center. Hierarchy is imagined mostly in relation to the center or the major. It is not entirely clear if the two or more local or transversal spaces (the minor or Global South spaces) may also share a hierarchical relationship as the counterclaim to hierarchy in such a relationship is presented in simply obviating the authority of the "center." It is, to use Gikandi's comparison of the politics of the center, merely a "temporary detour" that returns us to the "prison house" of authority (in Gikandi's case, Europe or European philology) (2011, 255). Or it simply overlooks tensions and contradictions within the major, as Ngugi warns. Doing so shifts from Shih and Lionnet's critique of Deleuze and Guattari's coding of minor literature in relation to major literature (a vertical disposition), to the relationship between two or more minor literatures, "minor-to-minor" (away from the dominant major) (2005, 8). For a more rigorous exploration of transnationality, I would argue not only that these minor, lateral, or transversal constituencies may not themselves be bereft of internal hierarchies but that two or more "major" cultures may also constitute a transnational relationship. Thus, I aim to focus on transnationalism as a relationship between geographies—religions, races, ethnicities, languages, classes—in an effort to recast the space of any given geography and examine equalities and inclusions.

Like "minor transnationalisms" that politically circumvent the center to connect with non-Western concentrations of power, the relatively radical concept of "dissident relationality" encompasses an "anti-manichean practice" or "internal expressions of anti-imperialism" that recovers friendship between unlikely actors, across dangerous borders (North–South; colonizer–colonized) (Gandhi 2006, 14). Dissident relationality, argues Leela Gandhi, emerges as "the lost trope of anticolonial thought," instantiating generative possibilities of rethinking such forms of "given community" as family, fraternity, genealogy, filiation to posit "transnational and affiliative solidarity" (2006, 10). To these ends, Gandhi focuses on

> multiple, secret, unacknowledged friendships and collaborations between anticolonial South Asians and marginalized anti-imperial "westerners" enmeshed within the various subcultures of late Victorian radicalism. (10)

Gandhi sees socialist utopianism or "late Victorian radicalism" as having compelled a minor group of Westerners—Mirra Alfassa, C. F. Andrews, Oscar Wilde—to foster "extra institutional" or "unofficial" collaborations and deep friendships with such colonial subjects as M. K. Gandhi, Manmohan Ghose, and Sri Aurobindo to subvert colonial divisions or the "hygiene of oppositionality" at the height of fin de siècle colonialism in the nineteenth century. At the same time, these figures also critiqued anticolonial nationalist formulations that reinstated Manichean polarities, thus "positing alternatives" to the dull, replicative, and repetitive polarity of colonial and anticolonial nationalist thought in the pursuit of their political vocations.[36] What drew these "civilizational allies" together was their common politics—merging socialist transnationalism and utopian thought—to envision an uncompromising "cosmopolitan solidarity" that eschewed forms of "given community" (9). The radicalism of such dangerous alliances, I would say, is attenuated by the practice of politics in places that were not as unsafe (colonized lands) and with politically influential counterparts (elite, popular leaders) who were not as marginal as these Westerners were at the center (or Europe). C. F. Andrews and Mirra Alfassa, in particular, were by Gandhi's own admission "marginalized westerners" who moved from the center toward a location where their politics would be relatively safe, encouraged, and welcome. More important, these anticolonial visionaries collaborated with figures who were unsurprisingly far from the margins of anti-imperial politics. They were its stars—the face of the politics they championed—M. K. Gandhi, Sri Aurobindo, Rabindranath Tagore—all prominent luminaries of the struggles for self-determination. Such pairings and the locations of such alliances did little to threaten the precarity of their minority visions of social Utopia.

Rather than a daring boundary-crossing act that unites kindred spirits, transgeographic feminism participates as a spatially distant presence, thus rebalancing the power inherent in the location (Global North, center, or Dirlik's fragmentation of the production of hegemonies locally) of interlocutors. Like the inextricable twining of local and global, as Grewal and Kaplan analyze with acuity the postmodernity of scattered hegemonies, the spatially distant present, as I conceive it, operates in several ways to bring about a rebalancing of unequal power relations to destabilize the hegemony of the dominant hierarchies. First, a spatially distant presence bears a resemblance to events in transnational relationships but may not dominate those relationships. As I will elaborate in chapter 3, E. E. Sule uses examples of the Gulf War, the Liberian War, and the Iraq War in his novel *Sterile Sky*, but these international events never dominate the tenor of the way the people of Kano, in northern Nigeria, understand violence in their own city. The residents of the city actively evoke these events of violence as a way to explain their own problems; however, these events never serve as reference points for their own problems of interreligious strife. If an event is explicitly referenced, it may not serve as the privileged interlocutor, or "the organizing principle," to evoke Gikandi (2011, 256) again. The event may be acknowledged, but ideas and influences may not flow from it toward the constituents of a transnational relationship that are deemed peripheral, weaker, or marginalized. To evoke again the idea of locational feminisms as discussed earlier, "the politics of location," is apposite here. Caren Kaplan suggests that the deployment of the term "woman" can depend "upon who utilizes the concept in what particular context" (1994, 138). Feminism can "function as a marker of Western interest in other cultures and signals the formation of diasporic identities" (138) or, adds Kaplan, mark "important *shifts* in discourses of location and displacement" (138, emphasis added). Deconstructing "any dominant hierarchy or hegemonic use of the term gender" is the work of a politics of location (139). That is why when Peter Morey refreshingly analyzes such concepts as Islamophobia or an "anti-Muslim prejudice" in recent world literature, he rightly draws attention to the market for the Muslim that protracts a discourse on Muslims, implicating *both* writers and readers in the prolific critique and reception of Muslims (2018, 10). Morey states:

> A market for the Muslim . . . means that texts from around the world that engage with the existing political articulation of "the Muslim problem" contain the right elements, and offer some kind of "authentic" pseudoanthropological insight. (6)

Morey thus urges us to be "more historically aware of the provenance of the terms and values we employ to approach texts by and about Muslims (as well as by culturally different writers and about people more generally) (11). Yet the politics of location comes into play precisely as the dozen or so novels that Morey adroitly analyzes centralize Islamophobia in the *West*. The authors—John Updike, Monica Ali, Nadeem Aslam, Leila Aboulela, Hanif Kureishi, Amy Waldman, and Khaled Hosseini, among others—are all located in the West, implying an exploration of the prejudice from the vantage point of writers in the Global North as the term continues to hold sway in the center without consideration of iterations outside the boundaries of Europe and America. Keeping the center intact and its hold over such prejudices, Morey's reading of Kamila Shamsie and Nadeem Aslam's work merely *extends* the center to other lands in the analysis of the *longer* histories of anti-Muslim prejudices. Admittedly, the project remains anchored in puncturing "Western complacency and superiority" by crossing space and time, the authority to produce the sign, to contest anti-Muslim prejudice, is centered in the West (2018, 27). The location of politics amplifies such questions about Muslim literature as the timing of the production of Muslim literature (pre- or post-9/11, for instance); its circulation and reception (literature in dominant philologies such as English and French travel more widely); and finally, its connections in transnational relationships. Does Muslim literature reproduce the dialectics of dominance and equality, or might it never come into contact with its thematic and aesthetic counterparts outside the West or in a medium other than English or French? To probe these specific questions of transnational interactions of Muslim literatures, as I discuss in subsequent chapters, the

Global North is rendered as the "distant presence" where it may not base its authority in transgeographic relationships.

Like Gandhi, Mary Louise Pratt explores "models of community" in "contact zones" or social spaces where "cultures and societies clash, meet and conflict with each other, often in contexts of highly asymmetrical relations of power such as colonialism, slavery, or their aftermaths as they are lived out in many parts of the world today" (1991, 34).[37] Partly in contrast to the idea of Benedict Anderson's imagined communities (where people who have never even met each other will have at least an image of a "communion" with them), Pratt does not simply examine community (37). Rather, she delves into *the style* of imagining a community, for it reveals the different strategies employed by communities to adapt, invent, and select influences from the dominant partner in the relationship. Pratt denominates this process "transculturation" (36). Transculturation elastically encompasses the style of community models and the various kinds of relationships within such groups. I would only particularize transculturation as a rebalancing act in unequal relations that serves to reorient not only the influence of the dominant group but also bypass it, surprise it, or correct its misguided perceptions, as I will read in the stories of Adichie, Aboulela, and Abubakar in chapters 2 and 3 respectively.

Perhaps the most recognizable space where dissident relationality, transculturation, and minor transnationalisms unfold in everyday and aleatory interactions, exchanges, and encounters is the marketplace. It instantiates, as Khairudin Aljunied states, "Muslim cosmopolitanism" or human connections in "affable interreligious and intercommunal exchanges" (2016, 3). Even such hidebound spaces as Kelantanese societies reveal "contact zones" as non-Muslims absorb the habits of the dominant Muslim culture around them—eating with hands, for instance—to blend with the Muslim landscape (12). For the sake of business transactions, Muslims and non-Muslims, avers Aljunied, suspend—if momentarily— antagonisms, biases, and reservations to ally with each other and merge with the broader geography of multireligious interactions. Such unplanned and informal contacts flatten out rules, impositions, and even policies and laws about cultures and traditions (3, 8–9, 13). Just as the marketplace is also a place of social interactions, the character of cosmopolitanism is more than the idea of being in the world. It is the contact zone of aleatory exchanges and relationships that celebrates "diversity, peace and respect for people of all faiths and beliefs" (14), much like the markets in Indonesia, Singapore, and Malaysia. Ultimately, these four concepts—"minor transnationalisms," "dissident relationality," "contact zones," and "Muslim cosmopolitanism"—thread the governing idea of *ummah* as I emphasize it in this book, namely a network of exchanges, encounters, and relationships bonding transgeographically across and within classes, ethnicities, races, nationalities, and religions.

The *Ummah*:
Transgeographic and Transnational Meanings

Ummah means "community" or "nation" in Arabic. Its salience as the common thread of religion among Muslims in the world—superseding national, racial, and ethnic affiliations—has acquired more semantic valence than any of its other meanings. In the Qur'an, the *ummah* is mentioned in a variety of ways but underscores the commonness of the religion, or as Frederick Matthewson Denny notes, as "a religious dimension at its center" (1975, 39). However, Denny points to the trajectory of the meanings of the term, "in the Qur'an the *ummah* concept itself develops from a general one, applying to non-Arab groups, too, toward a more exclusive one which is limited to the Muslim community" (36). For instance, in chapter 23, verse 52, the Qur'an states: "And verily this Ummah of yours is one Ummah and I am your Lord and Cherisher, therefore fear Me and no other," meaning there is one God for Muslims, and this feature unites them into a community of believers. But the Qur'an also uses the word *ummah* to refer to the communities of other faiths, Jews and Christians (2:213; 10:41). Likewise, the *ummah* of Muhammad is also recognized by their common devotion to one God (3:110). As Denny then explains, the word in the Qur'an changes not so much in meaning as "having its meaning progressively augmented," toward the full perfection of the prophetic message.[38] Scholars like W. Montgomery Watt (1956) express a similar idea by stating, "*ummah* was the sort of word that could be given a new shade of meaning; and it also was capable of further development subsequently" (240).[39] Historically, too, as Abdullah al-Ahsan (2007) plumbs its sixty-four occurrences to frontline the capacious use of the term in the Qur'an, ranging from its meaning as "the whole of humanity" to "the exempler [sic] of an ideological group of people," the *ummah* is invoked in the Qur'an even in a transhistorical realm, meaning the followers of the prophets of all time, across periods, and even as the lifetime of a community (607–608, 609). As a conceptual construct for transnational feminisms, the *ummah*, however, remains a somewhat poorly theorized and problematic framework for discussing Muslim women's engagements with the self and world. While I discuss the *ummah* in the context of feminisms in detail in chapter 1, I should mention here briefly some of the most common critical limitations associated with the concept of *ummah*: namely the racial, national, and ethnic fragmentations within the Muslim world that overshadow the rich engagement with strategies that broaden its connotations.

Equally compelling are arguments that despite racial and class inequalities in the Muslim world, the concept of *ummah* exercises considerable affective influence on Muslims, especially for collective political action. Dave Gunning (2010), for instance, understands unity in the *ummah* as "'homogeneity' from 'shared religious practices,' producing a sense of shared identity and a political solidarity against acts of oppression" (66). Gunning reads sameness of religion as unity, the absence of which seems to thwart the idea of *ummah* itself. In fact, Gunning's interpretation of the term is buoyed by Lord Meghnad Desai's statement that there is no "real *umma* at all" owing to a lack of homogeneity across the Muslim world (107). Similarly, as mentioned briefly earlier in this introduction, Jamillah Karim cites the example of race as a factor of disunity between South Asian and African Muslims in America. The Pakistani woman (Sanjana) in the opening example in Karim's study, for instance, claims to downplay race when interacting with other Muslims, and rather naively, in Karim's opinion, imagines the *ummah* as united over faith, a viewpoint that Sanjana's African American counterpart and Karim do not share.

The Muslim *ummah*, even during Muhammad's time was diverse, disparate, and fragmented. It nursed hardly any illusions or aspirations of homogeneity and uniformity bereft of social divisions: preexisting tribal and filial ties, wealth disparities, pre-Islamic customs, conspiracies, and token conversions to avail of political and social benefits under the new constitution. This *ummah* deeply influenced political relations and considerations despite the religion acting as an encompassing equalizer. Piety, as is commonly noted in Islam, is the ultimate yardstick of difference, and the religion only emphasizes pious behavior over other pursuits. It does not claim the nonexistence of other such divisions, discriminations, and disparities as class, race, or gender-based differences that abound across and within Muslim societies. Nor do these differences weaken or disunite the *ummah*, as they were pervasive even during Muhammad's time as amply documented in countless *hadith* on Muhammad's adjudication of disputes, differences, and discriminations over religions, clans, tribes, families, classes, and numerous other divisions. Disparities in wealth, status, and standing subtend crucial articles of faith in Islam. The example of *zakat* or the obligatory act of charity attests to socioeconomic disparities even among Muslims. The injunction to perform the pilgrimage or *hajj*, likewise, is also incumbent on personal wealth and the financial ability to fulfill this article of faith. Sylviane Diouf most aptly historicizes the *ummah* in America by highlighting its class-based (slave), racial (black), ethnic (West African), and interreligious (non-Muslim) topologies by stating that "as much as Muslims in the Americas were part of the *ummah*, they were also part of the enslaved world, and non-Muslims not only were well aware of their presence but were sometimes influenced by Islam and its followers" (2013, 7). The nonrecognition of race by Muslims—as in Sanjana's case, in the example cited by Karim—may not imply a nonrecognition of other social categories and the boundaries drawn by them. Sanjana may not privilege race as a basis of difference and discrimination. But that does not mean she is unaffected by other social divisions such as class, ethnicity, or language and subcultures within each of these broad categories of identity.

The *ummah* remains despite or perhaps because of its fragmentations. *Al-Hujurat*, verse 13, in the Qur'an delineation *ummatic* diversity. Abdulla Yusuf Ali's translation of the verse (49:13) reads, "O mankind! We created you from a single (pair) of a male and a female, and made you into nations and tribes, that ye may know each other (not that ye may despise (each other).".[40] The "constitution of Madinah," elucidates al-Ahsan, that was specific to the establishment of the Muslim community in Medina where Muhammad's followers recognized him as the chief officer of Medina, also acknowledged preexisting tribes, Yathrib and Quraish, allowing "for both tribal and geographical identities" (2007, 611, 612). Thus, while the distinctions between the believers (Muslims) and the others (in this case Jews) were clear, their cohabitation in Medina was also a fact of the document—"an act of peaceful co-existence and cooperation," explains Al-Ahsan (2007, 612).[41] Admittedly, *ummah* in the context of the Medinan verses, developed a distinctly religious character as belonging to it changed the "individual's loyalty from tribe to *ummah*," as the primacy of Islam over tribal loyalties "broke this tribal barrier and replaced blood ties with universal ideals" (613, 614). Yet belonging to the *ummah* on the basis of religious belief did not exclude or isolate cohabitation, exchange, encounters, and dialogues with non-Muslims. Like Ismail al-Faruqi, the most essentialist subscribers to an Islamic state assert that the state exists to fulfill God's will or a "God-dictated" law predicated on cooperation and different identities (2000, 188). al-Faruqi states:

> God constituted humans into tribes and nations for purposes of identification and cooperation. Sovereignty in the Islamic state belongs to the law . . . this divine law prescribes for the state the mission to transform the world into the likeness of the patterns, or oughts, revealed by God. (188)

Following Muhammad's death, the meaning and nature of the *ummah* changed once again, observes al-Ahsan, becoming one with the "institution of the caliphate" and subsequently with a variety of other forms of community in terms of its understanding and realization (615). If the *ummah* is understood as a community with all its disjunctures in tribes, nations, and races, as the Qur'anic verse in *Al-Hujurat* suggests; if its meaning underwent gradual transformations following Muhammad's death, then new ways of thinking about it in transgeographic linkages that aim not at homogenizing Muslims but at emphasizing their interactions with others through such strategies as exchanges, dialogues, and contacts must also emerge. As I discuss this feature of the *ummah* as a human community in more detail in chapter 1, if taken to connote only a uniformly homogenous or heterogeneous set of interactions the concept of *ummah* will present interpretive pitfalls in capturing the variations of its meaning. It is the deployment of the variety of the *ummah*'s meanings in Muslim women's everyday activism to redefine the self and consequently the nation and transnation that I foreground in the chapters that follow.

Each of the chapters attempts to theorize and uncover Muslim women's *ummah*-building strategies and rebalance power inequities. In "*Ummah* and Friendships: Transgeographic Inscriptions of Transnational Islamic Feminisms," the first chapter, I redefine the transnational by tracing the development of transnational feminism in women's studies in the American academic context. I point out the limits of transnational feminism when identifiable only in formally legislated venues and policy gains in blindsiding, as Leela Gandhi puts it, "affective cosmopolitanism" as it crafts a vision of things to come, imperfect, improvisational, and even immature in the context of the politics of its time (2006, 17, 18, 19). Compounding this impasse is the consensually accepted goal of solidarity that fails to work out the following theoretical question: how can solidarities map themselves equitably and inclusively across national boundaries and also across classes, languages, ethnicities, and other affiliations? The chapter examines critical tendencies within Islamic feminist theorizations that echo feminist conceptualizations of the transnational as a cross-national experience, thus limiting the possibilities of alternate frameworks of community. To rethink the transnational then, this chapter integrates four strategies—"dissident relationality" as developed by Leela Gandhi; Mary Louise Pratt's "contact zones"; "minor transnationalisms" as theorized by Françoise Lionnet and Shu Mei Shih and "Muslim cosmopolitanism" as coined by Khairudin Aljunied—to plumb transgeographic feminisms. Chapter 2, "Windowed Encounters: Gazes, Times, and *Ummah*," reads the three different versions of Chimamanda Ngozie Adichie's largely unnoticed short story, "A Private Experience" (2008) that also appeared as "The Scarf" in 2002, along with Mariama Ba's well-known novel *So Long a Letter* (1979) and Abubakar Gimba's novel *Sacred Apples*. The chapter analyzes the motifs of communal violence, marital discord, and Islamophobia using the concepts of "dissident relationality" and "contact zones" as *ummah*-building strategies. By reading the lateral or transversal exchanges and dialogues in the encounter between two Muslim and Christian Nigerian women against the backdrop of a religious mob in a marketplace, the chapter posits possibilities of transnationalisms with interlocutors other than the West. In the suggestive metaphor of the window, opening out to the riotous marketplace, and framing in a materially and historically unequal encounter, the chapter proposes a respatialization of cross-national feminism as an ongoing and simultaneous/conjunctural conversation transgeographically. Along similar lines, Ba and Gimba illustrate the idea of community transhistorically through the trope of marriage and interrelated dialogues and exchanges that serve as windowed encounters across religions and nationalities. These windowed encounters or *ummah*-building strategies, I argue, enable Muslim women to strategize solutions in their marriages and daily lives. In particular, in Gimba's novel, the main character, Zahrah, revises her conceptions about marriage by dialoging with her Christian friend, Miriam, who is married to a Muslim. This interreligious marriage and friendship functions as a model of and for the *ummah* and the Nigerian nation-state to redefine the boundaries of its social structures.

In the last two chapters of this study, I continue exploring transgeographic relationships in comparative readings of African and Southeast Asian literatures. First, in chapter 3, "Intimate Bonds: Marriage, Race and *Ummah*," I take up the idea of "contact zones" again to delve into the direction of the flow of information, "theory," and influences in the metaphor of mixed marriages as a way of rethinking transnational feminism. I focus chiefly on E. E. Sule's novel *Sterile Sky*; Leila Aboulela's short story "Majed," Pearlsha Abubakar's short fiction "Maghrib," and her essay, "'Naunu Na Kaun Yan?' (What's Happening to You?)" All three writers metonymize transgeographic relationships through the trope of interreligious marriages to respatialize broader cross-national issues of Islamophobia as conflicts within national boundaries between Christians and Muslims and colonial and postcolonial histories. Chapter 4, "The Sterile Womb: Nation-Space, Polygamous Relationships and Ummah," focuses on women's strategies for countering domestic violence, sterility, polygyny, and vulnerable sexualities in a selection of rarely discussed short stories, including Anna Dao's "A Perfect Wife," Jemila Abdulai's, "#Yennenga," Pearlsha Abubakar's "Ayesha's Pretty Hate Machine," Arifa Macaqua Jamil's "Sakeenah," and Abidah el Khalieqy's "Road to Heaven." Through a close reading of these works of fiction, I focus on problems that are not always societally solved but remedied through everyday activisms or internally defiant strategies, thereby countering cross-national imaginaries of Islam, imperialism, and patriarchy. These imaginaries are balanced with such internal realities as filial and psychological constraints that cannot be legislated and easily mapped onto landscapes of feminist praxis. Such a delinking of feminism as a state-related or legislative activity resonates with the popular yet simple call made by Nurcholis Madjid ("Islam, yes; Islamic parties, no") to delink religion from nationalist and identity-based politics in Indonesia in the 1970s (Arimbi 2010, 108; Rinaldo 2013, 42). The most compelling reason for highlighting spaces other than state-legislated and sponsored ones is to underwrite the subjectivity of the *ummah* in constructing religious identities.

In sum, *The Space of the Transnational* rethinks the sites of transnational feminist experiences and epistemologies. The new sites of action—transgeographic in character—present informal and everyday subjects whose work risks erasure and oversight. In removing these subjects' work and gendered experiences from the orbit of transnational vocabularies and formulations of solidarity, the writers in this study foreground a topological inscription premised on more equitable cognitions of self and others. These equitable relationships, as I will show in the following pages, are instanced through Muslim women's *ummah*-building dialogues, encounters, and relationships with other faiths; their *ummah* building recasts the relationship of gender to the family, community, and nation as mixed, plural, and interreligious spaces. As the nation is respatialized, the space of the transnational is also reshaped both supranationally and subnationally. In exploring these relationships, this book, along with the texts it studies, works to reorient the flow of information, "theory," and influences to a different set of interlocutors and equitably rebalance power relations between historically and materially unequal sites. Most of all, the aim is to rethink solidarity as a goal of transnational feminism by centering the concept of *ummah*. More than a global community of believers, *ummah* comes to name the simple, oftentimes aleatory contacts, dialogues, conversations, short exchanges of words, and chance meetings that shape community such that it inhabits our everyday lives. The ambient feeling that community is found everywhere redesigns the logic of gendered citizenship, women's agency, and transnational feminism. My examples of community-building efforts from African and Southeast Asian fiction and nonfiction show that Muslim women strategize to solve the gendered problems that cross-national forms of feminist solidarity have too often left in place.

Chapter 1

Ummah and Friendships

Transgeographic Inscriptions of Transnational Islamic Feminisms

> In the past decade or so, new frameworks of knowledge production have emerged to destabilize the binary structure of comparative methodology by continually emphasizing the highly politicized nature of identity formation in modernity.
>
> —Inderpal Grewal and Caren Kaplan, "Transnational Practices and Interdisciplinary Feminist Scholarship: Refiguring Women's and Gender Studies."

As an example of aesthetic cosmopolitanism, Khairudin Aljunied points out the unique merging of two religions—Islam and Christianity—in the architectural composition of the Hajjah Fatimah Mosque in Singapore:

> The mosque's minaret is a duplicate of the church spire of the century-old St. Andrew's Cathedral not far from it. Not only that, slightly slanted, the minaret has also been dubbed the "Singaporean version of Italy's leaning tower of Pisa." (29)

While Aljunied attributes this hybridity to the "inclusivist" culture of Islam and Muslims, such sights in fact reveal a spatial topology of two or more faiths that exceed inclusivity. In other words, the church stands physically distant from the mosque. Yet its architectural presence within the minaret respatializes the distance so it exists within the minaret as its duplicate—inscribed in it and difficult to separate. Also reoriented in this respatialization from coexistence (close to each other, marked by spatial distance) to existence within each other are the directions of the flow of influence and information: or quite simply the appropriations of influences, power, and ideas, from Western Christian designs (the cathedral) to Eastern Islamic constructions (the mosque). These appropriations—how the influences are received and what the colonized do with these influences—also respatialize power relations. Such architectural aesthetics of faith and communities are not uncommon. A much older and more popular example of unusually respatialized relationships, notes Barry Flood Finbarr, is that of the Umayyad mosque in Damascus that also houses within it the shrine of John the Baptist. Muslims and Christians have worshipped here for centuries.

Along these lines of reimagining transnational relationships as respatializations of power relations, in this chapter I attempt a theoretical redefinition of transnationalism as transgeographic intercourse between two or more such geographies as classes, languages, ethnicities, or religions to address inequalities, exclusions, and misrecognitions of feminist agendas of the Third World or Global South. I approach this redefinition from two angles. First, I point out the implicit prioritization of issues in current formulations of transnational feminisms and the abiding influence of this consensual prioritization on theorizations of transnational Islamic feminisms. Secondly, and more importantly, I focus on the direction of information, "theory," influences, and interlocutors to rebalance materially and historically uneven powers in transnational relationships (Grewal and Kaplan 1994, 2). To these ends, this chapter is divided into three main sections. The first section highlights the limits of transnational feminism by tracing its genealogy, unfurling primarily in the sites of movements, organizations, and activist spheres. In the second section, in particular, I underscore the striking discursive similarity between Islamic and transnational feminisms to foreground the lack of critical self-reflexivity and the risks of normativizing a discursive practice. This discursive impasse, as I also argue in the second section, is responsible for the underarticulation of *ummah* as human community—a heterogeneously federated community—that is both essential and operative for understanding Muslims today. To move out of this impasse, I connect such concepts as "contact zones," "Muslim cosmopolitanism," and "dissident relationality" (or "dissident friendships") to Muslim women's *ummah*-building gestures of dialogues, exchanges, and encounters for solving gendered problems, not simply because they foster solidarity or coalitions but because they enable a more inclusive theorization of transnational feminist activity. Most importantly, these *ummah*-building strategies perform the key task of reorienting "theory" or the flow of information and influences from hegemonic structures of power to materially and historically weaker sites. I conclude this chapter by underlining the governing idea of this book: that a respatialized transnationalism rests on neglected sites of knowledge production and practices—imperfect, improvisational, and even immature—outside of formally legislated policy gains in everyday and aleatory encounters, dialogues, and relationships. Highlighting them abets a redefinition of the temporal and spatial subjectivities of transnational feminism.[1] I begin with a brief overview of transnational feminism to engage with its roots in two basic features—formal movement building and organizational mobilizations, underpinned by solidarity and the consensus over the unstable character of transnational feminisms.

Limits of Transnational Feminisms: Genealogies, Spaces, and Stable Instabilities

The impetus for a transnational feminist spirit and space can be traced to international conferences and conventions sponsored by powerful international organizations since the early 1980s. In the vein of anti-imperial and decolonial ferment, these conferences have (also since the 1980s) bravely anticipated and battled the onset of globalization.[2] Most notably, theorists cite the UN decade for women (1976–1985), the UN Conference in Kenya in 1985 and in Beijing in 1995, and transnational political organizations such as the European and African unions, including agencies such as the UN and organizations that pioneered the organizational impetus for uniting women's voices across national borders.[3] Sociologist Myra Marx Ferree calls this increased mobilization of feminist issues "the democratization of feminism" in that movements now involved greater participation from "ordinary citizens and social movements, not merely governments and elites" (15). Since Mohanty and Alexander's foundational theorization of transnationalism as a potent tool for countering global capitalistic dominance, and since gradually devaluing such theoretical vocabulary as "sisterhood," "international," ("adhering to nation-states"), and "global" ("prioritizing northern feminist agendas"), transnational feminism emerged as the preferred lens for feminist praxis, premised on comparative, relational, and historical conceptions of women (Nagar and Swarr, 2010, 4).

But this transnational growth in feminist issues was far from uniform or linear. It was contested, interrupted, and contradictory in character even as transnational feminism sought to remedy the inadequacies of "global sisterhood" and international and global feminisms (4). It differed from its predecessors in that it was willing to accept diverse and "new modes of subjectivity" from uneven relations, as Inderpal Grewal, Akhil Gupta, and Aihwa Ong recognize in transnationalism, the "uneven and unequal exchanges and effects [that] generate new modes of subjectivity and political activity" (1999, 655).[4] Similarly, Nagar and Swarr point to transnational feminisms' ability to attend to diverse shades of globalization and the formation of subjectivities in relation to globalization (2010, 5).[5] And Briggs, McCormick, and Way (2008) detailed its numerous meanings in "globalization, neoliberalism, colonialism, and internationalism" to denaturalize the term and focus on its cross-disciplinary score. As such, the definition of transnationalism that has endured is the one proposed by Briggs et al, "as much as it belongs to the worlds of free trade agreements and export processing zones, transnationalism belongs to genealogies of anti-imperial and decolonizing thought" (628).[6]

It is odd then that despite the often contested, contradictory, and unstable forms of transnationalisms, the theorization of transnational feminist experience rather stably and uniformly constellates around an unchanged set of themes, actors, and sites of knowledge production. It tenaciously privileges a lexicon of solidarity—linkages, alliances, and connections. Despite insurmountable and glaring chasms, incommensurabilities, and strangeness, even impossibilities, transnational feminist theorization unflinchingly aims for "understanding and solidarity," asserts Piya Chatterjee (2009, 132). "Epistemological divides are geopolitical divides," Chatterjee pithily suggests, underscoring irreconcilable differences between various geographies (communal, regional, national of other kinds). And yet these cross-border divides seem fluidly connected by an "imagined bridge" between scholarship and activism, resting on "leaps of faith, hope and tenacious optimism," capable of coalescing ethical and just solidarity across borders around feminist causes (132). Consequently, a three-point pattern emerges around transnational feminisms—topoi, actors, and sites. First, the set of topics or "feminist issues" as Amrita Basu calls them:

> cluster around familiar themes: women's legal and political rights, violence against women, reproductive choice and abor-

tion, sexual freedom, employment opportunities and discrimination, and women's political participation and representation. (2010, 10)

Second, the actors of knowledge production in transnational feminism are, as Manisha Desai and Nancy Naples delineate transnational feminist activity, "grassroots organizers" and "transnational activists" who advocate through transnational networks to link global politics with local struggles (1992, 33). Finally, the sites of transnational feminist praxis are clearly identified as organizations, networks, and movements. Myra Marx Ferree (2006) points out that feminism and feminist movements are often used interchangeably (18).

When Wendy Harcourt and Rawwida Baksh ask, "What are the different spaces from which transnational feminisms have operated and in what ways?" the frame for feminist praxis predictably and unambiguously emerges around advocacy, campaigns, and actions for transforming inequalities between men and women (2015, 4):[7]

> Transnational feminist movements are understood as the fluid coalescence of organizations, networks, coalitions, campaigns, analysis, advocacy and actions that politicize women's rights and gender equality issues beyond the nation state, from the 1990s, when deepening globalization and new communications and information technologies (ICTs) enabled feminist to connect readily with and interrogate their localities and cross-border relations. (5)

More precisely, Basu frames the aims of transnational feminism as not in abdicating, relinquishing, or conceding foundations, objectives, and constituencies but on balancing tensions between constituents and establishing strong foundations:

> the challenge women's movements encounter is achieving a productive balance between alliance and autonomy in several spheres. This entails first, attaining *strong foundations within the national context while forging links* with international and transnational forces. . . . Women's movements have been most successful when they have engaged the state, through

> contestation and collaboration, without abdicating their own identities and constituencies . . . women's movements have been best served by forging strong linkages with other social movements and groups within civil society without relinquishing their own objectives and identities. (2010, 3)

The clarification of the platforms and methods of transnational feminist praxis thus presages "alliance building" as its key aim (3).

Nevertheless, like its predecessors—global feminisms and international feminisms—transnationalism, too, faces a number of glaring challenges and ineluctable divides. Chief among its limits are exclusions and erasures of historical and material inequalities that provoke dichotomies between knowledge production and practice. Nagar and Swarr's interrogation of the sites from which knowledge is produced, to the sites of its practice, thus calls for collaborative praxes between voice, authorship, and representation to address such dichotomous distances:

> We suggest that interweaving theories and practices of knowledge production through collaborative dialogues provides a way to radically rethink existing approaches to subalterneity, voice, authorship, and representation. (2010, 2)

Blurring the distinctions between theory/method, individually/collaboratively produced knowledge, and academia/activism to "combine struggles for sociopolitical justice," as Chowdhury joins in to formulate the theoretical imperatives of transnational feminism, also underpins the sedulous aim of bridging inequalities in power relations (2011, 7). However, in *Women's Movements in Global Perspectives*, Basu notes that the literature on women's movements:

> ignores women's movements in the postcolonial world, considers women's movements products of modernization and development and assumes sameness in the forms of women's repression and women's movements cross-nationally.[8] (1)

Secondly, leaps from particularistic to universal lead to a stretch from the most particular to the most universal, as Basu states, "In fighting for what appears to be particularistic goals—finding their voices, setting their own agendas, and creating their own social spaces—women's movements are seeking the most universal objectives" (19). It was in response to the blanketing of these uneven and asymmetrical relationships in search of universal common grounds that Chowdhury's timely study intervened to "reverse" transnationalism and unearth "exploitative" connections as transnationalism operated between major and minor domains (13). Still, conversations between women in Third and First World countries take place cross-nationally or as a relationship between the center and periphery, local and global, or major and minor. Even attempts to establish models of "bidirectional flows" that reify "comparative, multiple, overlapping and discrete oppressions rather than . . . hegemonic oppression under a unified category of gender" inadvertently lapse into a reaffirmation of hegemony in that they produce a subjectivity in relation to the center (Grewal and Kaplan 1994, 19).

To use just one example to illustrate the failure of "bidirectional flows" of theory, I highlight Grewal and Kaplan's emphasis on the onus of critiquing transnational oppression on American feminists in the US-sponsored war in Afghanistan. Grewal and Kaplan argue that American feminists failed to foster "transnational feminist alliances" to oppose US state intervention (20):

> When the United States gave billions to General Zia to fight the Soviets in Afghanistan, the United States propped up a regime that was inimical to women. U.S. feminists need to fight against this kind of aid on their home ground instead of abstractedly condemning Islam as the center of patriarchal oppression. (19)

Likewise, the sponsorship of international Christian fundamentalism by the Republican Party, they state, also oppresses women through "funding and development practices that structure reproductive and other politics" (20). In the fervent endeavor to foster cross-border transnational alliances, the burden of critiquing the "representation of culture within a hegemonic framework," falls back on women in powerful sites who are enjoined to fight structures, reinstating hegemonic appropriations of feminist critique (20). Carole Boyce Davies's statement that "cultural theorizing is often done by those with the power to disseminate, generally male scholars (more recently white women and Black men)," reiterates the well-known but underacknowledged hegemony of the power of theorizing by white women, meaning women in centers of power and privilege (1994, 13).

Why is the force of critique in other sites not powerful enough to censure the US war on Afghanistan? In power relations, then, who critiques power also codes power and maintains it divisively. There exist robust censures of US foreign policy and Christian fundamentalism in transgeographic sites as I will show in my reading of African and Southeast Asian literature: these are not simply protests against foreign policies but imaginative recalibrations of spaces of power. Yet, Grewal and Kaplan's transnational feminist model rests on the "concepts of multiple peripheries" that tie the domestic politics of a world power such as the US to its foreign policies through "multiple, allied, solidarity projects" (1994, 20). Why should the West, as I questioned earlier (citing Friedman), be used as a measure against which all other realities are understood? (2015, 4). How would such allied solidarity account for the inequality in material conditions between American feminists and their Third World counterparts? In other words, how can women facing uneven, asymmetrical, and dissimilar material conditions—economic and educational—be expected to craft solidarity projects? Solidarity projects, as I show throughout this book, cannot be articulated without revising the spaces of self in relation to broader sites such as nation and transnation. As I analyze in chapter 2, what would alliances look like between illiterate subaltern women and upper-class women? While Grewal and Kaplan rightly note that "location is still an important category that influences the specific manifestations of transnational formations," I ask the following: how does alliance building realistically develop amid such locational asymmetry? (1994, 16). Most importantly, is locational assymmetry mapped onto broader landscapes? A consequence of what Maitrayee Mukhopadhyay calls "implicitly consensual priority issues" around which feminists are expected to rally—especially when feminists acknowledge the challenges of breaching incommensurabilities—is the notable omission of such feminist frameworks as *ummah*. As Alidou rightly points out, the idea of *ummah*—a religious identity—is central to transnational Muslim feminism as it goes beyond one nationalistic or ethnic identity that limits the possibilities of a transnational Islamic feminism (2005, 6). Yet, as Alidou argues, the hegemonic tendency to exclude Black Muslim women on account of nationalistic and racial grounds persists in theorizations of non-Arab Muslim women: of their experiences, ambitions, and (most of all) of their goals in feminism. More important, such hegemonic tendencies reproduce the challenges that feminists decry in transnational intercourse between unequal locations, namely the nonrecognition of differences and the production of knowledge in elite and politically motivated centers by an equally elite and the particularistic demography knowledge producers. Alidou defines such an oversight as the reproduction by Muslim feminists of the "colonial division" of knowledge production (5). This is most evident in the aura of epistemic authority about Muslim women as I will elaborate in the next section.

Spaces of Transnational Islamic Feminisms: Mirroring Transnational Feminisms

In this section, I contend that the template for knowledge production or epistemic authority on Muslim women in North American and European academies is briskly critiqued, reproduced, and circulated in unchanged frames of analyses.[9] In other words, Islamic feminisms are deputized for feminism, failing thus to chart their own paths, revive their own vocabulary, and explore their own episteme. A handmaiden to non-Muslim feminisms, Islamic feminisms replay the dangers of inequality. To argue this, I adumbrate the force exerted by a handful of theories on Muslim women, constipating discussions on transnational Islamic feminism. Mohanty and Alexander attribute this blanket extension to the undeniable linkages between the social and class demographic of knowledge producers, the subject of their theorizations and the kinds of analytic tools deployed (1996, xvi). Consequently, the "Islamic template for gender equality," as Badran (2010) calls it, is remarkably similar across a large number of studies on Muslim women around the world in their use of referents that are cultivated in an exclusive and elitist environment, thus deepening the gaps between the locations of knowledge production and the subjects of that knowledge (25).[10] Thus, as Badran posits, Islamic feminism emerges as a transnational and delocalized movement for equality between women's rights, state feminism, and Islamic revitalizations (2010, 113). Wherever it is applied, asserts Schroter (2017), Islamic feminism manifests itself in women's struggles for reform in Islam, thus stating that "one of the cornerstones of Islamic feminism is modern reformist Islam," alluding to its coincidence with the birth of CEDAW in 1979 that radically established the equality of genders (116, 117). Using Amina Wadud and Asma Barlas as the two most prominent examples of such transnational reformist feminism in Islam, Schroter claims that the American environment provides ample context for Amina Wadud to carry out her work on reform, thus ensuring that global feminist theories maintain the agendas and the convenience of these agendas securely in northern spheres of knowledge production.[11] Equally theorized as such, Muslim women's relationship to the nation-state also resembled the subordination to the male nationalist narrative. Schroter states, "Social reforms and women's emancipation were thus intrinsically linked to the achievement of national independence" (2017, 113). While Islamic feminism is a contested concept, what remains uncontested, or only ostensibly contested, are the two following features. As a discourse, Islamic feminism promotes only those relationships that engage with state-legislated and political expressions of women's experiences and, second, as unfolding only within organizations and activisms with well-defined goals. Informal and everyday strategies that I call *ummah*-building gestures remain unmapped in theorizations of Islamic feminism. It is therefore not hard to miss the parallels with transnational feminist theorizations, as Schroter twins the births of Islamic feminism as an anticolonial movement and the struggle for national independence in countries of the Islamic world (2017, 113).

The epistemic authority of a handful of theorizations is thus established in the consensual acknowledgment of the influential contributions of Leila Ahmed, Lila Abu Lughod, Saba Mahmood, Margot Badran, and Ziba Mir Hosseini, considered pioneers of Islamic feminist scholarship and widely acknowledged for their foundational and path-breaking academic insights on gender in Islam, particularly in the North American academe. Common to all these studies are several striking features that moot questions on self-reflexivity, sites of knowledge production, and the normativization of discourse on women. But first, we will broach the geographical focus, namely the Middle East or Arab world. An entire discourse on Muslim women, now uncritically reproduced as "Islamic feminist scholarship" in institutions of higher education in North America, centers on the histories and agendas of women who constitute the smallest proportion of Muslims in the Islamic world: the Middle East. This is not a new development or observation. As I have argued elsewhere, Islamic feminist theorizations in one part of the world—mostly Arab and Middle Eastern states—have come to stand in for the rest of the Muslim world (Edwin 2016).[12] Similarly, Ousseina Alidou comments on the scarcity of scholarship on Muslim women in regions that are not "ethnically Arab dominated" (2005, 5). To paraphrase Alidou, if, as feminists believe, that gender is shaped by ethnicity among a torrent of other intersectional factors, then one must ask how ethnically Arab women who are also Muslim can serve as models for the study of Muslim women who are not ethnically Arab but Wolof,

Swahili or Hausa, Malay or Moro? Occasionally, when attention is shifted to lesser-analyzed regions of the Muslim world, namely Africa and Asia, the mode of analysis also remains focused on Muslim women's formal and state-controlled platforms for reform and women's rights. At play even in Islamic feminist discourse are, as Mohanty and Alexander put it, the "contradictory ironies of invisibility and hypervisibility"; erasures; appropriations of the work of women of color and Third World women or token inclusions that silence the work of women who are not white, middle-class, or heterosexual; and to spotlight the problem of the direction of the flow of information, "theory," and influences (1997, xv, xvi, xvii). These contradictory ironies are ongoing, and their genealogies continue to hold sway over knowledge production on Muslim women.

Sufficient scholarship and discussion on Muslim women's victimization have been produced that the formulation of Lila Abu Lughod's now-famous rhetorical question "Do Muslim women need saving?" instinctively evokes the erudite rejoinder that they don't need saving any more than non-Muslim women. But unaddressed by such rhetoric is the equally invidious danger of Islamophilic behaviors to defend and idealize Muslim women's experience that are as corrosive as Islamophobic reactions. Sadia Abbas cautions:

> The "problem" of the veiled woman in Europe and America has generated a series of theoretical responses whose fascination lies primarily in their sinuous, creative, usually more philic than phobic attempts to deal with the anxiety generated by the veil and by the Islam it is taken to signify. (2002, 45)

Thus extending Abu Lughod's question, I ask if Muslim women also need saving from theorizations constructed in one part of the world that are uncritically applied "transnationally" in another, thereby reinstantiating the colonial gloss that masked inequalities and drove structural asymmetries in the flow of theory and ideas from the First to the Third Worlds and from the Global North to the Global South? It is perhaps eagerness for cultural diversities bordering on philic fervor that historical particularities are lazily examined and spatiotemporally spread to all Muslim women. If knowledge about women is contingent on its production (and the spaces of its production), I might add that where theorists have lamented the dichotomies between the sites of knowledge production (elite and privileged institutions of the First World) and the subjects of this knowledge (underprivileged inhabitants of the Third World), then Muslim women do need saving from the entire theoretical apparatus that produces even well-meaning knowledge on them, as such endeavors are absent of critical self-reflexivity. The example that readily comes to mind is that of Saba Mahmood's path-breaking analysis of Muslim women in Egypt. To apply to it my question of transnational linkages, what would transnational possibilities and practicalities of conflating a pietistic movement in Egypt, the *dawa* movement (such as the one Mahmood studies) look like with the historical *yan-taru* movement revived by Nana Asma'u in the nineteenth century? (Mack and Boyd 2000). How can such experiences within the Muslim world, across transhistorical or national boundaries, converse through translations, extensions, and parallelisms to map onto a broader landscape of transnational feminism in Islam without gaping dispiritingly at the incommensurabilities of transnationalism? Again, here, until translated across linguistic and conceptual divides, bridged across disciplinary boundaries, and mapped onto broader geographic spaces, methodologies of producing and receiving knowledge production—the Islamist piety or *dawa* movement and the *yan-taru* movement—would remain distant from each other in transnational imaginaries of Muslim women's agencies.

Ummah as Human Community

To the extent that it is traced on cross-national relationships, the *ummah* as a conceptual tool is also poorly understood in Islamic feminist theorizations. It is certainly not my intention here to romanticize interfaith intercourse as a space for rethinking transnationalism; for as is well known, a number of restrictive measures by Islamic states vis-à-vis the politically "protected classes" or *dhimmis* point to the tense and bellicose complexion of interreligious topologies. Denny maps these relationships as ranging from tolerant, condescending, prohibitive, and even harsh. He states, "Although the letter of Islamic law regarding the dhimmis was somewhat harsh, the application of it varied greatly from place to place and period to period." (2016, 76). A number of analyses examine race and ethnicity as spokes in the wheel of *ummah*. With regard to the American *ummah*, Jamillah Karim studies two ethnic groups—African Americans and South Asians in America—"not ordinarily linked" to explore the interplay of racial and religious identities (2008, 6). She concludes,

"America's legacy of racial inequality frames not only race relations in the American *ummah* but also its ethnic makeup" and "the American *ummah* is challenged by race and class inequities" (4,7). Even though as an African American Muslim woman, she imagines sameness with other Muslims through religion, Karim constructs differences through race, and these differences are further refracted by ethnic and class differences (9). Karim is right in pointing out racial and class disjunctures between African American and South Asian Muslim communities in the United States. I would also argue that Karim's conceptualization of the *ummah* is limited to its meaning of community united by religion (6). Overcoming differences of race, class, language, and nationalities is not unique to the American *ummah*. These disjunctures are more pronounced in immigrant communities and further deepened by differences in language, ethnic ties, filial bonds, and many such unmappable affiliations that make Muslim selves complex and contradictory.

As I mention in the introduction, Karim cites the experience of a Pakistani Muslim woman, Sanjana, who upholds in the *ummah* the idea of Islamic bonding above racial and national divisions, stating that "when I am at the masjid [mosque], I don't see Pakistani or Indian or Arab, [only Muslim]" (2). Sanjana may deny the existence of race in her sense of Muslim unity, but she may also be overlooking class and ethnicity (not to mention colonial histories) as ineluctable factors in shaping Islamic identity, even in her own context as a South Asian Muslim from Pakistan. In other words, race is but one category of discrimination and oppression facing an *ummah*. Race is also the fundamental organizing factor in American society and politics. Its absence in Sanjana's sense of community does not imply the absence of other equally destructive forms of social organization and structuring that are frequently deployed oppressively such as religion, ethnicity, class, or gender. These conversations such as the one Karim cites in her study of African American, Pakistani, and Eritrean women do not hamstring the *ummah* if the *ummah* is taken to mean a community unified in faith in one God and Muhammad's prophethood. That is why Karim's use of 9/11 as an example, which was for African American Muslims only "one part of a set of ethnic histories making up the American Muslim experience," would also apply to South Asian or for African Muslims: for them, it may be said, 9/11 was also but one part of a broader set of more painful histories constituting their identities and positionalities as Muslim, underlying the dense crosshatch of ideas and orientations that make up the *ummatic* fabric (9–10). For many South Asian and African Muslims, in fact, European colonialism was protracted in its intensity and duration as a harrowing and psychologically debilitating experience, irrevocably marking their lives and experiences as Muslims. Just as African American Muslims straddle the nightmares of racism, civil rights, and slavery in addition to their Muslim identities, Muslims from formerly colonized societies continue to negotiate their identities based on their histories and encounters with imperialisms, as well as growing capitalistic neoimperialisms. Ejaz Akram recognizes the multiple histories in *ummah*-consciousness when he states that most Muslims did not cast lots for the world to be the way it is today and remain "uncomfortable with this political arrangement that arose out of their colonial past" (2007, 394). The nature of the *ummah* then, in a given context (e.g., America) carries not the challenges of unity leaning toward uniformity but that of recognizing similar forms of discrimination and oppression to strategize solutions for the idea of human community. What can be concluded, as Akram aphoristically underlines, is that the *ummah* as a concept in the Muslim world is both "essential and operative"—one that weaves Muslims as diverse as Chinese and Moroccan into a single "ummatic fabric" (389, 397).

The excessive attempt to purify and present Muslim practices as sanitized versions of human praxis has less to do with the way the Muslim world actually exists in its divisions and distinctions and more to do with a fervent aspiration for solidarity as is also common in transnational feminist theorizations. I would like, therefore, to stress the considerable latitude in the meaning of *ummah* and its existence to underscore the diverse semantic appropriations by highlighting the arguments of two relatively conservative Islamic thinkers. The noted Islamic scholar and exegete, Ismail Raji al-Faruqi, for instance, argues that the word *ummah* itself is untranslatable in English in that none of its common translations—nation, community, or people—do justice to its exact meaning in Arabic (2000, 105).[13] In fact, al-Faruqi refers to the *ummah* as "the world *ummah* of Islam," suggesting that it is united in the commonness of religious belief (Islamic monotheism) but that it is "a weak constituent of world order," interminably refracted and "divided against itself," and "at loggerheads with other *ummahs* on all its frontiers" (xiii). As an Islamic state, suggests al-Faruqi, *ummah* is distinct from a nation-state. He underlines its heterogeneity within a federally autonomous structure and bemoans the disappearance of the "*ummah wasat*" (median community of all peoples of mankind) (Qur'an 2:143). He intimates:

> The Islamic state was not a state in the national sense of the term current today. It was not a homogenous whole, a nationally integrated unit, as community in the *gemeinschaft* sense of the term, whose *raison d'être* was the defense and service of itself as the measure of all things. It was a strong center supported by a defence force and an *ummah* of Muslims, as well as a federation of autonomous religious communities, each of which was endowed with religious, social, political and economic institutions of its own. (187)

To redress the disappearance of the median community of humankind, al-Faruqi advocates a reconstruction of the spatiotemporal structure of the *ummah* that he denominates as "space-time" and urges Muslims to actively embrace such a reconstruction using the vision of Islam (xiii, xiv). Important here is that al-Faruqi conceives of *ummah* as a construction of community that is no less than an "interference" and a proactive step: although this is not an act of defiance or invasion but a task that crystallizes the "vision of Islam as relevant to every moment of human life" (xiv). At one point in the same study, he invokes the word *ummah* to mean society (93). So encompassing is the understanding of the term that al-Faruqi also applies it through the universalism of the Sharia, understood as Islamic law, uniting in a "truly universalist brotherhood in which all men are members," either by virtue of birth or by "a free personal ethical decision to enter into the world fellowship of the law" (119). Seyyed Hosein Nasr's view similarly distinguishes between *ummah* and nation-state in the context of a "world with many communities" (2002, 162). Acutely cognizant of the political disunity and cultural fragmentations of the Muslim world today, Nasr understands the *ummah* not merely in a political and economic sense but in "unforeseen ways" socially and culturally (163). Like al-Faruqi, the idea of *ummah*, suggests Nasr, even when it reached its most exclusivist meaning in terms of Muhammad's followers, did not ignore the fact of cohabitation with other faiths.

The *ummah* is at its most useful when used for engaging the Enlightenment and post-Enlightenment concept of the nation-state as it reanimates many debates surrounding alternative conceptual frameworks. If the special quality of the *ummah* as a community that transcends divisions enables it to defy the constraints of the nation-state boundaries, then it also holds true following Nasr and al-Faruqi's elaboration of the term: that the *ummah* is greatly constrained within the nation-state owing to incommensurable differences of race, language, class, and ethnicity. Diversity, I am arguing, bears underlining regardless of boundaries. The idea of *ummah* as a human community pertaining to a planetary society, encompassing all of creation and constituted by a number of autonomous communities, presents precisely such a framework to address uneven relations in transnational feminist networks. One way then to respond to Karim's concerns about the dilution of the *ummah* in relation to gender in Islam is to draw from Khadija Elmadmad's insights on addressing the current refugee crisis and human rights for Muslim women. Elmadmad recommends a topological understanding of Muslims in the world today when underscoring the gendered nature of the human rights catastrophe as Muslim women constitute the majority of refugees and victims of displacement today. They also remain, avers Elmadmad, more vulnerable than any other category of women with regard to asylum, employment, and education.[14] As a model for solutions then, Elmadmad turns to Islamic law and principles as *complementary* to extant secular and international laws for increased sensitivity toward the unheeded plight of Muslim women refugees. She suggests the following:

> Coordinate more closely the efforts of the various humanitarian organizations in the field. Joint action by both Muslim and non-Muslim NGOs should be encouraged . . . Use Islamic rules and principles on asylum and *aman* more extensively in law and practice. (1999, 270)

Her legal strategies encapsulate the topological nature of measures—joint efforts, coordination between "International Islamic NGOs," and current humanitarian organizations such as the International Committee of the Red Cross (ICRC). The important point here in the critical conversation on fragmentations is, as Karim analyzes the conceptual understanding of *ummah*, that the same Qur'anic injunctions are received on varying levels of prioritization and both communal and individual levels in different parts of the world. Perhaps best summed up by Amina Nayel, the definition of *ummah*, if taken to mean a political notion cultivated in an attempt to bring Muslims together as one nation, is always in jeopardy from other cross-cutting boundaries of race, culture, ethnicity, and class difference (2017, 135). As seen above in the interpretations of some of even the most conservative thinkers (al-Faruqi and Nasr), the *ummah* is contingent on the cooperation and presence of heterogeneously federated autonomies. The eager elision of differences to forge transnational solidarity or an equally eager generalization of Muslim women's experiences, as I discuss in the following section, undermines the transgeographic potential of the *ummah*.

Diversity as Tokenism: The Transgeographic Potential of *Ummah*

It is certainly not by accident that the fragmented homogeneity of the Muslim world is subordinated to the overinvestment in unity and solidarity that hampers the understanding of the *ummah* as heterogeneously federated communities. Fearing differences as signs of disunity, academic feminism on Islam surfaced most recently in the fervent and unprecedented critical reception of Saba Mahmood's highly influential sociological inquiry on Muslim women, *The Politics of Piety*. The unparalleled celebration and application of Mahmood's work in academia worldwide in recent times testifies less to the contribution it makes to feminist theory than to the topic of its inquiry: Muslim women. The sheer force of its critical acclaim alone raises crucial questions about the politics of scholarship in women's studies in America, as the study has become indispensable to scholarship on Muslim women. Although it focused on a relatively small geographic region, Egypt—and an even smaller movement within that region, namely the *dawa* movement, which is shaped by a specific historic moment and context of Egyptian society—the study is now required reading on Muslim women. What implications does such a reception have for transnational feminism? The example of Mahmood's study is not the only instance of whitewashing asymmetries in feminist scholarship on Muslim women to consensually prioritize agendas. In particular, Mahmood's work is based in the very site that Karim and Aljunied also identify as encapsulating collective life in Muslim communities: the mosque. As is well known by now, Mahmood investigates "piety activists" who "aim for a "regulative sensibility" that can imbue every aspect of daily life taking its inspiration from the "Islamic theological corpus" rather than a "modern secular ethics" (2005, 46, 47). Alarmed by the increasing marginalization of religion in daily life or the "secularization" of Islam in that it is increasingly relegated to "folklorization" of worship, the *dawa* participants aim for the transformation of the separation of the spheres of life—economic, legal, educational, and familial (47). Scores of mosques in the Egyptian capital, where Mahmood conducted her fieldwork over a two-year period, participate in the *dawa* movement, with some mosques marking attendance of no less than five hundred women. Mahmood's skill lies in ensuring that Islamic topics as understudied and unfamiliar to Western academia as *salat, hijab, dawa, saum*, and an entire lexicon on Islamic theology is rendered remarkably approachable and critically affordable via a framework that is all too familiar to Western academic audiences. To do this, Mahmood filters these concepts through the theoretical lens of subject formation, bodily discipline, and societal norms on gender as propounded by arguably the most influential thinkers in Western intellectual history: Judith Butler, Aristotle, and Michel Foucault.

I am interested in extracting the transnational valence of such a powerful Islamic feminist critique. As such, the very subject and site of Mahmood's investigation of feminist knowledge production—the mosque participants and the mosque sites—remain unconsidered in that they offer important clues about the transnational validity of Islamic praxis. Thus the transgeographic location of Mahmood's fieldwork cannot be overlooked as it is based on no less than six mosques lodged in neighborhoods ranging from affluent and middle class to the poorest parts of Cairo. The granular descriptions of three mosques in particular—Umar, Ayesha, and Nafisa—underscore the transgeographic distance between classes, levels of education, linguistic sophistication, incomes, and lifestyle choices of the mosques' visitors. Ayesha and Umar mosques, Mahmood tells us, stand "at two *extremes* of the Cairene socioeconomic spectrum" in that they are characterized by a wide variety of attire and occupations of women, from housewives, students, working women to retired professionals (41, emphasis mine). While the Umar mosque is air conditioned, opulent, and upper middle class (reflecting the affluence of its surrounding neighborhood), the Ayesha mosque is located in one of the poorer neighborhoods where the women are not as well educated as those in the Umar mosque in that they are from a "working class" background and have had fewer educational opportunities (42). To balance these transgeographic class-based extremes, Mahmood includes another mosque, Nafisa, as a middle ground between the Umar and Ayesha mosques—made up of housewives and students. The visitors to Nafisa mosque, Mahmood tells us, pursue a strict adherence to female modesty in that most of the attendees wear the full body and face veil (*niqab*) and consider themselves to be more pious and virtuous than their counterparts in the other two mosques (43). Also starkly disparate are styles of lesson delivery, preaching, and learning at the three mosques, ranging from the fire and brimstone sermons to the gentler tones of lecturing and from the animated discussions between teacher and students to a quieter reception of the lectures (42–43). What can be discerned in this sweeping panorama of three socioeconomically heterogenous mosques is that women's views and engagements with Islam are irreparably fragmented across age groups, educational levels, time commitments, tastes in dressing, and perceptions of piety and self.

Mahmood extends this fragmented socioscape to the variety in optics, practices, and habits. With regard to the veil itself, Mahmood notes the fractures and fissures in that the veil is considered by some as important because it is a marker of "identity, culture, and civilization, primarily by well-known spokespersons of the Islamist movement" (52). For others, particularly for women in the piety movement, the veil is an important marker of religiosity but "insufficient" if it does not "enable" the "cultivation of Islamic virtues in the entirety of one's life" (52). Mahmood thus calls for a spatially and temporally focused approach as "micropractices" over a "universal modern process" as the same topic may vary spatiotemporally across sections of society and over time (52). She specifically cites the wide reception of the theological and doctrinal issues on "self-reflection," "self-reflexivity," and "modes of reflection" that have changed over time in classical, historical, and discursive invocations where ordinary women can discuss religious topics and students, and where working women also participate in public discussions on religious issues in their lives (55). Accounting for the diversity in opinions among public figures—Heba Saad Eddin, Adil Hussain, and Hajja Faiza of the piety movement—on the topic of the veil, Mahmood suggests studying

> how each of these views need to be analyzed in terms of the larger goals toward which it is teleologically oriented, the different *practical* contexts in which each type of reflection is located, and the consequences each particular form of understanding has for how one lives practically, both in relationship to oneself and to others. (56)

But the purpose of a gimlet eye for the demographics of the three mosques, we soon learn, is to make the same mistake that is now commonplace in feminist theories, especially with such politically charged themes as Islam and gender for critical consumption in the United States. With one sweeping sentence, Mahmood dismantles the diversity of her subjects that she painstakingly details to illustrate their demographic diversity:

"Despite differences among mosque groups, though, the participants all shared a concern for what they described as the increasing secularization of Egyptian society" (43). That is, Mahmood presents such a disparate tapestry of class, education, age, taste, self-perception, and occupation only to equalize them by concluding that women across class, intellectual, and practical differences were unified in the movement. One wonders why the wide-ranging diversity of unpredictable, idiosyncratic, and contradictory contexts is painstakingly sketched if not to trace it on a broader canvas of Muslims across the globe. After all, Mahmood approaches Islamic revivalism as a movement "across the Muslim world" (52). How can one for the sake of semblance uniformly unite heterogeneous practical contexts and even extremes in class, beliefs, opinions, and practices? If these factors influence even religious identities, practices, and avid habits, how can religious practice, itself a broad spectrum of histories, languages, ethnicities, and behaviors, unite or level differences across other cross-cutting differences? Women may overlook class to unite for a common cause, while others (as Chowdhury points to paradoxes within feminist practice) retain class to secure benefits even at the cost of that common cause (2010, 170–171).

I now turn my attention to the enduring disjunctures in gendered experiences in an attempt to underscore the understudied asymmetrical presence of disparities in class, ethnicity, and belief that are whitewashed in case studies of Muslim women in the service of a unified theater of feminist activity. The gaps or paradoxes I aim to underscore make visible the "invisible actors" in gendered experiences that remain unmentioned and unnamed especially in transnational networks of feminist activity. Chowdhury identifies this flow from West to East as "dependency chain" (5). Rebalancing this structurally unequal chain, she argues, means making visible those "invisible actors" and their goals that remain unmentioned in the network of international "humanitarian work in third world nations" (5). Their exposure matters for several reasons. First, these "invisible" Third World actors enable "better known, better-financed, and better connected institutions to make important interventions" (xviii). Second, exposing these invisible subjects, avers Chowdhury, affirms that they "may have had other goals that were subsumed by the global progress narrative of victim-survivor-activist" (xviii). Such transnational enabling not only resists erasures and exclusions but also posits different goals. Most important, visibility emphasizes women's differences in classes, languages, ethnicities, and religions to map onto cross-national differences in varying degrees and forms, including not at all (14). The paradoxes I discuss in this section amplify these reasons to rebalance the unequal dependency chain.

The first paradox highlights the unusual relationship between the state and gender. In congruence with the first paradox, the second contradiction concerns women's subordination and agency, and the third paradox pertains to the perception of interlocutors in the expression of gendered agency—West or East? The unusual relationship between the state and gender—returns us to Tickamyer and Kusurjiati's comparative study of two rural regions in Indonesia to underscore the gaps between women's social power, economic control of wealth, and state-legislated and patriarchal expectations of gendered roles. On similar lines, Rachel Rinaldo's (2013) examination of Muslim Indonesian women exposes one of several gaps or "gender paradoxes," where Muslim women work, study, and enjoy relative physical and spatial mobility despite restrictive state ideologies and patriarchal norms in the largest Muslim country in the world. In describing the motivation behind her study, Rinaldo observes an atmosphere of "unparalleled political freedom"):

> In a country where women are often encouraged to fulfill traditional expectations as daughters, wives, and mothers, these same women were proving to be impassioned agents for reform. Women swelled the ranks of rallies calling for change, mobilized food deliveries for the poor, organized commemorations of one of the country's female heroines, and demanded an end to violence against women after dozens of Chinese-Indonesian women were raped during the riots that accompanied the regime's demise . . . In addition, many younger women were becoming committed to Islam as they joined activist alliances. (1)

Similarly, Mahmood (2005) states that the piety movement or the women's mosque movement seeks to "imbue each of the various spheres of contemporary life with a regulative sensibility that takes its cue from the Islamic theological corpus rather than from modern secular ethics" (47). The piety activists thus endeavor to make Islam more meaningful in everyday life through a range of topics—clothing, spiritual habits, daily conduct, charity, education, entertainment, speech, and household management—that render the theological sources of religious ritual publicly practicable, thus posing a threat to secularism that maintains the distinction between public and private spheres. Consistent with conventional perceptions of the nexus of Islam, patriarchy, and the state in the control of women, such movements would ordinarily be associated with religious "fundamentalism" and "subjugation of women" as they enforce and maintain women's subordination in society (5). Paradoxically, however, the piety activists aim to engender "Islamic awareness," which makes it a threat to the state (48). It is in this sense—as a threat to its authority—that the state closely scrutinizes the *dawa* movement and even deeply distrusts it. But the *dawa* movement is not the only threat to the state's sovereign authority that the state fears (76, 83–84). There is also the perceived threat of discursive control of the theological corpus that causes much friction between two orthodox centers of power (75). The paradox, in other words, pertains to qualifying the role of the state and its relationship to women's agency, when in such cases of women's orthodox movements, the state is at loggerheads with other such regulatory bodies as itself. If gender's relationship to the state is examined through a lens that spotlights the state's control of gendered minorities, then gaps between the politics of control and the politics of internal refractions between such governing bodies as the state and religious organizations (the *dawa* movement in this case) remain unnoticed.

Similar gaps become visible in the second paradox I wish to discuss in the imputed tensions between women's subordination and feminist agency. The subjects of the piety movement, Mahmood tells us, "occupy an uncomfortable position in feminist theory" because of the perception that they promote and will their own subordinate status (4–5). They consolidate patriarchy instead of opposing it. Mahmood therefore suggests that agency must not be understood only in terms of subordination and resistance but focus instead on how subjects are shaped by it and how they engage with it when conditions permit (17). The paradox lies in assuming that women do not will their subordination and the ascription of an inherent opposition to subordination to feminist theory. Mahmood angles her argument by basing it on the general presumption that women's voluntary subscription to a highly orthodox form of Islam, involving the conservative practices of veiling, praying, and adopting bodily movements that discipline, subdue, and control the self, is perceived by feminist theorists as inimical to feminist interests. Such a presumption leaves unnoticed the blindspot about the reflection of such willful "bondage" as an extension of women's sociopolitical and material conditions in society (1). In other words, what is inadequately connected in Mahmood's attribution of feminist agency opposing their subordination within feminist theory is the nexus of that agency opposing its subordination and women's general sociopolitical and socioeconomic subordination in society. For instance, Rinaldo (2013) observes that despite the pervasive presence of patriarchal norms and regulations, it is *paradoxical* that Indonesian women enjoy relative freedom of movement and freedom relating to education and work opportunities (1). From this statement, we should ask the following: why would women oppose their subordination if they enjoy considerable freedom? Mahmood presumes a contradiction (that women practicing orthodox Islam aligns with their social position but would contradict assumptions of feminist theorists) to set up the contradiction (women in the piety movement will their subordination), in order to expand the conception of feminist agency. Mahmood thus positions her argument on the presumption of this generalized contradiction. This positioning enables her to state the obvious: that women's voluntary participation in a movement that seeks to uphold and maintain male authority should be surprising (which of course it is) to feminist theorists in the Western academe. She proceeds by imputing the assumption in feminist theory that "there is something intrinsic to women that *should* predispose them to oppose the practices, values and injunctions that the Islamist movement embodies" (1, 3). Unsurprisingly, therefore, if women do enjoy unparalleled political freedom, as Rinaldo asserts, *despite* widespread patriarchal controls, why should one assume an inherent opposition to disciplinary norms as the brakes on gendered freedom are effectively neutralized by women's access to educational and other opportunities? The presumption that women's natural disposition to freedom should animate their pursuit for freedom in society is the rhetoric that Mahmood observes as absent in the piety movement: this is because women in the piety group produce their subordination and do not fight it. Thus, Mahmood attributes women's opposition to their subordination as the premise of feminist theory's critique of the piety movement and uses that imputed inherent opposition to subordination to posit that women within the *dawa* movement in fact will their own subordination. Mahmood is thus able to argue that her inquiry on gender in Islam not only uncovers for Western audiences such willful embodiment of subordination as a rare and unique discovery but it also enables an appreciation of Muslim women willing their own subordination, something that Western feminist theory must critically embrace in their understanding of Islamic feminism.

Would aligning the wider context of their gendered social subordination with the piety movement not provoke the question on their position in society if the women did not participate in the movement?

Would their absence from the movement overturn the broader condition of their gendered subordination in society? Has religious practice, even if imposed on women, anything to do with the existence and maintenance of patriarchy that exceeds it? Or are gender theorists only examining the predictable connection between religion that is serviced by patriarchy to maintain control over women's agency? Religion itself, as Islamic and other feminist theorists have long argued, is not viewed as producing women's subordination, nor does it mitigate women's access to sociopolitical gains any more than nonaffiliation with it. Religion, as Sangari and Vaid economically describe it, is a systematic servicing of scriptural texts in the construction of nationalism and class-based reform that emerges as the bedrock for a universalized reconstruction of womanhood (1990, 10). Religion, therefore, is but one piece of the larger matrix of forces that collude to suppress gender. I would argue that patriarchy not only exceeds domination via religious control, but it also perpetuates itself through a multitude of other visible and invisible means to subordinate gendered agency.[15] As such, women's participation in feminist praxis that produces their subordination is inconsequential to patriarchy and their nonparticipation in a movement such as the piety movement.

The third paradox concerns the perception of audiences in the expression of gendered agency. I aim to show through this paradox that literary spaces—writing, circulation of literary texts, and translations—in fact uncover important strengths for rethinking transnational feminist experiences. The problem I am alluding to—that of audiences—returns me to one of this book's framing questions, which concerns the direction of the flow of information, "theory," and ideas in transnational feminist theorizations that keep historically and materially unequal relations intact. There is no denying that Mahmood is deeply conscious of the reception of her work in the West. She preponderantly engages with pioneering theorists—Butler, Foucault, and Aristotle—who have defined the fields of cultural, women's, and philosophical studies in Western academia. The problem metastasizes from the assumption that non-Western feminisms would find this unproblematic as Mohanty and Alexander, Grewal and Kaplan, among others, have unceasingly critiqued the production of Third World women as shorn of agency, exposing the glaring absence of Third World women of color in institutions of higher education in the West, coupled with the sense of "alienation, dislocation, and marginalization that often accompanies a racialized location within white institutions" (Mohanty and Alexander 1996, xiv). Hinting at the same, Abbas poses a vital question to interlocutors: "Are arguments *between* Muslims simply irrelevant?" (2014,

50, emphasis added). As noted earlier, Mohanty and Alexander alert us to the class demographic of the knowledge producer and the analytic tools used by researchers comfortably located in knowledge-producing centers in the West (1996, xvii). Despite the widespread attention that cross-national transnationalism can attract to women's causes, discourses and concepts in gendered justice reinscribe preexisting inequalities (xvii). For transnational Islamic feminist theorization, not just the themes that metonymize Muslim women but an entire body of knowledge about Muslim women is created and reinscribed using categories for an audience, forcing Muslim women's experiences to be read through a lens of Western grammar of gendered experiences.

In again questioning the direction of the flow of information and "theory"—who is it pointing toward?—a paradox emerges when this question is conflated with a corresponding challenge facing Global South literature and transnationally, or as Mukoma wa Ngugi (2018) puts it, its conversations with other African literatures. Ngugi broaches the important topic of translation or conversations between literatures, especially between African literatures, thus also raising the important point about the direction of the flow of ideas or influences and audiences. Ngugi highlights the absence of literary structures that impede the writing and translation of literatures between African languages comparatively. The preferred audience (English-speaking) guides the preferred medium and emerges glaringly at the time of communication and conversation. The structural challenges or "voids," then, that maintain the "unmappability" of African writing point to the possibility of imagining spaces of conversation not oriented in the direction of the dominant North (Apter 2019, 196). Similarly, as B. Venkat Mani notes, lodged on the axis are such chasms as "unknowability," "inscrutability," "inaccessibility," and "illegibility" that cannot be bridged in the service of agendas by historically and materially powerful constituents no matter how globally migrant the world has become (2017, 11–12).[16]

"Unlikely Alliances" and Spaces: Contact Zones, Dissident Friendships, Muslim Cosmopolitanism

In this section, I pause the discussion of topologies to highlight the properties of relationships between different constituents. Are they equal? Does information flow in one direction? What would the sites of knowledge production look like where such dynamics are studied? I examine, in particular, contact zones, Muslim cosmopolitanism, and dissident friendships to attempt to answer these questions. As briefly discussed earlier, Mary Louise Pratt puts forth the idea of a "contact zone" and extends it to the "model of a community" to study the topology of relationships between dominant and dominated groups (1991, 34). According to Pratt, contact zones are

> social spaces where cultures meet, clash, and grapple with each other, often in contexts of highly asymmetrical relations of power, such as colonialism, slavery, or their aftermaths as they are lived out in many parts of the world today. (34)

Reversing the flow of influences from dominant to dominated groups, and rendering visible the unnoticed work of actors in less powerful sites, Pratt underscores "transculturation," or a "process whereby members of subordinated or marginal groups select and invent from materials transmitted by a 'dominant metropolitan culture'" (36). Pratt thus focuses on the power that subordinate groups exert in their reception of ideas and influences in that they determine what gets absorbed from the dominant culture even though they may not have control over what gets communicated (36). Subordinate groups also determine the uses of such knowledge. Pratt's topological observation of a "contact zone" thus shifts focus from simply asymmetrical relationships between dominant and marginalized groups, colonizer and colonized, master and slave, to the agency of the dominated group. It asks to consider more than the direction of the flow of ideas or "theory" (from the center to the periphery). It asks instead to examine what the subordinate group does with the idea of "theory."

Resembling "transculturation" is Khairudin Aljunied's "Muslim cosmopolitanism" as the "agency of the laypersons" (2016, xvii). In an effort to shift focus from cosmopolitanism as a function and product of European and global processes such as digital circulations to more informal and quotidian forms of life in marketplaces and mosques, "cosmopolitan localism" alludes to scales—macro and micro, where the latter epitomizes the informal agency of the layperson and locally committed subject, while the former is a representative of dominant globalization. People of differing backgrounds produce and reproduce cosmopolitanism either spontaneously or regularly through different kinds of strategies—"fostering interest," "mutual agreement," "sealing the deal," and "the production of market acquaintances," such that sellers and buyers may even become close to one another in the interest of long-term ties and regular patronage or "loyalty" to the seller (8, 9–10). Muslim cosmopolitanism in sites of everyday informal encounters and exchanges is often unrehearsed and unpredictable. They function as fluid spaces of interaction where "the ability to speak and communicate in an open, calm and warm manner constitute everyday Muslim cosmopolitanism in Southeast Asian markets," writes Aljunied (8).[17] Aljunied identifies in such unrehearsed strategies cosmopolitan tendencies. Rules of market space interactions and sociability, intimates Aljunied, are rarely congruent with religious views and practices. "Political Islam does not necessarily influence the shape of Muslim cosmopolitanism in the marketplace," meaning that despite their religious differences, Muslims, shopkeepers, and vendors interact with others on a scale that bespeaks *ummah*-building tendencies of connecting and dialoguing with others (12, 13). While Karim notes in mosques divisions and differences between Muslims that pose threats and challenges to the unificatory impulse of *ummah*, Aljunied's cosmopolitanism finds the marketplace and mosque to be a "contact zone" of transculturation, or "places that enable different faiths, persuasions, ideologies, and temperaments to interact" (25). The mosque, then, for Aljunied, stands as a cosmopolitan space of difference that enables people of diverse persuasions, ideologies, and temperaments to interact. The unity of beliefs, in other words, is not enough to determine the *ummah*.

Muslim cosmopolitanism comprises a dual spiritual imperative—that of opposing hatred in the sustenance of plural viewpoints. Thus, "Muslim cosmopolitanism" inscribes such *ummah* ideals as Muslim inclusiveness, shared goals, tolerance, dialogue, and openness while upholding the idea of diversity precisely because diversity is also, argues Aljunied, a spiritual imperative where Muslims are accountable to all humankind (xxi). He thus states:

> Much like Islam as a belief system and a cultural reality, different individuals and groups may understand and express cosmopolitanism differently in accordance with the demands of their milieus. They are, however, bounded [sic] by the shared conviction that Muslims are accountable to all of humankind and that they learn from each other and from the 'other.' Purveyors of Muslim cosmopolitanism contribute to the making of plural societies, ensuring that peace, harmony and mutual respect are upheld just as they unceasingly oppose the forces of hate and disunity. (xxi)

For Aljunied, Muslim cosmopolitanism and its community-building ideals are like Islam—discrepant in space and time. However, this shared conviction of accountability to humankind, insists Aljunied, does not presume stability or coherence—it needn't. Rather, the variations of its plurality are underpinned by the shared conviction of the well-being of humankind.

The most striking example of transgeographic relationships that Aljunied offers is the location of the Chulia mosque in Singapore's bustling Chinatown, in the midst of "markets, businesses and all things non-Muslim," only a few meters from the oldest Hindu temple in Singapore, "Sri Mariamman Temple" (24). The "contact zone" of the mosque and the Hindu temple in Chinatown respatializes the transnational as transgeographic. Aljunied is not alone in evoking the unique example of the Hindu temple in Singapore. Malaysian writer Dina Zaman penetratingly describes her visit to the iconic sanctuary in her nonfictional account, *Holy Men, Holy Women* (2017), as part of her stated attempt to forge friendships even with people of other religions and beliefs, pivoting on the Islamic concepts of migration and *ummah*. In an earlier account, *I Am Muslim* (2007), in particular, Zaman claims that fostering community through friendships, dialogues with others, exploring new cultures, and getting to know others or *taaruf* derive from *unsur tawadlu/tawadhu* or elements of humility in Islam. Zaman (2007) intimates, "Those familiar with *unsur tawadlu* will understand that it is *taaruf* for Muslims to learn about their sisters and brothers in faith as well as their friends of other religions and beliefs, and forge friendships" (34). Buoyed by these noble impulses to research comparative religion, Zaman nevertheless admits that for most Malaysians like herself, a place of worship from another faith merits no more than a glance or a five-minute look at the most (30). Thus, she bravely documents her awkward dialogue with the caretaker of the Sri Mahamariamman Temple in Chinatown, Singapore. Mr. K, as she chooses to call the Hindu custodian, assumes that Zaman is Christian. On learning that she is Muslim, he immediately makes clear that he does not like her religion because they kill animals and that he is vegetarian (31). Despite the dissident encounter and tense exchange, Mr. K graciously enlightens Zaman about the history of the temple and the minutiae of its construction. Zaman concludes the awkward exchange by expressing an interest to return later and continue her "friendship" with Mr. K, who promises to teach her about his religion so she may know his people (32). This strained exchange to forge friendships, Zaman eventually realizes, was unexpectedly challenging in its intention to learn about the faiths of others (32).

At work in Zaman's attempt to forge friendships are alternatives to political and conventional notions of community similar to Liz Philipose and Elora Chowdhury's timely reworking of "dissident relationality" as "dissident friendships" that suggests that structural power and "imperial imagination" do not control the horizon of possibilities (3). Borrowing the term from Leela Gandhi, dissident friendships defy "narrowly defined agendas" and constitute an "openness to the other" even at the risk of reproducing inequality (Gandhi 2006, 3, 4). Combining the fluid, unrehearsed, and unpredictable interactions that Aljunied observed among Muslims with anti-imperial reproductions of race and dominance, along with Zaman's evocation of the principles of *unsur tawadlu* and *taaruf* or forging unlikely friendships to know other faiths, dissident friendships are formed

> across political boundaries and structural power that demonstrate the power of affect and emotional bonding to counter divisions. National, racial, imperial, class, gender, and "enemy lines" fail to keep people from crossing lines in friendship. (3)

These divisions, maintains Chowdhury, in her sterling analysis of women's "consensual and complicitous" maintenance of patriarchy, are nevertheless essential as "enriching resources, epistemologically, politically and personally" (2016, 161). Thus Chowdhury and Philipose underscore the value of dissidence in relationships as counterparts dare to reach out to each other across hostile and dangerous divides of structural power—national, racial, imperial, class, gender—to defeat the monopolization of subjectivities by political boundaries in the act of fostering friendship (3). Both dissidence and friendship are maintained not with the aim of facilitating solidarity but with the aim of inveighing hegemonic, colonial, and racial structures of power and imperial imaginations of lives. From these "unlikely alliances" and associations emerge "multiple and sometimes contradictory subjectivities" in communities of support, write Chowdhury and Philipose (3, 4).

Literature as a site of feminist knowledge production throws into sharp relief the "multiple genealogies of feminist practice" (Mohanty and Alexander 1996, 26). It complicates feminist knowledge production with data that is not even factual but notional at best—data that is not easily mapped onto the transnational feminist landscape. While the subjects of Chowdhury's study—grassroots feminist movement of victims of acid violence—are real and engage in activism that directly redounds to social justice, can such a claim be made for women such as Adichie, el-Khalieqy, or Arifa Macaqua Jamil, among others, whose characters are imaginary and don't explicitly engage in social justice practices via community-based and activist models? Furthermore, not all of these writers of fiction are known to engage with social justice groups. If premised only on, as Basu terms it, the tensions between "alliance and autonomy," the flow of information between sites delimited as global-local, center-periphery, and Global North and Global South, which are mutually constituted, then it is impossible for a transnational feminist relationship to include writers with no proposed solutions to social injustice through movements and memberships to formal venues of social justice, as myriad forms of socially and empirically dense feminist expressions remain invisible, unmapped, and unaccounted for in internally refracted frameworks: the nation-state (2010, 3). My attempt to comparatively analyze African and Southeast Asian Muslim women pushes the analytical limits of mapping knowledge production on just two counts, regionally and linguistically, among numerous others. In the chapters that follow, my reading of Abida el-Khalieqy's "Road to Heaven," for instance, interrogates how violence and abuse map onto the transnational landscape when strategies lie in nonmovement-based solutions? Equally, the story remained unmapped linguistically until its translation into English. Even so, el-Khalieqy's work is not popular in academic circles or courses on feminism in the United States or Europe, judging from informal surveys to observations of academic scholarship—databases, monographs, book collections, syllabi—on feminism in institutions of higher education in North America and Europe. In Arifa Macaqua Jamil's "Ayesha's Pretty Hate Machine," and Anna Dao's "The Perfect Wife" (also a translation from French), how would polygamy map onto a transnational landscape when reactions to it vary between helplessness in the face of emotional betrayal to revenge for betrayal? How would interreligious marriages in Leila Aboulela's "Majed" and Pearlsha Abubakar's "Maghrib" converse transnationally when they involve such transgeographic dissident responses as interfaith marriages and identities? How would such responses or experiences map onto the critical landscape of women's studies if theorizations of gendered experiences engage only social justice and equality instantiated in movements and alliances cross-nationally? As Basu suggests, women's organizations and movements grew out of the failure of the postcolonial state to accommodate women's rights despite their active participation and endorsement of self-determination in anticolonial struggles (1995, 15). Thus, it is from this failure and disappointment of transnational movements to account for the work of "invisible" actors, as Chowdhury describes the work of grassroots organizations and activists, that unpredictable, unrehearsed informal struggles powerfully foreground the multiple genealogies of knowledge production, as women articulate greater consciousness of their experiences that cannot be mapped onto formally organized and cross-national spaces.

The danger lies not in excluding or erasing differences—that is a danger one must live with. The danger lies instead in assuming that a geographic space—religion, class, ethnicity, languages—does not rebalance inequalities between sites, weakening the reimagination of the "bidirectional flows" of influences and ideas (Grewal and Kaplan, 1994, 14). As such, not all feminist activity engages official pronouncements or policies in their relationship with Islam. In the literature under analysis here, the aleatory dialogues and encounters engender a space of women's transnationalism outside of engagements with the nation-state, not literally beyond its borders but even within them, to point to unnoticed and unconsidered geographies of feminist causes. In fact, women's relationships with the state and external agencies of activism emblematize the conflict between nation-state, kinship, and filial affiliations. Basu's example of the success of the "thappa" brigade in India in procuring rights for women by engaging the state (but stopping short of developing into a full-fledged movement) amply illustrates this dissonance. Fearing reactions from the family, intimates Basu, women controlled and scaled back their feminist rights agendas as their activities risked jeopardizing kinship ties embedded in inheritance rights and laws, thus illustrating an example where the "excessive reliance on the state to enact public measures supporting gender equality" clashes with the "consciousness of inequality within the home and family" (15). Earlier, Rachel Rinaldo's observation of the "gender paradox" evoked such dissonance between state-based and patriarchal expectations of obedience and the reality of women's participation in public activities in their daily lives. In the chapters that follow, I focus therefore on such paradoxes—disjunctures and dissonance—that emerge from women's informal strategies and solutions through aleatory encounters, exchanges, and relationships to build community with others and that remain hard to map when transnationalism is conceived solely as a cross-national relationship.

Chapter 2

Windowed Encounters

Gazes, Times, and *Ummah*

> One's relationship to windows now changed in the city. A window was the border through which death was possibly most likely to come. Windows could not stop even the most flagging round of ammunition: any spot indoors with a view of the outside was potentially in the crossfire.
>
> —Mohsin Hamid, *Exit West*

> Literature is the home of nonstandard space and time.
>
> —Wai Chee Dimock, *Through Other Continents: American Literature across Deep Time*

In this chapter I examine Chimamanda Ngozi Adichie's largely obscure short story "A Private Experience" and its first iteration "The Scarf," and read them with two longer narratives on gendered attempts at transnationalizing community, namely Mariama Ba's classic novel *So Long a Letter* and a lesser-known novel *Sacred Apples* by Abubakar Gimba. The two shorter analyses in this chapter, of Ba's classic novel and Gimba's lesser-known novel, that accompany a longer study of Adichie's short story combine the rich and timely illustration of religious topologies and community building. All three works of fiction narrativize Muslim women's claim that Islam is a multihistorical and multispatial topology involving non-Muslims. In other words, the trope of *ummah* that unfurls in all three works of fiction signifies across religious spheres to delineate the broader politics of Africa and its place in the world. Equally, they are powerful discussions on the history of identity politics in African societies that have been brought to bear upon the current conjuncture on the transnationalization of gendered causes. The simultaneous worlds of social imagination and material and political realities are most iconically evoked by Mariama Ba in her classic novel *So Long a Letter* in the figure of Jacqueline and in her polygamous, multireligious, and multinational marriage. I thus discuss interfaith relationships as Ba channels her idea of Africa and gender through the space of Jacqueline's marital bond. Gimba, in comparison, is more direct in his attempt at redefining the space of the nation as a plural and mixed matrix of interreligious interactions. Adichie's relatively unknown story is likewise transnationally global both in its structure and narrativization, as it signifies across boundaries. It instances the transnational by folding in the cross-national space within transgeographic relationships. This comparatively obscure story, in both its earlier iteration "The Scarf" (2002) and the current version, "A Private Experience" (2008), is structurally and thematically pivotal in its multiply overlapping emplotment of transnationalism. Anthonia Kalu's illuminating analysis of the African short story divides the genre into two main types: "the traditional oral narrative and the written contemporary short story" (2016, 375). The latter, suggests Kalu,

> presents important aspects of different African communities' narrative ethos and practice, helping to illuminate contemporary African literature's project of building connections between Africa's precolonial past and its colonial and post-independence cultures. (375)

Indeed, "A Private Experience" builds connections between religions and between Africa's precolonial past and its colonial and postindependence cultures by focusing on a chance meeting between a Christian and a Muslim woman in an ostensibly enclosed space during an ethnic mob scene in Kano City, a northern Nigerian town.[1]

"A Private Experience" is not Adichie's first attempt to grapple with religion in general and with religious relationships in particular. She does so in a number of works in her longer and better-known oeuvre, particularly in *Half of a Yellow Sun* (2006) and *Purple Hibiscus* (2003). Adichie first attempted to deal with the theme of this short story by writing it under the title of "The Scarf" in 2002. And Ba's classic novel is not commonly analyzed for thematizing transnationalism and even less so for a spiritual transnationalism enshrined in the idea of *ummah*. Abubakar Gimba and his oeuvre are virtually unknown to readers outside of Nigeria. Together, these tangential contours of literary writing—the reputation of the writer, the popularity and critical purchase of certain themes, and the popularity and circulation of some works more than others—are useful indices for measuring the thrust of transnationalism in theorizations of transnational feminisms. I begin with an analysis of Adichie's story, followed by shorter segments on Ba's use of transnational feminism in the tangential figure of Jacqueline and Gimba's illustration of interreligious relationships in dialogues and encounters between Christian and Muslim women in Nigeria.

Because the trope of the window in Adichie's story connects the spaces of the shop and the marketplace, I read the meeting of the two women as a "windowed encounter" that affords both a framing and a viewing, functioning thus as an expanding, transparent, and inverted metaphor for a number of relationships, namely Islam in relation to other faiths in Africa; Africa's place in the world; and African Islam's place in the Islamic world (and more broadly, the world at large). The window also inverts the view by framing global topologies in the interfaith encounter of the two women. Using the window as the central metaphor that anchors and loosens the space and time of the encounter at once "projective and recessional," as Wai Chee Dimock terms it, I tie these simultaneously open and closed spaces of the shop, the window, and the marketplace with equally concurrent and multiple temporalities (flashbacks, the present encounter, and the future) to highlight such *ummah*-building gestures as dissident relationality, contact zones, and Muslim cosmopolitanism where perspectives and attitudes toward identities and realities respatialize the transnational, to evoke Dimock again, "against the official borders of the nation and against the fixed intervals of the clock" (2006, 3, 4). Although the Christian and Muslim women have their own stereotypes and prejudices about each other, unfurling dissident relationality as a strategy for working out their meeting, this "unlikely alliance," as Gandhi terms it, between associates of differing communities is also "potentially transformative, personally and socially transformative, and in many cases subversive" of imperially maintained opinions (Chowdhury and Philipose, 2016, 3). Dissident relationality requires listening to differences, as Chika gradually does, crossing over and exchanging but also retaining boundaries that shape identities, as the Muslim vendor does. This chapter redefines both transnationalism and *ummah*.

I spot *ummah*-building gestures in the women's nonlinear or conjunctural gazes on themselves and on each other—dialogues, flashbacks, and introspections—in the three works of fiction under analysis in this chapter that reconfigure the meaning of *ummah* from a group of believers to a group of people with a "set of ideas or an ideology," as observed by Abdullah al-Ahsan, and as stated in the Qur'anic verse 10:19: "And (know that) all mankind were once but one single community (*ummatan wahidatan*), and later did they begin to hold divergent views" (2007, 607). Al-Ahsan also notes that *ummah* is used in the Qur'an to "describe a well-knit group of people" in addition to the "beliefs of such a group of people" (607). It is in this sense of a well-knit group of people who cohabit with others but not necessarily sharing their beliefs—yet connecting with them as the Muslim woman in Adichie's story connect with the Chika through several *ummah*-building strategies—that I read these strategies as a rebalancing and revising of their relationship to foreground the rebalancing between historically inequitable relationships between Christians and Muslims. The social power that Chika possesses in her superior class and education slowly dissipates as the illiterate Muslim vegetable vendor rebalances it in the course of their exchange. An important component of this rebalancing, I will demonstrate, is also performed, in particular, through Adichie's building of the latest reprisal of the story in 2008 on its prior iteration that debuted as "The Scarf" in 2002. I do so by reading both versions of the story and by focusing on three spaces that exemplify "simultaneous worlds" as Caren Kaplan denominates spaces that push onto each other—the space of the shop itself, the marketplace outside the shop, and the window of the shop that frames the meeting of the two women inside the shop peering out at the marketplace (Kaplan 1994). Allusively, "The Scarf" and "A Private Experience," enable an understanding of the transnational as windowed, for both iterations exemplify Adichie's rebalancing and revising of relationships in the unusual conflation of two versions of the same piece of writing on religious topologies.

I conclude the discussion of the story by commenting on Adichie's portrayal of solidarity in the two women's actions at the conclusion. The story is told by Chika, an affluent, educated Christian university student in her early twenties. Chika and an older Muslim woman, a vegetable vendor, are forced to take refuge in an abandoned shop as an ethnic mob convulses in Kano City. Chika is visiting the town with her sister, Nnedi. The sisters stay with their aunt, who is a government official. The riot in the marketplace erupts when a Christian shopkeeper involuntarily drives a scooter over a copy of the Qur'an.

Adichie's engagement with religion in "A Private Experience" is unusual in that she first wrote it as "The Scarf" in 2002, and it also appeared two years later in 2004 under its current title before finally being published as "A Private Experience" in a collection of stories, *The Thing around Your Neck* (2009). When the story is the subject of critical analysis, however, it is reductively read as a mere meeting or clash between a Muslim and Christian woman who misunderstand each other. It is also to the latest version of the story (2008) that most critics turn when mentioning Adichie's cursory attempt at reflecting on religion. As such, Adichie's longer publications, her "accomplished novels," as Aghogho Akpome calls them, enjoy greater critical attention (9847). Her novels, states Rose Sackeyfio, comprise a "window into lived experiences of contemporary African women" (2013, 104). When Adichie's characters are described as being "transformed by unfamiliar environments, tensions and contradictions with new spaces," critics usually mean the protagonists that populate her novels and the experiences of such protagonists in an explicitly crossnational sense, explaining perhaps the reason for the scant attention to some of the same forms of transformations in unfamiliar relationships in "A Private Experience" (104). Maitreyi Misra and Manish Shrivastava, for instance, celebrate Adichie's work for its insights on "dislocated individuals striving hard for cultural assimilation in the host country" (2017, 187). Her characters, they assert, are essentially "diasporic" and encompass the cross-national rubric of relationships as "either coming from Nigeria to America, or getting back to Nigeria from America" (187). As critics settle firmly on the transnational as a theme in Adichie's other stories—"The Arrangers of Marriage," "Imitation," and the title story "The Thing around Your Neck"—"A Private Experience" can often be overlooked, as the story does not fall under any of the more popular critical labels of transnationalism—gender discrimination, immigration, racism, or postcolonialism. But this neglect of the short story is symptomatic of a larger anxiety in African literatures that has insufficiently tapped the literary and imaginative potential of this literary form. Ernest Emenyonu cites Charles Nnolim, who bemoans the critical negligence of the short story, calling the genre "stillborn" (2013, 1). Critical neglect of the African short story is perhaps the reason why the ability of the short stories under analysis in this section to transact globally remains underexplored.

Peter Kalliney's observation elaborates Kaplan's idea of simultaneous worlds that push into each other both thematically and actionably, as activist writing on transnationalism and globalization. Charting the aspirations of contemporary African writers to be part of a mobile literary archive globally and transnationally, Kalliney notes a "subtle, but distinct, shift in the Anglophone African novel" in the late 1980s "with a trend toward more self-consciously global narrative perspectives" (2016, 411). Even when a metropolitan publisher such as Heinemann served as an intermediary between African writers and their audiences, African novels were read as "primarily national in their thematic concerns and narrative devices," writes Kalliney (411). The shift, observes Kalliney, has occurred in writers since then who "push against the imaginative boundaries of the nation state" (411). I would add that Adichie's short story, though not a novel, is a robust contender for the transnational canon in its imaginatively feisty use of many of the narrative and thematic devices that Kalliney notes as representative of this shift in African writing that shaped African fiction in a global context—memory, travel, narrative objects, displaced persons—encapsulating African fiction's transnational thrust (2016, 411, 414, 417).[2] Ernest Emenyonu's reading also decodes Adichie's unique transnational message that links "difficult realities" shaping "a new world of understanding as they give expression to realities people know and human commitments and awareness they need to know" (1). As a writer committed to multiple roles in her work of challenging, teaching, educating, and creating social awareness about human actions, for Emenyonu, Adichie is, like the traditional Igbo writer, "the educator, entertainer, philosopher, and counsellor" (2017, 9, 12). Not unlike Achebe's influential call to African writers to reshape their societies, Emenyonu and other critics see Adichie following in Achebe's aesthetic and engaged footsteps to help shape a new world of understanding.[3] Of interest then in this story is not only the factual exemplification of interreligious tensions but also the link, as Aghogho Akpome argues, between social imagination and material and political realities (2017, 9848).

Shadows, Extensions, Expanding Frames of the *Ummah*

To argue that the meeting between the Muslim and Christian women—a windowed encounter—foregrounds projective and recessional gazes, space and time, metaphorizing relationships of two religious groups—I turn to James Ferguson's book *Global Shadows: Africa in the Neoliberal World Order*. Ferguson examines Africa's exclusion from global discussions on politics and economics and its treatment on the margins of global processes (or as the title of his book suggests, "the neoliberal world order") (2006, 3). Ferguson's deployment of the word "shadows" in the title of his book is evocative not just of the perception of Africa's place on the globe—on the margins of global discussions, not fully acknowledged—but also of its inseparability from the world. Ferguson describes the shadow as a "bond and a relationship . . . an attached twin," or doubleness that "is not simply a negative space, a space of absence; it is a likeness, an inseparable other-who is-also-oneself to whom one is bound" (17). In other words, it is pointing to "relationality" that is not apart, distant, or spaced between two constituents but of two constituents attached within each other and as extensions of one another (17). Adichie, too, is concerned with Africa's place in the world, of seeing oneself as outside the center. As we shall see, she alludes to this "place in the modern world" in examples of media depictions of the mob in the story. In an interview, she voices these metaphysical and psychological exclusions, the peripheral place of Africa, outside the center and the lack of metaphysical validation of the self by looking "somewhere else":

> We Africans may have become well versed in performing the rituals of nationhood—the flags and borders and anthems that keep a people ostensibly united—but what has made other modern states succeed is a faith in its own idea of what it is and its place in the world. We are a people conditioned by our history and by our place in the modern world to look towards "somewhere else" for validation, to see ourselves as inhabitants of the periphery. I am not merely referring to political expressions like "Third World," but to the phenomenon of being outside the centre in ways more subtle than mere politics, in ways metaphysical and psychological.[4] (Adichie 2010)

Africa in this story is depicted differently than in her novel *Americanah*, where America or the West is integral to the performance of Africa. Stephanie Li suggests, "Any performance of Africa is inextricable from an accompanying performance of American life" (2018, 24).[5] Rather, in this story, Adichie redirects attention from the West as the privileged venue of exchange, to paraphrase Boehmer, to the periphery, in an attempt to explore a conjunctural space where Africa, a trope of the periphery, is also inseparable from it (2005). As a trope of the self, the shadow stakes ground internally and externally or conjuncturally as it passes over borders. This twin relationship of the shadow with the self and also as an extension of the self accentuates the preoccupation with "Africa and its place in the wider world," of broader questions or large-scale issues (Ferguson 2006, 6). Ferguson writes that he is concerned with:

> "Africa" as a category through which a "world" is structured—a category that (like all categories) is historically and socially constructed (indeed in some sense arbitrary), but also a category that is "real," that is imposed with force, . . . a category within which and according to which, people must live. . . . I want to ask how that place-in-the-world functions in a wider categorical system and what this means for the way we understand an increasingly transnational political, economic, and social "global order." (5)

More than the dialectical relationship between Afro-pessimism and Afro-optimism about a continent or by proving what Africa is instead of what it is not, as Mbembe cautions, I blend the window and shadow to focus on the windowed meaning of shadow—a dark nothing to mirror, not the nothingness of Africa, the dark continent, as Ferguson notes, but the gaps in our understanding of Africa (2002, 10). Just as there is a "shadow" government, a shadow economy, and a shadow social order accompanying the formal sectors of the economy and political systems in Africa (one that we incompletely grasp), Africa itself serves as a shadow to the world, never quite centralized in discussions about the world but without which discussions of the world are essentially incomplete (Ferguson 2006, 15, 17).

Likewise, we may think about Islam in Africa as interconnected and of the topology of this sociality as inscribing expanding frames within it. Inversely, to study African Islam and Muslims through keywords like inequality, aspiration, and rank in the world is to recognize that this lexicon, as Ferguson underlines, is also widely employed to allude to Africa and its place in the globe (2006, 19). If transnationalism is read simply as Africa's relation to the rest of the world, to interrogate its place in the world, we risk missing not only the expanding transgeographic relations that Adichie dramatizes in this story but also overlooking the reversals in the flow of information, "theory," and influences that preciously rebalance unequal relationships as a result of a respatialized transnationalism. To understand dissidence in such relationships as the ones Adichie dramatizes in the story is to see it through the metaphor of both the window that inscribes multiple geographies—class, religion, language, ethnicity—and the shadow that is attached but can also pass over borders while remaining attached to the body. The shadow in particular, connotes two important analogies that I elaborate below with the idea of "mimetic semblance" or a "former time," a "former self." The shadow bespeaks spaces that are at once unnoticed and hard to spot. The shadow can also mean spaces that are easily breached.

A shadow functions as a "former self" and unsettles the "reified certitudes" of the other, as Jisha Menon has suggested in her study of the performance of violence in literature between religious, ethnic, and national communities in South Asia during the political partition of India and Pakistan (2013, 21). Using the idea of "mimetic semblance," Menon evokes a "former time" or a "former self" that does not dissolve difference into sameness but rather exposes the doubleness of the self, the nonidentity of the self with the self, thus fracturing the unity and uniformity on which civic and religious nationalisms depend" (5, 21). Evoking Dimock again, what is at work here is "irregular duration and extension, some extending for thousands of years or thousands of miles, each occasioned by a different tie, and each loosening up the chronology and geography of the nation" (2006, 4). To this end, it is useful to see that the *ummah* is not a smooth and successful venture at first. It passes through the women's subjectivities based on their classes, religions, and perceptions of the other to loosen their sense of time and space in the articulation of the relationship of self to the other and to the nation. To briefly recapitulate the three spaces that I discuss to illustrate a respatialized *ummah*—the shop, the marketplace, and the window—I underscore each space as the precise moment that fractures certainties around religious and civic identities. The shop is a closed space where the encounter unfurls to reveal temporally (historical inequalities) and spatially (class inequalities) disparate feelings. The two women are spatially separated by class, religion, ethnicity, and language as they are temporally united or separated by a history of these differences. The space of the shop allows them to confront these historically driven social conflicts in a private way. The window serves as the conjuncture of these spaces. As it frames in the shop of uneasy dialogues and encounters, it also exposes the space of the marketplace—the site of the mob—spilling over the private meeting of gender, religion, and classes within the shop into a wider space of encounters.

The Space of the Shop

The enclosed space of the small, abandoned shop is no bigger than Chika's walk-in closet, "Chika climbs in through the store window first and then holds the shutter as the woman climbs in after her. . . . The store is small. Smaller than Chika's walk-in closet back home" (Adichie 2009, 43). In both—the physical space of a place safe from violence and a comparison of the shop to Chika's closet, alluding to her upper-class affluent status—Adichie inscribes broader class-based tensions between Christians and Muslims. The window thus allows the reader to peer through its frame and extricate the colonial vestiges of class divisions that underpin the differences in education and classes of the two women, resulting also in the religious divisions found in the story. These divisions, however, are far from straightforward disparities that pit one group over another and continue an unchanged power dynamic between disparate communities. In fact, as Moses Ochonu's historical inquiry of Christian-Muslim relations in northern Nigeria shows, Muslims in northern Nigeria were not always ethnically or economically marginalized. Ochonu studies the repoliticization of a dueling relationship between Muslims and Christians by uncovering the unfamiliar history of a process by which the colonial administration in Nigeria cultivated a class of "African subcolonials," or paradoxically "native aliens" or "socially advanced African outsiders," to prepare them to govern the "backward" Africans for indirect colonial rule (Ochonu 2014, 3).[6] Ochonu not only deconstructs but also demystifies the notion of indirect colonial rule as simply the imposition of a class of people tutored in colonial ways to govern other groups. By pausing on the preexisting divisions in this religiously plural society, Ochonu highlights the politics on which the British capitalized by preparing a group of subcolonials who were not appointed to preserve difference, as was the case for colonialism in the rest of Africa, but to dissolve it through a paradoxical "native alien subcolonialism" of sociopolitically conscious superiority (8). The reification of this brand of colonial rule, as it paved the way for a full-blown implementation of the more widely known politics of indirect rule, was the placement of the ethnically Muslim groups, the Hausa-Fulani, as subcolonial agents who, although instituted to ostensibly dissolve differences, used instead religious difference to preserve superiority over their subjects. Unlike in many other parts of Africa, the British, states Ochonu, in fact, "faced the actual difference of religion and ethnicity" in northern Nigeria

(9). The allure of dominance thus drove them to deepen "ethno-cultural difference" through this subcolonial class of "presumably 'progressive' Africans from proximate 'civilized' ethno-religious communities as drivers of surrogate colonial rule," writes Ochonu (3). Thus, from slave-raiding invaders into the middle-belt regions, to tax collectors and agents of British imperialism, the Hausa-Fulani, predominantly Muslim agents, contributed to a lesser-known middle belt "sociopolitical consciousness" that is on full display in Adichie's story in the two women's observations and comments about each other's class, religion, and ethnicity (2009, 4). It is this historically complex emplotment, both precolonial and colonial, of a fluctuating sociopolitical psyche, rather than a straightforward relationship based on linear and unchanged historical inequities between two ethno-religious groups, that Adichie unravels in the story as Chika climbs into both psychological and physical delimitations of the exiguous space of the shop and of her views.

In placing the meeting within the closed shop, where the women confront long-standing historically driven variations and fluctuations of ethno-religious inequities, Adichie also seems to temporally spatialize relationships within national boundaries. Even when indicative of cross-national or "transnational" problems such as Islamophobia and religiously motivated violence, Adichie inverts the window to provoke commentary on transgeographic relationships. Given the story's multiple versions, it would not be unrealistic to diachronically parallel its revisions with the developments in the world following 9/11 that revived Islamophobia more pervasively in recent times, followed by US President Trump's ban on travelers from Muslim-majority countries.[7] This rise in Islamophobia is often equated with America's push to establish its foreign politics globally, including militarization, capitalism, and global dominance. Revathi Krishnaswamy (2008) describes this tendency as "imperiality" where shortly following 9/11 there was a move to merge "the American nation-state with the state of the globe" (12). Adichie's encounter in the story and her commentary on interfaith relationships then relocate not only the space but also the interlocutor from global or cross-national sites to subnational and transgeographic spaces, suggesting that the post-9/11 world might not have experienced its politics as intensely as America. Moreover, the rest of the world might not be responding to 9/11 and its afterlives in the same way as America. This internal turbulence, contained by the walls of the shop, comes to a head most tangibly in the motif of the mob.

Space of the Marketplace

Khairudin Aljunied signposts the marketplace as an important place for seamless "affable interreligious and intercommunal exchanges" communication and "fluid interactions or the ability to speak and communicate in an open, calm and warm manner" (2016, 3, 8). It is a place, he avers, where "antagonisms and biases between peoples of differing backgrounds and origins are suspended and sometimes forgotten to give way to forms of talk that can have mutual benefit to both buyers and sellers as well as to locals and strangers" (13). However, in Adichie's story, the marketplace becomes a site of unbridled violence—a travesty of the idealistic cosmopolitanism that Aljunied observes in Southeast Asian marketplaces. Yet, Adichie's message in the story is not limited just to the marketplace as a space of cosmopolitanism. It is, as Aljunied gestures to the extension of the marketplace or the marketplace itself as an extension of other interactions, dialogues, and exchanges. The marketplace, then, is less idyllic in Adichie's story if its focus is taken to be a reductive encounter or the exchange between the two women. As Aljunied states that "political Islam does not necessarily influence the shape of Muslim cosmopolitanism in the marketplace" (Aljunied 2016, 12). Adichie, on the other hand, shelters the two women in a shop but frames the two oppositional spaces—shop and marketplace—with a window to delve into the projective and recessional politics of Christians and Muslims in Nigeria as they respatialize relationships against the official borders of the nation and the fixed intervals of the clock (to evoke Dimock) (12). As such, Adichie flips the idea of seamless, affable communication, untouched by political violence, in the conflict outside the shop that is enacted, if with stronger intensity, and pushed to its limits by the private experience inside the shop's walls. This occurs not as a separate space—as a site of the privileged interlocutor that risks reproducing the inequality characteristic of historical and material imbalances—but as cosmopolitically projective and recessional spaces outside the window (the marketplace) and the one inside it (the shop) that fold in broader conflicts.

Not only the window but the unnamed narrator of the story also moves the narrative out of its linear temporality through past, present, and future. The narrator's voice also troubles the spatialization of the shop and the marketplace. It would seem that the market serves as the backdrop of the mob. However, it is the encounter that serves as the backdrop for both the marketplace and the mob. This respatialization—diegetic and physical—is precisely an *ummah*-building technique that exposes Chika's revised view of Muslims and rebalances inequalities. I will discuss this in detail in the next section. Here, I focus on the projective and recessive temporality of the narrative as it pauses on the space of the marketplace and the ways in which the private encounter spills into the space of the pitched battle outside. Diegetically, by projecting into the future, we learn that Nnedi is still missing, perhaps dead. In Adichie's story, this temporal projection overlaps with the spatial projection of the marketplace to situate interreligious conflicts in Nigeria: "The reactionary Hausa-speaking Muslims in the North have a history of violence against non-Muslims," and "Hausa Muslim zealots attacking Igbo Christians, and sometimes Igbo Christians going on murderous missions of revenge" (Adichie 2009, 49). The most recognizable and well-known feature of this interreligious conflict, however, is said to be the ascension of Boko Haram, a militant religious organization founded in 2002 as a school and youth center for Muslims in Maiduguri. Roman Loimeier's assessment of Boko Haram is insightful here in broadening the framework of understanding Adichie's story from the narrow ambit of a perceived indictment of Boko Haram's activities that remain more widely circulated in Western media.

For the purpose of my analysis, this brief detour helps in probing the framework of transnationalism—and charting the flow of influences and "theory" and the West as privileged interlocutor—that Adichie relocates transgeographically through this story. More importantly, this brief discussion on the background of Boko Haram also corrects the misconception that is widely circulated in Western media outlets: that the terror outfit was formed to attack only Christians. David Shariatmadari (2012) somewhat incorrectly wrote the following in the *Guardian*:

> Boko Haram, whose name means "western education is forbidden," emerged in Maiduguri, in Nigeria's north-east, in 2002. *Since then* it has mainly carried out attacks on Christians in northern or "middle belt" states (emphasis added).

Loimeier states that an improper understanding of the "true character" of the organization can misleadingly result in "narrow-minded" approaches to the social roots of interreligious relations in northern Nigeria (2012, 138). For one, Loimeier details the complex history of religious reform in northern Nigeria, tracing its more recent origins to the *Yan Izala* movement in the 1960s. Boko Haram, asserts Loimeier, did not form out of nowhere. The radical group is certainly not the first of its kind either, he clarifies, comprising a long history of dissent and disagreement over theological positions on education, employment, social structures, and institutions by Boko Haram's founder, Muhammad Yusuf, and his teacher, Jafar Mahmud Adam. These disagreements, notes Loimeier, took the shape of protracted speeches, sermons, debates in pamphlets, CDs, and cassettes over a number of years, culminating in Yusuf's disavowal of the Nigerian state and the sultan of Sokoto (the nominal head of Nigerian Muslims), aligning himself increasingly with Wahhabi positions on politics (149). It was only in 2003, when the theological disagreements of the two prominent figures became public, did the followers of the respective schools resort to violence, including attacking police and security personnel, thus leading the Nigerian public to label Yusuf's outfit as the "Nigerian Taliban," a label quickly adopted by the Western media (150).

Only some years after the publication of "The Scarf" (2002) and "A Private Experience" (2008) did Boko Haram begin diversifying its strategies of violence by attacking churches, especially Pentecostal churches. Up until then, the outfit was known primarily for "drive-by" attacks or "hit and run" shootings at targets, mostly police stations and security personnel (151). Moreover, the history of Christian-Muslim strife predates its increased association with Boko Haram extremism. Even Sufi leaders in the 1960s and 1970s deplored the *Yan Izala* for indicting fellow Muslims instead of attacking what they considered to be "the real enemy"—or Christians. In the context of the story under analysis, then, a recent report by the Council of Foreign Relations predictably focuses more on Boko Haram's common sites of attack, namely churches and mosques:

> Boko Haram frequently attacks churches and mosques. Through 2014, Boko Haram targeted churches more often than mosques. In its messaging and public statements, the group has closely linked Christianity with the West, Nigeria's secular government, and ethnic groups from other parts of Nigeria that are often perceived as rivals for local influence.[8] (Campbell and Harwood 2018)

As inferred from Loimeier's analysis of the history and motivations of the Boko Haram movement, Adichie makes no explicit mention of Boko

Haram in the story, nor does she tie the local events of Christian-Muslim violence to such wider problems as Islamophobia even though the havoc wreaked by the religious mob that she describes in detail is not unlike the carnage wrought by the extremist group, parading, for instance, the severed head of a man caught driving his scooter over a copy of the "Holy Koran" (2012, 46). Instead, her explicit avoidance of any ascriptions of interreligious conflicts to a local (Boko Haram) or global (9/11) scale suggests the folding of a transnational issue—religious intolerance, extremism, and violence—within the mob in the marketplace. In other words, she spatializes internal violence within a more immediate problem to explore interreligious topologies through a framework other than the transnational one offered to understand interfaith tensions. This framework, as I analyze in the next section, provides a more accurate and inclusive way to understand interfaith relationships.

Rebalancing Power: The Space of the Window

In this and the next section, I show that the windowed relationship rebalances power between groups perceived as marginalized on account of their religion or class as in the case of the Muslim woman in the story. I focus on several techniques by which power is rebalanced—the vendor's responses that redress presumptions of class and religion; the shuttling of time between past, present, and future perceptions; the vendor's act of praying; and the various iterations of the story itself that I examine in greater detail in the following section. The windowed encounter fosters *ummah* in the Muslim vendor's initiative to connect with Chika as a member of another community bound by a common humanity. This encounter respatializes the meaning of *ummah* from just a group of Muslim believers, thus expanding its meaning to include non-Muslims. Adichie describes the present and futuristic doubleness of the window: "Later, Chika will learn that, as she and the woman are speaking, Hausa Muslims are hacking down Igbo Christians with machetes, clubbing them with stones. But now she says, "Thank you for calling me." . . . Thank you" (2009, 44). The window frames in not only the doubleness of the self (based on past times and past selves), but it also exposes the self's double standards temporally—"later," "But now"—as Chika thanks the woman for saving her life, thereby fostering a connection and unfurling a revision of her views to contrast the communal bloodshed outside. In this way, the window loosens its historically and socially constructed prejudices in the present exchange between the two women, reiterating the doubleness of Ferguson's evocation of the shadow as "an inseparable other-who is-also-oneself to whom one is bound," reminding the self of gaps, margins, and darkness in its own construction of the other, and not of the other as a negative or an absence (17). The doubleness of the window's frame is also enhanced by the nonlinearity of the story's structure as it dispels the deposition of power by shuttling back and forth between the past and the present in the lives of the two protagonists and even historically about Nigeria and British colonialism.

In a rare analysis of the story, Carmen McCain holds that the story is told from Chika's perspective who disparagingly views the Hausa vendor, never learning her name, and misrepresenting her actions of praying as the Hausa woman removes her scarf to spread it on the ground to pray (2014, 108, 109).[9] The story, concludes McCain, is told from the perspective of an elite, upper-class, and privileged Christian:

> Chika spends a lot of time imagining how different the Hausa woman's life is from her own, but she asks the woman very little—not even her name. Adichie's representation of the woman in her story is sympathetic, but it is not accurate. Apparently, neither she nor her Western editor actually know enough about Muslim or Hausa women to correctly portray how they pray. The title "A Private Experience" draws on the language of privacy in Islam but leaves us only with a sense of Chika's experience and not that of the Muslim woman who helps hide her. Such a focus is only one side of a much larger story. (166)

Like McCain, Gladys Denkyi-Manieson reads the story as a demeaning gesture by the elite woman toward the illiterate Muslim woman:

> Two women (one a medical student and the other an onion seller) are trapped in a room when riots spark up in Kano market. The latter woman, an illiterate Hausa Muslim in her small ways tries to comfort the former, a literate. But as has become the customer of the 21st century African elite woman, she begins to demean and downplay the intelligence of the illiterate onion seller who has saved her life. Chika, the Med-

ical student is forced into reality when the illiterate woman begins to query and subtly challenged [sic] her knowledge of medicine. (2017, 54)

Admittedly, the relationship starts out with Chika having the upper hand, stereotyping the Hausa vendor, learning very little about her, and internally deriding her ignorance and crude appearance. Denkyi-Manieson is right about the challenge to Chika's stereotype, as is McCain about a "larger story." However, as Denkyi-Manieson also adds, the "illiterate vendor" begins to challenge Chika's smug knowledge and self-assurance because of it (54).

Rebalancing in the context of African women's writing is not simply about reversing the direction of the flow of influences and information to the weaker of the constituents in a transnational relationship. It is about recognizing that the periphery can have other interlocutors and be poorly informed about the center.[10] This is why the vendor remains vague about Chika's sister despite learning her name. Moreover, the Hausa woman's unpretentious questions to Chika reveal unconventional knowledge of things that in fact rebalance power between the two women. Toward the end, for instance, it is Chika who calls the vendor's daughter by name ("Halima"), although the vendor remains unnamed. To rebalance the namelessness as vagueness or a lack of interest in the other is to see that it is the vendor who repeatedly refers to Chika's sister as "sister" despite knowing her name early on in the story as Chika has told her: "My sister. Her name is Nnedi" (Adichie 2009, 46). Indeed, she rebalances the unequal relationship by challenging Chika's assumptions about her, but she cannot challenge Chika's education: she is unable to match this due to centuries of class-based disparities. These chasms cannot be breached, not even by an "imagined bridge," which Chatterjee sights between incommensurabilities. Yet, these gaps can be engaged via such dialogues, exchanges, and encounters to rebalance relationships by focusing on sites other than the dominant center. These chasms show that the center (or Global North) is not the privileged venue of exchange or a privileged interlocutor. On offer here is a rebalancing of relations as an *ummah*-building technique in that it revises Chika's thinking about ethnic and religious conjunctures in her country. The *ummah*-building gesture is not to be read in the sentimental act of kindness by the Muslim woman who saves Chika's life but as operant in the revisions to Chika's thinking of Muslims and the consequent rebalancing of power as Chika realizes that she has misjudged the woman's levels of knowledge and wisdom.

Class and Religion

When the Muslim woman pulls Chika from the crowd scrambling for shelter, she cares less about being thanked for saving Chika's life and wastes no time in letting Chika know that she lost her necklace: "My necklace lost when I'm running" (43). Understandably, the upper-class Chika measures the woman through barriers that she is unable to shake off throughout the story: "Probably plastic beads threaded on the piece of string," she says to herself, when told about the necklace (43-44). The barriers multiply. The Muslim vendor appears to Chika, marked by her religion—"Northerner," "narrowness of her face," "strong Hausa accent," and "Muslim because of the scarf" (44). Chika's constant comparisons of class—her vacations in New York, her Burberry bag, and her expensive jewelry being strikingly different from the vendor's cheap plastic necklace and her nylon bra—further deepen divisions. Chika is keen on revealing that she is Christian but can do so only if this information about her identity accompanies her affluent class—the "silver finger rosary" in telling contrast to the cheap beads when imagining the necklace that the Hausa vendor says she has lost (44). The window—framing in the encounter and looking out at the mob—doubles as a frame of Chika's opaque thoughts and gaze. The space of all of Chika's external impressions of the woman on account of her cheap clothes, underclothes, accessories, unschooled language and accent, religious symbols, and appearances is consolidated in the internalization of her opinions of the woman as a poor and uneducated Muslim. It doesn't help Chika's impression that the Muslim woman is more concerned about her vegetable stall that she leaves hurriedly in the riot, wondering what will happen to it.

The vendor nevertheless rebalances power by ordering Chika to sit, advising her on the wait time, and updating her on the mob: "Sit . . . we are waiting here a long time" (46). She has a better sense of their surroundings. In broken albeit economical English, she says, "This place safe," "Close window," and "Outside is danger" (44, 45, 52). The vendor also possesses a better instinct than Chika, who perceptually conditions her impressions of the woman through material possessions and appearances. As the women talk about education, Chika has already judged the woman as inferior. She reveals to her co-occupant that she is at university studying medicine and instinctively "wonders if the woman even knows what going to university means" (49). She narrows the gulf between the two classes as she asks about Chika's "clinicals": "In school you are seeing sick people now" (48). Chika "averts her gaze so that the woman will not see the surprise" (48). In many instances the Muslim vendor has surprised Chika, making the smug upper-class medical student revise her opinions of Muslims. These revisions will solidify as the omniscient narrator peers into the future and the past to inform the reader, "Later Chika will learn that as she and the woman are speaking." (44). Projecting into the future, the narrator states, "Later she will see the hulks of burned cars" (45). Several times, the narrator looks upon this encounter and prospectively tracks corrections that Chika will make to her impressions of the vendor and all that the poorly educated Muslim woman symbolizes within this constrained space, where the air, like Chika's own thoughts, is allegorically stale, putrid, and dusty—in need of urgent ventilation or revision (45).

Shuttling of Time

This prescience—Nnedi's death—parallels Chika's own perceptual change in the encounter with the Muslim woman, and that will prepare her to confront the loss of her sister. The narrator presages the conclusions to the story and the questions in the protagonists' minds as they wonder about their loved ones lost in the mob. As the narrator indicates, "Later, the family will offer Masses over and over for Nnedi to be found safe" and

> later, when Chika and her aunt go searching throughout Kano, a policeman in the front seat of her aunt's air-conditioned car, she will see other bodies, many burned, lying lengthwise along the sides of the street. (52, 53)

This inscription of transnationalism within a transgeographic as a "distant presence" becomes increasingly clear in the way Chika imagines the radio coverage of the mob:

> She will listen to BBC radio and hear the accounts of the deaths and the riots—"religious with undertones of ethnic tension" the voice will say. And she will fling the radio to the wall and a fierce red rage will run through at how it has all been packaged and sanitized and made to fit into so few words, all those bodies. (53, 54)

She will also contrast her encounter with her reading of the mob in the *Guardian* that "the reactionary Hausa-speaking Muslims in the North have a history of violence against non-Muslims" by remembering that she has "examined the nipples and experiences the gentleness of a woman who is Hausa and Muslim" (55). However, this self-revisioning will take place also during her encounter with the vendor when she lies about her mother's use of remedies to soothe cracked nipples during breastfeeding. The narrator observes:

> She hardly lies, but the few times she does, there is always a purpose behind the lie. Now, she wonders what purpose this lie serves. . . . Later, she will wonder why she lied to the woman, why she felt the need to draw on a fictional past similar to the woman's. (50)

On her part, Chika revised a past, having realized the inequalities of their classes and the jagged histories that have widened these gendered gaps. This diegetic disclosure fosters a "bond" with the woman (50). She continues to connect with Chika as she prepares for the prayer.

Act of Prayer

The act of praying protracts the rebalancing of power between the two women as Chika has a direct experience of an act that cuts to the heart of her ill-conceived assumptions about Muslims. It rebalances power precisely because it provokes the distinction between "religion as faith" and "religion as a demarcator of difference" as Ayesha Jalal has described the function of religion today (2009, 16). When the vendor starts praying, the ritual functions as a demarcator of difference for Chika. The prayer unfolds through Chika's prejudiced and ill-informed eyes whose unstinting subjection of the Muslim woman to her entrenched stereotypes continues unmitigated as the latter prays. In the story, as the woman prays, "Chika looks away. She knows the woman is on her knees, facing Mecca, but she does not look. It is like the woman's tears, a private experience, and she wishes that she could leave the store" (52). Chika's exposure to this private experience encapsulates two things. All along she has subjected the woman to her gentrified prejudices, but the act of the woman's directness and ease of praying, like her unexpected knowledge of "clinicals" causes Chika to avert her gaze, unable to reconcile the thought of the woman on an equal footing as the woman gradually levels the field, not with education that she cannot match or sophisticated English that she cannot speak. Secondly, Chika's averted gaze is suggestive of her reluctance to learn while the Muslim woman feels no inhibitions in praying in front of Chika. The sanguine instincts that the vendor exhibits in saving Chika, commanding her to sit and wait in the shelter, asking her about her clinicals and the ease with which she converses with Chika, is absent in Chika's clumsy thoughts and mannerisms toward the vendor. Once again, the vendor appears far more sanguine than her co-occupant. It is through the diegetic tracking of Chika's changed opinions by the narrator's view and gaze that the reader discerns in Chika a revision of opinion. Toward the end of her observation of the prayer, the ritual unravels as religion as faith:

> "I wash and pray," the woman says ... the woman clumsily washes her hands and face at the tap, then removes her scarf from her neck and places it down on the floor. Chika looks away. She knows the woman is on her knees, facing Mecca, but she does not look. It is like the woman's tears, a private experience, and she wishes that she could leave the store. Or that she, too, could pray, could believe in god, see and omniscient presence in the stale air of the store. (52)

In addition to being a compulsory ritual, the *salat* (or canonical prayer) is also a source of meditative relief for stress as the woman uses the moment to calm herself from worrying about her daughter's whereabouts in the riot.

Lila Abu Lughod describes the distinction between religious ritual and the political theorizations of Muslims in that rituals do not necessarily explain political actions or motives for a number of practices that have come to define Muslims and Islam in the global imaginary. Abu Lughod connects the numerous requests for talks on radios and college campuses she received following the US war in Afghanistan to three uniformly posed questions by journalists and her hosts to explain the short steps from ritual to politics and prejudice. "Do Muslim women believe 'x'? Are Muslim women 'y'? Does Islam allow 'z' for women?"[11] writes Abu Lughod (2002), elucidating a fitting response to the uniformity of these questions:

> What is striking about these three ideas for news programs is that there was a consistent resort to the cultural, as if knowing

something about women and Islam or the meaning of a religious ritual would help one understand the tragic attack on New York's World Trade Center and the U.S. Pentagon or how Afghanistan had come to be ruled by the Taliban. (784)

This distinction between religious rituals and political theorizations of a community is sufficient to explain Adichie's purpose in the story to separate the private (shop) from the political (marketplace) but illustrate the incommensurability of the sources of experiences. The misconstrual of rituals as political explanations is captured in the depiction of the vendor's prayer. Adichie uses *salat* as an example of rituals that do not explain the mob outside but rather is a means of understanding the other as a constituent of the mob. Similarly, the Muslim woman's ability to pray even at such a tense moment underscores the distinction between not only the private and the political but also the equally private and internal tenor of Chika's perceptions, thus doubling and erasing at the same time the differences between the violence outside and the gradual, reluctant, and involuntary revisions inside Chika. This multiple spatial gaze—class, religion, and gender—has most valence for the theorization of the transnational as an inscription within the transgeographic for understanding the other.

The descriptions of the viewing of the woman's prayer inscribe multiple connections—the private experience of the vendor's spirituality, the unfolding of Chika's prejudices and a recalibration of her stereotypes, and the extension and inscription of this private experience with the riotous violence on the street outside the store. Adichie illustrates this projective and recessional experience in the expression "a private experience" (Adichie 2009, 52). For whom is this experience private, the woman or Chika's stereotypes? Which experience is private—the prayer, the encounter, Chika's revised thinking, or Chika witnessing the woman praying? Conjuncturally then, three things—the doubleness of the personal act of praying despite the violence outside, the personal revisions of perceptions of the other, and the public act of spectatorship of this private prayer—enable an overturning of the public and impersonal acts of violence between the two communities by centralizing the personal, human, and internal dimensions of relationships between fraught communities. In this sense, Adichie's double-edged depiction of multispatial private and public spheres is instructive of the relationship of gender to the nation, mediated as in this case by the relationship of gender to a multireligious or multiethnic community, or multitransgeographic relationships.

Against this overtly explicit balancing of Chika's stereotypes and prejudices, from not even asking the woman's name, and continually subjecting her to a smug gaze, Adichie's purpose gradually emerges—dispelling Islamophobic reactions in collusions of the media along with upper-class Nigerians, layered with historical fissures that continue to rent the social fabric of multireligious societies. Chika's stereotypes of the Hausa woman, of being illiterate, poor, and ignorant, have influenced her feelings in eschewing the media accounts of the violence she has witnessed firsthand. In Chika's gesture of slamming the radio against the wall as an international/transnational radio channel attempts to cover the experience of ethnic violence in Kano City, we find the respatialization of the transnational—its impersonal and distant account of violence—in an experience that Chika has lived. The transnational then and its account—the BBC and the *Guardian*—become a distant presence with their few words where the actual borders and barriers were crossed by Chika and the Muslim vendor in a dusty, smoke-filled shop. Like the smoke and dust, the transnational BBC permeates the experience as a presence but does not occupy a central position in a relationship that shifts the space of the transnational to a more transgeographic or proximal encounter, exchange, or dialogue. Chika's refutation of the BBC and the *Guardian* is also meant to search for an alternative for a common humanity, redefining the *ummah* also as a community of humanity that perhaps prompted the Muslim woman to reach out to Chika at the start of the story when saving her life and changing the direction in which Chika was originally running toward the direction of the small shop that eventually saves their lives.

Rebalancing Two Stories: "The Scarf" (2002) and "A Private Experience" (2009)

Adichie registers an insistent focus on revising and consequently rebalancing relationships. This is not only the case of the vendor's unintelligent questions and her gradual equalizing of power from but also in the various versions of the story, starting with "The Scarf" in 2002, then in 2004, and finally in 2009 in its present iteration as "A Private Experience." This insistent focus on revising the story mirrors Chika's perceptual change to foreground rebalancing relationships. A more compelling sign of rebalancing as self-revisions can be found in a comparative reading of the two versions of the story, appearing first as "The Scarf" and then under the current title. In an insightful study of Adichie's portrayal of religion, Daria Tunca comparatively analyzes Adichie's first two novels, *Half of a Yellow Sun* and *Purple Hibiscus*; her stories "Father Chinedu" and "Miracle"; and her lesser-known poems published under her Americanized name, "Amanda N. Adichie," along with the various versions of "A Private Experience" and even her play, *For Love of Biafra*. Tunca (2013) tracks Adichie's "juvenilia," and "indecisions" on her "views on religion," and her "crisis of faith" (51, 52, 55). I would say that the reward of delving into Adichie's ruminations on religion lies not only in charting her indecisions and evolutions but in examining the self-revision that arises from the treatment of religion in relation to other faiths, suggesting perhaps an understanding of oneself that transpires only topologically. Unusual then in this corpus of Adichie's writing on religion is the interplay of religion with other systems of belief, namely Islam (in her second novel) and in the various versions of "A Private Experience." Reading "The Scarf" first, Tunca makes a clear division between class and religion by attributing the entrenchment of differences between the two women to class or "social status" and not to religious backgrounds or ethnicity (2002, 52). While Chika is chauffeured around in her aunt's car, notes Tunca, the vendor takes two buses to work—details that are present in the first version of the story but not in its latest version. Admittedly, Adichie compounds these divisions in descriptions of the two women's accessories—"plastic beads threaded on a piece of string" is the first class-based thought that Chika harbors toward the woman in the latest version of the story but not in the first iteration (2009, 43–44). She follows up this impression with "a lower class woman who puts money in her bra, a trader whose mind is not occupied with questioning abstract ideologies or case studies, but with the price of groundnuts" (28).

However, the relational exploration of religious beliefs in these two stories occasions a rethinking of the transnational and its space over time as interethnic relations in Nigeria were linked to tensions on a broader scale. For instance, in both iterations, Adichie anchors identity to ethnicity and religion. She notes, "Even without the woman's strong Hausa accent, Chika can tell she is a Northerner from the narrowness of her face . . . and that she is Muslim, because of the scarf" (44). Although modified, this observation in the first iteration of the story contains the same conjunctural references to religion, ethnicity and language (Adichie 2002, 26). Another clue lies in Nnedi's statement in "The Scarf" where she says, "Christianity is our most nominal and colonised [*sic*] identity"

(29). This statement appears thus in "A Private Experience": "Rosaries are really magical potions, and I don't need those, thank you" (2009, 52). Tunca reads the latter statement as more provocative than the first one. But in its direct attack on the imperial provenance of the religion, with its attendant class distinctions and ethnic fissures that have devolved into unspeakable acts of violence in present-day Nigeria, I see Nnedi's earlier statement as far more inflammatory and intuitive in its description of the current dispensation. Reading the latest version of the story (2009) as a progression in nuance and a tempering of the earlier reductive stereotype of only class distinctions, rather than as a revision, is enabled by Nnedi's candor, "I don't need those," whereas the earlier version of the story lacks such directness.

Yet, Adichie is known to indict institutionalized forms of religion in both Islam and Christianity. In her public denouncement of both Christian and Muslim institutions in fomenting violence, years after the publication of the two iterations of the story, Adichie reportedly tells the following to the *Guardian*:

> Christian leaders must continue to preach peace and togetherness so that Christians do not retaliate, Muslim leaders must strongly and repeatedly condemn the violence against Christians and make it clear that Boko Haram does not represent Nigerian Islam. (Shariatmadari 2012)

Both of Nnedi's statements thus can be read relationally without the second one canceling out the previous one even in a chronological sense where Adichie first recognizes the historical imperialism of Christianity and its nominal effect on Nigerians and then disclaims them by rejecting religious symbols as supernatural solutions. Carmen McCain makes the astute observation that Adichie is ignorant of Muslim practices in that she allows her character to remove her scarf and use it as a prayer mat, something that a more knowledgeable writer would have avoided. This also reveals Adichie's self-awareness of her ignorance or voids in knowledge that need breaching through such encounters and exchanges that would heal historical and material wounds (2014, 108, 109).

This focus on self-revisions through the gaze on the other—the doubling that Menon (2013) identifies in the self from a previous time ("a former self")—can be discerned in the changing titles of the two pieces (21). In the title of the earlier version, Adichie uses the word "scarf," a metonym for Muslim women, and by extension for Islam, to evoke Abbas again (McCain 2014, 159). In replacing the title, perhaps Adichie revises her own perceptions like Chika does in realizing that she has misunderstood and misread the Muslim vendor. The titular revision rebalances relationships as Adichie now steers her understanding of religion in terms of public-private and experiential demarcations, separate from the state and official politics that are used to explain and justify a religion and its practitioners, and different from the earlier impersonal and metonymic stereotypes used to appraise Muslims. Such self-revisions inhere with the transformation of certainties, weaned on prejudices and stereotypes, to uncertainties nursed by personal experiences, as proffered by Adichie in the two versions of the story. Chika in the earlier story is "certain that the woman can tell she is Igbo and Christian" (Adichie 2002, 26) whereas in the latter version, "Chika wonders if the woman is looking at her as well, if the woman can tell, from her light complexion and the silver finger rosary . . . that she is Igbo and Christian" (2009, 44). A similar revision occurs from "Chika is certain the woman has no clue what it means to study medicine or political science" in "The Scarf" (2002, 27) to "Chika wonders if the woman even knows what going to university means" in "A Private Experience" (2009, 47). Most of all, such revisions point to the rebalancing of relationships that occur not only through the vendor's gestures of using her scarf to nurse Chika's wound but, as seen in the previous section of this study, through Chika's self-corrections of her prejudiced optics of the Muslim vendor.

Solidarity and *Ummah*-building Strategies

An abiding goal of transnational feminist theorizations is solidarity. Despite incommensurable differences, feminist theorists firmly advocate solidarity as the most effective way of fighting fragmentation that seeks to defeat feminist struggles. My aim throughout the present project is to rethink solidarity as a goal of transnational feminist organizing. Mohanty and Alexander state, "Working in solidarity with different women of color was at times insufficient to entirely subvert acts of racial fragmentation aimed at separating women of color from each other" (1996, xiv–xv). Reading this can mean that women must unite despite differences, or as Mohanty and Alexander assert, women must commit themselves to "feminist communities founded on different grounds," and such a commitment would automatically aspire to solidarity (1996, xv). Ultimately, feminists must unite even if not around the same goals. Chowdhury has suggested that even dissident friendships aspire to solidarity and are interchangeable with alliance and community because they are premised on "human connection" (2016, 163). But as Andrew Shryock (2010) warns, "When 'friendship' is subordinated to the demands of sameness—whether conceived in national or human terms—it can be just as coercive, just as prone to misrecognition, as the sentiments of hostility is meant to correct" (9). Shryock thus recommends approaching relationships beyond the politics of enemy and friend particularly as they pertain to issues of Islamophobia, terrorism, and Islamophilia in a politically charged global context. Shryock lists the factors at stake in assessing the situation today—colonial histories, the dangers of inverting Islamophobic impulses to produce their opposites in "the image of the Muslim as friend, as a figure identified with the Self" and "impervious to nuance" (10). Predicating human connections and communities on solidarity thus entails the danger of reproducing the forced attachment to goals and principles that risk reproducing the hegemony that the principles of solidarity are meant to counter.[12] Two facts in the story point to a revised framing of solidarity for transnational feminist issues.

First, the absence of specific invocations of any named interreligious tensions itself underlines Adichie's refusal to foreclose the women's interactions as a response in solidarity to conflict. Second, the Muslim vendor climbs out of the window the following morning. The act of climbing out symbolizes the possibility of leaving open the outcome of such encounters. The Muslim vendor's parting words to Chika are, "Wash your leg well-well. Greet your sister, greet your people," to which Chika will also reply the same, "Greet your people also. Greet your baby and Halima" (2009, 56). Eve Eisenberg underlines that in her longer work Adichie is "able to think through and model alternative routes to authorial 'interpellation'" but in the short story the restriction on its length "frees Adichie from the obligation to provide closure of positive, resistant, 'politically efficacious' answers" (2013, 9, 10).[13] Read in this vein, solidarity in this "unlikely alliance," between Chika and the vendor is "potentially transformative, personally and socially transformative," as Chowdhury and Philippose describe unlikely friendships in that Chika becomes gradually aware of gender differences and differential oppression (2016, 164). By framing the women's private encounter within the shop whose only outlet is a window, the optics of the frame signify going beyond the reductionist relationship of tolerance and conflict that aims at "challenging the notion that Muslim-Christian difference is inherently conflictual" (Nolte, Ogen, and Jones 2017, 257). Shryock's insistence on the study of Islam beyond the politics of enemy or friend decodes the topology that Adichie delineates in this story for she draws no such conclusions of reconciliation or revision, leaving open the possibility—the window—where two women have interacted with one another, and introspectively and retrospectively faced their own stereotypes, prejudices, and shortcomings.

Windowed Topologies of Religion and Nationality in Africa in Mariama Ba's *So Long a Letter*

As a literary attempt to claim community in Africa, Mariama Ba's classic novel *So Long a Letter* focuses on identity politics in African societies. While Ramatoulaye, the narrator of the novel and Aissatou, her best friend and interlocutor, are definitely the main characters in the story, it is through a brief detour to introduce Jacqueline that Ba centralizes a much heavier question on community in her newly independent country, Senegal.[14] Published in 1979 in French as *Une si longue lettre*, Ba's novel remains a monumental narrative for its deeply personal ruminations on a multitude of topics related to gender and national identity. It continues to dominate literary discussions even today. As I discuss in this section, Jacqueline's example enables Ba to generatively explore the possibilities of a human community, a preoccupation she enthusiastically announces early on in the novel to merge her promising future with that of her young nation. This is especially so as Ba metaphorizes the family as nation when she states that the success of the nation depends inevitably on the family (1981, 89). The family, however, and consequently the nation for Ba, emerges as a space structured by the politics of the majority religion in Senegal, Islam, and by patriarchal privilege. Thus, the type of family that Ba evokes is assumed to be of one or the other class (rich or poor); one or the other level of education (aware or unaware); traditionally and conventionally bound by marriage (separated or united) (89). The kind of nationalism she therefore envisions for marriage, family—and by extension, community to subtend—underlines her frustration with a culturally, religiously, ethnically homogenous nation space. In this landscape, Jacqueline can be said to exemplify Ba's experimentation with the possibility of a different brand of family that determines the success of the nation space.

Ba uses heterogeneity as a trope to discuss the nation. She calls her protagonist the "first pioneers of the promotion of African women," embarking on "an uncommon destiny" to twine the futures of the young nation with that of a newly educated class of young women (14, 15). Ba contextualizes Senegalese society and its heterogeneity to signify across national boundaries, going beyond Senegal to the rest of Africa and universally beyond as she ponders on the possibility of national and transnational religious communities and even across time. Ba thus charts the transformation of her newly independent country in such social updates to construct a topological narrative of relationships with other systems of belief, structures of organization, and patterns of habits. Ramatoulaye alludes early on to postindependent Africa as "autonomous republics" at school in that the girls from various African nations appear the same, except for the "specific racial features" (15). Ramatoulaye thus cultivates a vision of the world and "universal moral values" for the construction of a "new Africa" and the "promotion of the black woman" (16). Across time, Ramatoulaye tracks the changes in the Fann Hospital and its exact location:

> on the road to Ouakam, near the university, where medical students do their internship as they do at the Aristide le Dantec hospital. This hospital did not exist at the time Mawdo Ba and Samba Diack studied at the school of Medicine and Pharmacy. (43)

Braided in this discourse of a new Africa are spatial snapshots—new buildings, landmarks, developments in the newly independent country, novel structures and systems replacing older ways—that reveal Ba's intention of narrating the story of a new Africa. In fact, János Riesz (1991) argues that the novel is essentially about education as it traces the transformations from colonial to postcolonial Senegal through modifications in professional training for teachers, vocational training for students both traditional and modern, with all their benefits and drawbacks (29). Thus Ramatoulaye compares new choices for professions and schooling as the "trowel is spurned" for book learning (18). Again, through this dual mapping of past and present, nostalgia and future, tradition and modernity, Ba undertakes a topological exploration of diverse social systems.

It is against this eager anticipation of a "new Africa," modifying an older one, that Ba uses marriage as a trope of encounters and exchanges to enthusiastically explore the potential of a transgeographic community. Through the black woman, as Ba puts it, one can understand this new Africa and vice versa, thus also centralizing gender in this new society that is transforming in front of her eyes (1981, 16). However, Ba's new Africa is even more complex, layered, and bold. It must consider the tangential and non-Senegalese figure of Jacqueline. Once both Aissatou and Ramatoulaye have faced the shock of desertion and emotional betrayal at the hands of insensitive spouses, Ramatoulaye turns to a non-Senegalese, non-Muslim (Jacqueline's) experience to underscore the extent of emotional damage wrought by a national patriarchal order of a monochromatic culture. She does so to confront her disillusioned belief in the universal values of human connections. For Ba, the family, in this sense, cannot assure the success of the nation in the wake of such emotional and gendered upheaval in its midst. Jacqueline, "the Ivoirian," Ramatoulaye tells us, "disobeyed her Protestant parents and had married Samba Diack, a contemporary of Mawdo Ba, a doctor like him," stationed temporarily in Abidjan (41). Senegal, however, is a new world for Jacqueline, "a world with different reactions, temperament and mentality from that in which she had grown up" (42). Ramatoulaye believes that the national distinctions that may produce this temperamental difference stem from religious differences: "In addition, her husband's relatives—always the relatives—were cool towards her because she refused to adopt the Muslim religion and went instead to the Protestant church every Sunday" (42). Jacqueline is derisively labeled "*gnac*" (or backward) (from the hinterland) for all her willingness to "truly become Senegalese" (42). Furthermore, her husband's adultery and extramarital excesses drive Jacqueline to mental despair. She begins to lose her sanity and suffers from delusions and "neuro-vegetative dystonia" (44). She is admitted to the psychiatric ward but is also released soon after when diagnosed only with depression. She promises to fight back, leaves the hospital "re-animated," and gives herself a reason to live (45). Ramatoulaye recognizes it as a "happy ending" (45).

To examine transnational limits, Ba sets out to test her hypothesis on race, religion, and nationality. Ramatoulaye first experiments with race as racial sameness that alone would suffice to accept Jacqueline in Senegalese society (overcoming national boundaries). Racial sameness reaches across African nation-states, as Ramatoulaye frequently uses the term "black women" to describe African women. She then foregrounds Jacqueline's example as a Christian, Ivoirian woman beyond the visible identity of only her "blackness" to test her hypothesis of the definition of Senegalese that transcends the Muslim religion or common nationality. In testing her hypothesis of racial solidarity, Ramatoulaye stumbles at transnationalism when it is mixed with religion and realizes that the girls from Dahomey and Guinea are the same as her, but Jacqueline or Mireille are not. Why? Mireille is white, French, symbolic of the former colonizer, it may be conceded, but Jacqueline is not. She is a black African as Ramatoulaye reasons in her attempt to blur the national and ethnic distinctions when she saw no difference between the girls from Dahomey, Guinea, and herself. She wonders:

> A black African, she should have been able to fit in without difficulty into a black African society. Senegal and Ivory Coast have both experienced the same colonial power. But Africa is diverse, divided. The same country can change its character and outlook several times over, from north to south, or from east to west. (42)

Neither Jacqueline's nor Mireille's example in Ba's other novel *Scarlet Song* can be simplistically seen as Ba's despair with interracial tensions. Rather, they are to be seen as a scathing denunciation of a society's failure to envision interracial and interreligious communities, or the "universal moral values" that Ramatoulaye and Aissatou eagerly imbibed and envisaged as pioneers of the young nation at the dawn of independence from colonial servitude (15). The heady hope and feverish excitement of an optimistic future for a "new Africa" are not only crushed by the grim reality of gendered subordination as both Mawdo and Modou—also pioneers in their own right of a new class of educated African intellectuals—cruelly overlook gendered emancipation in their ambitious albeit patriarchally centered ambitions for a new Africa. The optimism is rudely dashed by Jacqueline's feeling of "mental alienation," rudely shattering Ba's idealism about the unifying values of racial unity (45).

Earlier in the novel, Ba intimates another transgeographic hurdle—class difference—in Aissatou's tragedy. Aissatou is from a lower class. Her father is a goldsmith. Mawdo's family is of noble and aristocratic lineage, a "Guelewar" (17). Progressively resolute in his aims and vision of a new Africa, Mawdo marries Aissatou despite his mother's vehement disapproval. He raises Aissatou "up to his own level, he the son of a princess and you a child from the forges. His mother's rejection did not frighten him," as Ramatoulaye recounts Aissatou's misfortune (19). Even as observant and dutiful Muslims, Ba nostalgically describes "Christmas Eve parties organized by several couples, with the costs shared equally, and held in turns in the different homes" (21). Nevertheless, the transgeographic gulf illustrated in Aïssatou's unfortunate experience, renders interfaith relationships, as Ba reads them, unfeasible even at a time of unprecedented national reconstruction and rebirth. Ba quickly extricates her vision of a new Africa from the one she had as a younger woman upon realizing that all visions of the new Africa will fail unless monocultural ideals are decidedly buried. She thus extricates transnationalism from fixations of national relationships and respatializes the new Africa within geographies of religion, class, ethnicities, and other such divides in that Jacqueline is not only an Ivoirian, not in addition to, but at the same time a Christian. Ba decisively rejects the forging of a transnational alliance only in terms of unifying national or racial differences. The question then becomes whether Jacqueline would be more welcome if she were a Senegalese Christian but not an Ivoirian one.

Like Adichie, Ba also presents the story of gender within the context of Africa's social history of racial, national, and religious differences and complicates it by conflating gendered experiences in Senegal with that of the Ivory Coast. But Ba layers the theme of gendered subordination with the example of Jacqueline's polygamous situation by illustrating Jacqueline's oppression on account of her religion and nationality and not only as a gendered victim of polygamy. Thus, with Jacqueline's example, Ba extends the discussion beyond national and religious lines and expands the terrain of transnational feminist discussion to explore the question of *ummah* or community in Africa's newly independent context as a topology that is at once subnational and transnational. She asks if Jacqueline would be more welcome as a *Senegalese* Christian, and trans- or cross-national. She also asks why the Christian, Ivoirian Jacqueline's *black* Africanness is not enough to welcome her into another black society. Thus Ba denounces her parochial society for oppressing Jacqueline, the Ivoirian and Christian, and bemoans the inability of the African continent to look within and beyond patriarchally instituted boundaries that women are able to overcome through religious and national intercourse, as in Jacqueline's case through her marriage to a Senegalese Muslim.

Interreligious Windows and Marriage in Abubakar Gimba's *Sacred Apples*

Abubakar Gimba's novel *Sacred Apples* (1997) is feminist in its purpose, as he dedicates it to women—to mothers, wives, "womankind," and "womanhood." The novel maps a woman's journey from psychological dependence on male guardianship in marriage to gendered self-determination in the figure of Zahrah. Zahrah divorces her overbearing husband Yazid for adultery and moves out of his home with their two children. Penniless and clueless about her future as she lived in Yazid's shadow, Zahrah quickly emerges from a state of psychological dependence on men to discover her own abilities. This is facilitated by Miriam, a Roman Catholic friend who is married to a Muslim (67). Over the course of the story, the Christian woman becomes "like her sister" (70). The conversations with Miriam serve as models for community that develop within national borders across geographies of religion. Zahrah actively claims this community with Miriam to understand her own stance on gender and society. As a result of this community, Miriam "had become Zahrah's role model as a woman: intelligent, assertive, and having a career" (66). Thus, Miriam's abetment of Zahrah's consciousness as an independent woman twins the novel's dedication to women and gendered self-determination as a statement on pluralism within Nigeria. This strong sense of communion and community with a Christian woman makes a double statement about the nation space that must be equitable on both religious and gendered grounds. Gimba's novel unambiguously exemplifies the idea that equitable and inclusive transnational organizing must proceed from this stance. Equally, solidarity, as seen in Miriam's and Zahrah's community, develops transgeographically across religions and genders first within national spaces. Furthermore, aesthetically, the novel's narrative on gendered consciousness unfolds as a dialogue, a multireligious exchange that illustrates Zahrah's gender consciousness. Like Ba's narrative that unravels in tandem with the transformation of the newly independent nation-state, Zahrah's journey of gender consciousness is traced on pluralism. In other words, the route to gendered consciousness is essentially through an understanding of other religions. Thus Gimba's presents Zahrah's psychological transformation as an exchange with Miriam.

A long series of conversations on gendered roles, rights, and responsibilities spurs Zahrah's gendered consciousness. She gradually revises her thinking about entrenched gendered roles after several conversations on gendered identity and roles. Zahrah feels light in spirit, much happier, stronger, and "more confident in herself" (86). Zahrah first encounters independence through Miriam's reference to the custom in Islam of taking the husband's name upon marriage. Miriam tells Zahrah that her Muslim husband suggested that she should "retain my father's name, and remain Miriam George. I thought he was up to something mischievous, till he showed me the place in your Book where it says, Call them by their father's name" (67). Zahrah compares this provision in Islam with her former spouse's unwillingness to let Zahrah keep her maiden name to expose the gap between religious decree with individual practice. The longest exchange deals with the conjugal contract as the first step toward an equitable community. Gimba describes the reality of rights and responsibilities:

> Most conjugal contracts get adhered to according to a dual mode of reading—one loudly, the second in very silent whispers. The rights of the husband and the responsibilities of the wife get a loud reading, while the rights of the wife and the responsibilities of the husband get an inaudible whisper. And the man always does the reading . . . often times, in the name of God! (66, 67)

Along the same lines, Zahrah recognizes sexually entrenched roles such as domestic labor that is promoted as women's responsibility, implicitly establishing men's rights or exemption from domestic responsibilities. She takes up, for instance, the paradox behind the commonplace label "working mother" to reflect deeply on the sexist perceptions of women's labor in society and boldly declares that the label "working mother is a euphemism for servitude . . . any mother knows that she has her plate full being just a mother. To have to work in addition to that is exploitation" (73, 74). Feminism for her is not an attempt to outdo men by imitating them but something that emphasizes women's differences. Resonant of the common theorization on African feminism that states equality but not sameness, Zahrah describes the value of homemaking: "Being a housewife is no less a full-time undertaking than being a doctor or pharmacist or nurse" (75, 84). Ba expressed a similar idea when she spotlighted housewives for the hidden economic value in a household and in society: "Those women we call housewives deserve praise . . . the management of the home is an art" (63).

In all three works of fiction one encounters a reinstantiation of the transnational as a presence in religiously and ethnically diverse meetings, exchanges, and dialogues within national borders. The private experience inside the shop in Adichie's story exposes the etiology of deep-rooted stereotypes while the other side of the window enacts this etiology. In

Ba's novel, likewise, Jacqueline's example serves as a window onto the topological histories of religions and national differences as Ba attempts to understand relationships between religions, nationalities, and genders. Essentially, in Jacqueline's failed interreligious and transnational marriage, Ba seems to be saying that the relationship is less about gendered subordination than about national and religious divides that hamper Africa's internal attempt at social progress. For Ba, transnationalism lies in foregrounding Africa's national pluralisms and embracing differences. She thus evinces Jacqueline's example to contrast the failure of her universal vision of nationless communities with the reality of bordered divides. Gimba's narrative on gendered consciousness unfolds throughout as dialogically generative of answers to questions on interreligious communities in the Bakhtinian sense of a dialogic novel. By expressing herself dialogically on gendered roles, self-determination, and psychological dependence, Zahrah reflects deeper on her internalized habits of gendered subordination to her former husband. She thus interpellates answers through this process and successfully revises her thinking to emerge much happier and lighter in spirit. This synchronous framing of encounters also rebalances power as the women cross colonially enforced and entrenched boundaries of class, religions, and nationalities. This trans-spatial and transtemporal movement foregrounds the refusal to close the relationship as acts of solidarity or clarifications, often poorly understood in transnationalism that is theorized as a relationship toward solidarity. These encounters become an expanding metaphor for reading multihistorical and spatial encounters between religions, genders, classes, and worlds. Rather than imagine these relationships as tensions at a time between two or more sites, Adichie, Ba, and Gimba stage multiply projective and recessional worlds within each other. As the women explore transgeographic relationships, gaze outside the windows of their boundaries, and gaze back at themselves and at each other—thus turning the relationships and tensions between lines of identity inward and outward—they revise and rebalance the narrative of the nation space as plurally gendered, religious, and communal.

Chapter 3

Intimate Bonds

Marriage, Race, and *Ummah*

I think I'm a better Muslim overseas than I'm at home.

—Dina Zaman, *I Am Muslim*

"The Family is a subversive organization [*sic*]. In fact, it is the ultimate and only consistently subversive organization [*sic*]. Only the family has continued throughout history and still continues to undermine the State. The family is the permanent enemy of all enduring hierarchies, churches and ideologies."

—Ferdinand Mount, *The Subversive Family: An Alternative History of Love and Marriage*

As a person born whole and separate from man, the Filipina legitimately owns her body and herself and can chart her own future and destiny

—Lilia Quindoza Santiago, "Rebirthing Babaye: The Women's Movement in the Philippines"

As a contact zone for "dissident relationality" and friendships, the space of marriage is a fertile trope for imagining broader relationships of self to *ummah* or community and nation-state (Gandhi 2006, 185). This chapter thematizes the motif of interreligious marriages as a syncopation of the monoreligious national space, suggesting its reimagination as a transgeographic network between religions and a reimagined relationship of gender to this pluralized, mixed, and interreligious nation space. To this end, I analyze Sudanese-Egyptian writer Leila Aboulela's short story "Majed" (1999), Nigerian writer E. E. Sule's novel *Sterile Sky* (2012), Filipino writer Pearlsha Abubakar's story "Maghrib" (2008), and her essay "Naunu Na Kaw Yan? (What's Happening to You?)"[1] The interarticulations of marriage with family, community, and parenthood in Islam—its contractual and emotional valence—coupled with the dichotomous duality of divorce as the most hated (yet permissible) act in God's sight underscores it as a space webbed with innumerable connections. Because the Qur'an also serves as the basis of juridical laws in Islam, marriage is angled as a legal contract, giving primacy to its contractual, technical, and clinical purchase, often eliding the emotional and multiple other sentimental, psychological, and physical contours of this intimate union.[2] What complicates this already interarticulated trellis of valence in marriage is mixed marriages, in that they problematize the status of women in relation to the state as "reproducers of the boundaries of ethnic/national groups," to evoke Yuval Davis and Anthias, where offspring of mixed—intercaste, interethnic, and interreligious—marriages may or may not accede to legal and other state-controlled benefits (1989, 9). For example, in Egypt, "a child born to a Muslim woman and a Copt Christian man will have no legal status," point out Davis and Anthias (9). In this chapter, I focus more closely on this recasting of the nation through mixed marriages in Islam as contact zones of transgeographic intercourse and dissidence. Ferdinand Mount has powerfully argued that in the Western and Christian tradition, family based on marriage is a subversive space as it poses a strong challenge to religious observance and to the loyalty to the state (1982, 27). Mount debunks the myth that family is an offshoot of the state and society and that the church and state upheld the ideals of the family. On the contrary, Mount shows that the family is a "source of trouble" to the state and that the two are in a constant battle for power over individual devotion, attention and favor (3). The idea of marital relationships as a contact zone of dissidence, subversion, and threat to official discourses is in some ways like Deleuze and Guattari's widely cited reading of Kafka's in *Toward a Minor Literature*.[3] Deleuze and Guattari read the imagery of doors—multiple entrances, main doors, and side doors—as a resonant trope of infinite connections. It matters little from where one enters, as "none matters more than another, and no entrance is more privileged even if it seems an impasse" (1986, 3). What matters is topology—*the ways in which these doors connect with each other*: "We will be trying only to discover what other points our entrance connects to, what crossroads and galleries one passes through to link two points, what the map of the rhizome is and how the map is modified if one enters by another point," they write (3). Also of interest is how each of these connections modifies the map itself of the castle or the hotel in Kafka's eponymous stories. As a zone of encounters, unions, exchanges, and dialogues, marriage modifies the Muslim *ummah* and the nation-state in that these spaces—ostensibly united in ideologies and beliefs—are themselves multiply refracted, especially in the case of mixed marriages.

Moreover, the relationship of scales—individual, family, community, nation-state—is not simplistically linear. In major literatures, the individual, family, marriage, and social milieu seamlessly merge with the political. They state:

> In major literatures . . . the individual concern (familial, marital, and so on) joins with other no less individual concerns, the social milieu serving as a mere environment or a background; this is so much the case that none of these Oedipal intrigues are specifically indispensable or absolutely necessary but all become as one in a large space. (17)

By contrast, in minor literatures, this connection between the political and the individual is not as natural, for its political aims must be more pronounced and connected with many more networks:

> Minor literature is completely different; its cramped space forces each individual intrigue to connect immediately to politics. The individual concern thus becomes all the more necessary, indispensable, magnified, because a whole other story is vibrating within it. In this way, the family triangle connects to other triangles—commercial, economic, bureaucratic, juridical—that determine its values. (17)

Because the relationship of gender to the nation in literature has been widely theorized in the construction of the nation as "feminine" (Anne McClintock reminds us that women's citizenship to the nation is mediated by her husband's citizenship), where gendered being remains submerged within the relationship of marriage. McClintock states, "A woman's political relation to the nation was submerged as a social relation to a man through marriage. For women, citizenship in the nation was mediated by the marriage relation within the family" (1993, 65). These comparisons of minor and major literatures to the nation underpin not only the interrelated scalar themes of individual, family, and *ummah* but also, as in the case of minor literatures, a range of other stories birthed from the contact zones of interreligious connections in marriage.

In this vein, the relationship of gender to a minority religious community within a nation becomes magnified and therefore indispensable, to evoke Deleuze and Guattari, in the literature under analysis here. For instance, Pearlsha Abubakar (2008) animates precisely "a whole other story" in a minor literature by Muslim Moro writers such as herself in her short story "Maghrib" and her essay "Naunu Na Kaun Yan? (What's Happening to You?)," where she particularizes the figure of Babaye in the Islamic context (Deleuze and Guattari 1986, 17). Abubakar draws from the indigenous Filipina myth—born from man in a simultaneous yet separate birth—to move effortlessly in and out of her family (the domestic community) to a transhistorical community dating back to Abraham (see Santiago 2018, 110–130). Tracing her multireligious family to the first family in Islam from which the world is born, Abubakar folds in the meaning of *ummah* as "ummah wahida," referring to "mankind as a total religious community," and deploys this overarching model to step back into the triangulation of her multireligious polygnous family to make sense of her multiply mixed self (2008, 51). These spatial (two families, two religions, two communities in relation to the nation) and temporal vibrations (the indigenous myth of Babaye, the biblical and Qur'anic families of Abraham, and her own families) rationalize Abubakar's situation, as they respatialize the transnational as a transgeographic presence within individuals. They also echo the Moro writer's multispatial relationship with Islam, national identity, and language in three overlapping spaces: as Moro identity in a Catholic majority nation space; as Moro literature where Muslim writers seek to express their own relationship to a national literature; and third, as a space of the modern nation-state in a society emerging out of Spanish and American colonizations. Coeli Barry points to the caliber of minoritization—gendered and national—of female Muslim Filipinos. Muslim Filipino writers, observes Barry, were struck by a "double consciousness" of their existence within the Filipino state (2008, xvi). They are aware, she clarifies, that Christians can "influence and even shape how Muslims live" (xvi). They are also aware that they are the "Other." Writing thus became an occasion to question the "prejudicial 'official' history" of their presence in the new nation (xvi). E. E. Sule settles firmly on the theme of mixed selves, marriages, and families to question the official history of a nation-state. In his novel *Sterile Sky*, Sule inscribes the transnational themes—the Gulf and the Liberian wars—within the violence in Kano City to mobilize the purpose of *ummah* or community as more than a transnational interaction. Indeed, it casts light over community as a transgeographic relationship, as modeled in the marriage between a Muslim woman and a Christian man. In the short story "Majed," here under analysis, Leila Aboulela similarly frames the anxiety of religious alienation and disorientation in marriage, not through the familiar and oft-critiqued trope of a Muslim immigrant in the West but by reversing it in the conversion of a white, European woman to Islam.

Key to questioning the official history of a nation-state, as these writers do, are two things: mapping the flows of information and influences and what dominated cultures do with the knowledge and information they receive or transculturate. It is, as Deleuze and Guattari have noted, relatively unimportant where one enters from or leaves but *how* the map of the castle is modified by the points that connect each other and which doors and galleries one has to pass through to get to another point. In transnational feminism, Nagar and Swarr (2010) remind us that international and global feminisms fail to sufficiently counter hegemonic relationships of power and agendas, "for prioritizing northern feminist agendas," and for "homogenizing women's struggles for sociopolitical justice, especially in colonial and neocolonial contexts" (4). Homogenizing, they point out, evacuates agency for social justice and ascribes powerlessness to the historically and materially subordinate. As such, transnationalism offers opportunities for organizing feminist causes and occasionally mitigates the "universalistic tendency of global feminism" (8). But as Chowdhury terms it, transnationalism is rooted in a "dependency chain" and "unequal power relations" in feminist structures of organizing, along with "complicated and uneasy alliances," particularly between nongovernmental organizations, of "powerful international NGOs" and "local NGOs" (2011, 1, 5). Uncovering the inherent inequality in "NGO linkages to international institutions," Chowdhury (2010) observes the simultaneous curtailment of the flourishing of perhaps more organic and radical ones" (5). Concomitant with this unequal relationship between "powerful international" sites and the less powerful ones is the direction of dominant philologies—the imposition of "technical skills like fluency in English language and drafting reports according to certain formats, rather than to adapt the organization's style to locally based needs" (3). Such asymmetries within the landscape of feminist organizing thus mobilize Pratt's (1991) concept of transculturation in "contact zones" that focuses not only on the direction of flow of information or influences—from Global North to Global South—but on their modification in the process of their reception by the slave or colonized. That is, what they do with the influence is the process of transculturation that is important to understand the reorientation of ideas underpinning a rebalancing of power relations.

Geographies of Spaces—Religion, Islands, and *Ummah*

My aim of reading mixed marriages is twofold. First, I argue that the writers under consideration in this chapter redefine domestic genealogies as mixed, plural, and multireligious, thus also redefining the relationship of gender to a nation that will be predicated on a mixed idea of its space. I briefly recapitulate Sangeeta Ray's deft analysis of the intimate relationship of gender to the nation through the construction of a rejuvenated Hinduism that othered first the Muslim and then women in the steady rise of Hindu national identity in the Bengali writer Bankim Chandra Chattopadhyay's feted novels *Anandmath* and *Devi Chaudharani*. Ray writes, "In his enunciation of the politicization of an Indian civil society through a rejuvenated Hinduism, the Muslims function as the supplemental remainder in an otherwise complete equation" (2000, 27). Gender was constructed in this contradictory and politically expedient context of a restrictive national political identity of "Hindu masculinity" that was willing to accept British colonialism as a force of positive social good to pose the Muslim as the absolute other and symbol of tyranny (27, 30). In Bankim's writing, as Ray (2000) points out, the relationship of gender to the nation was reliant on "the separation of the gendered other for the consolidation of the renewed male religio-political subject of Hindu nationalism" (30). In comparison, as I show in my reading of Abubakar's story "Maghrib" and in Arifa Macaqua Jamil's story "Sakeenah" in chapter 4, these writers contest not only the monoreligious, monolinguistic and monoethnic wavelengths of such theorizations of gender and nation but also the systematic othering of minorities as the supplemental remainder "in an otherwise complete equation" (27).

A brief glimpse of the geographical space and time of the Philippines suffices to explain these writers' motives in reconfiguring a nation contingent on its pluralism for its completeness. Thomas McKenna (1998) thus describes the islands of the only Christian majority nation in Southeast Asia as a double separation or distancing—from the northern parts of the archipelago and from each other linguistically and geographically:

> Muslims are geographically concentrated in the south of the country and are distinguished from Christian Filipinos not only by their profession of Islam but also by their evasion of three hundred years of Spanish colonial domination. Although Spanish colonizers had consolidated their hold on the northern tier of the Philippine archipelago by 1600, they never accomplished the complete subjugation of the Muslim South. Philippine Muslims are also separated from one another in this archipelagic nation by very significant linguistic and geographic distance. (2–3)

The spatial arrangement of the archipelago as multiple communities connected with and within each other illustrates the technique of recasting the nation space by reversing the flows of power, influences, and the directions of these flows or the "dependency chain." The reversal of direction, I want to point out, is not a simple change in direction back to the materially and historically dominated constituent of a relationship: the Global South or peripheries, in this case. Rather, reversal explores possibilities of other interlocutors, relationships, and a possibility solidly animated by transgeographic relationships. This impulse is echoed by McKenna's assessment of the Filipino Muslim community that was distanced from both Spanish colonial domination and also from each other owing to the archipelagic geography of the island nation. Pausing on the ways in which the Muslims/Moro Islands connect with each other in addition to or despite connecting with the Catholic center foregrounds Deleuze and Guattari's emphasis on *how* different entryways and pathways interact with each other. Equally, the reorientation of the direction of flow of ideas is especially salient in the notion of *ummah*: as Abdullah al-Ahsan notes that when the *ummah* acquired an added meaning during the Medinan verses, one of its features in the sense of Muhammad's followers, distinctly as his *ummah*, was, in fact, the change in direction of praying from Jerusalem to Mecca. This change signified a shift from older ways to newer ones, as it epitomized both a spatial turn from Jerusalem to the Kaba and an ideological formalization of a new identity for this small group. It mirrored in many ways the larger and more significant redirection in Islam, that of its birth, as the new faith turned away from pre-Islamic or *jahilliyya* society, emblematizing a shift from an old to an all-encompassing new order. Similarly, al-Ahsan invokes another meaning of *ummah* in the embodiment of the virtues of a community by one person in Abraham as the exemplar of communal qualities, "a model of the ummah itself, and could therefore himself be called an ummah," as generative of the meanings of the *ummah* (2007, 608). These two variant meanings of *ummah* are symbolic of the direction of flow of influences and ideas—a shift from one idea to another and of leadership that guides an *ummah* by encapsulating the qualities of the community such that the embodiment of qualities in the latter sense of *ummah* is also pivotal in rebalancing/redirecting power relations in the complex figure of a Western, Christian, and white woman, Ruqiyyah, in Leila Aboulela's short story "Majed." Through the fertile trope of marital and filial ties then, in this chapter I examine *ummah* as a spatially interarticulated trellis of relationships in the writing of Aboulela, Sule, and Abubakar. I consider the techniques used by these writers in their reconceptualization of the *ummah* through conversions, mixed marriages, and mixed religious identities of offspring of different religions, ethnicities, and nationalities as a way of strategizing against communal violence and domestic discord.

The first writer under consideration in this chapter, Leila Aboulela, reimagines the *ummah* as a solution to domestic problems through two main features of transgeographic feminism: the reorientation of the "dependency chain"—or the direction of influences, ideas, and interlocutors—and the space of the *ummah* in relation to national borders. This reorientation, as I have said, is not the simple change of direction from Global North to Global South. Rather, it is connecting with other interlocutors, as Deleuze and Guattari posit the relative unimportance of entering or exiting in favor of *how* each entryway connects with another in the eventual modification of the map. It is also useful to be reminded of Lionnet and Shih's model of "minor transnationalisms" that shift away from the center or the dominant major toward other sites of relationships. In other words, changing the direction means finding other points of connection. Both these features of the *ummah* can be glimpsed in Ruqiyyah who typifies the reorientation of the flow of information and influences and in the embodiment of its meaning in the same sense that Abraham embodied it. Because this embodiment is inherent in the person of a white, former Christian woman who embraces Islam, I will show in my reading of the story (untying therefore the national and ethnic connections of Islam), that Ruqiyyah embodies the meaning of *ummah* in the shift from older ways, from the East moving toward the West. This is especially important since her Sudanese-born husband, Hamid, is a lapsed Muslim. Unlike in Aboulela's other stories and her longer fiction, the direction of the flow of ideas, influences, and interlocutors in "Majed" takes place from West to East even though such categorizations (the West as a space of Christianity and the East as representative of Islam), as I argue elsewhere, inaccurately capture Aboulela's aims (Edwin 2013, 58–79). In "Majed," Aboulela counters this critical tendency that tethers Islam to a particular ethnicity, nationality, or culture, typically in the figure of disoriented, alienated, and isolated non-Western migrants. As a result, her transnationalism, I contend, lies not in the physical location of places, charted across national boundaries. Rather, it lies across all boundaries transgeographically. To this end, I focus on two major features of the *ummah* in Aboulela's story: first on Ruqiyyah and, second, on the change in direction of the flow of influences.

Culture, Nation, and *Ummah*: Directions of Influences, Ideas, and Interlocutors in Leila Aboulela's "Majed"

With little exception, critical reading of Aboulela's portrayal of Islam has focused on its persistent twi(n)ning with migration. The figuration of immigrants from formerly colonized societies moving West is common to several of Aboulela's novels, starting with *The Translator, Minaret*, and more recently in *Lyrics Alley*, along with her short fiction, "The Ostrich," "Tuesday Lunch," and "The Museum," among several new stories appearing in her most recent short story collection, *Elsewhere, Home* (2018).[4] Variously read as a writer who centralizes the healing power of religion for her protagonists in hostile atmospheres, Aboulela's characters operate within an Islamic logic of actions, prompting Ferial Ghazoul (2001) to famously declare her work "halal" (or acceptable by Islamic standards), migrating away from religion as an abstraction or empty rituals toward an inner harmony in a chaotic world. Her Muslim characters struggle to "grasp the essence of the religious experience" and find comfort in the "strength of spirituality" (2001). Three notable characteristics discernibly emerge in the twi(n)ning of Islam and migration. First, Islam most often appears as a source of comfort only to migrants. Put another way, Aboulela's *migrants* are nearly all Muslim. Aboulela's work is read as part of a "Muslim immigrant literature," as Waïl Hassan points out, "derived from Islam but shaped specifically by immigrant perspectives," pertinent chiefly to immigrant experiences (2008, 299). Secondly, following from this, Islam is read as broadly and generally interchangeable with culture, unfurling primarily in the space of "encounters between Islam and the West," or to substitute the two poles, the space of encounters can be described as variations of the same—an encounter between two binaries. As Hassan states, "Migrations between North and South, cultural perceptions, stereotypes, and the possibilities of building bridges between former colonizer and colonized" (298). When the two foregoing features are put together, the idea—Islam "for migrants only"—can be tracked in generally predictable directions of movement: that is, from East to West, Global South to Global North and fungible in these combinations of the colonized, Muslims, and Islam moving toward the colonizer, Christians, and Christianity.

Less noticed, however, and the focus of this analysis is Islam's pull as a new lifestyle choice for Christians in the West—for Muslims in "unsuspected spaces," as Hassan puts it—that did not exist in Britain in the 1950s and 1960s (299). Thus Aboulela's transnationalism must not be overdetermined by a universalized and placeless Islam, as it is less about cross-border movement in the sense of national borders and more about cross-geographic movements of religiosity. It lies less in a movement from East to West; from Scotland to Sudan or vice-versa, and more in the unusual directions and unsuspected spaces—unfolding in Scotland, the space of the former colonizer, a dominant space—where Ruqiyyah embraces Islam and meets Hamid, supposedly on his own terrain of beliefs and habits. The unusual space is of a mixed marriage. The fact that Ruqiyyah is already a convert when she meets and marries Hamid overturns the preponderant critical claim about Aboulela's writing on the intertwinement of Islam with nostalgia and migrant experience in a foreign land. It debunks the tendency to scrutinize Islam as an Eastern religion, embodied predominantly by migrants moving west. Ruqiyyah's conversion also challenges the gendered idiom of the double bind that Aboulela's characters (mostly always Sudanese and Muslim by birth) embrace Islam as an identity position to resist both a secular society and a romantic revival of Islam from the past in their homelands. Tina Steiner (2008) writes:

> Islam itself provides an identity position which can be harnessed
> by her characters in order to resist the hegemonic pressures

of assimilating into a secular present or of romanticising a particular past. (8)

For Steiner, Aboulela's Islam is revived by her characters only as a nostalgic evocation of past experiences, revived primarily when Muslims migrate, transnationally. She says:

> The shift from nostalgia to faith is not absolute, however, because despite Islam's transnationality, memories of home do resurface continuously, and are quite clearly linked to a faith that is carried into the present via past experiences. (2008, 14)

Similarly, Lindsey Zanchettin analyzes the theme of homesickness, migration, and Islamophobia in Aboulela's more popular short stories, "The Ostrich," "The Museum," and "Missing Out," arguing that migrants carry over faith from the past to heal loneliness. Zanchettin further asserts that "teaching Non-Muslims about Islam is a difficult task to undertake," and in so doing Aboulela demystifies the "us versus them binary" through Islam (2013, 46). As such, even Hassan's appraisal of Aboulela's work, when recognizing these unusual spaces of British converts (as the British convert Aisha in Aboulela's essay "Barbie in the Mosque" that Hassan analyzes), cannot escape the ascription of Islam in Europe to the presence of immigrants. Hassan (2008) makes the following two distinctions in Aboulela's fiction:

> Her work represents two historical developments since the 1970s: the Islamic resurgence that has attempted to fill the void left by the failure of Arab secular ideologies of modernity . . . and the growth of immigrant Muslim minorities in Europe and the United States. (298)

The figures of Aisha, therefore, and Aboulela (that Hassan rightly, if briefly, reads as unhinging the triad of "race, religion and nation") remain nevertheless folded within the larger theme of Aboulela's writing as fundamentally representative of *Muslim immigrants* in Europe and the United States, where crossing or migrating is "cross-cultural" but not "cross-religious" (298). Furthermore, accentuating race as grounds for discrimination and an emotionally more valent affiliation than religion, evinces such appraisals of Aboulela's plots as "interracial" relationships but never as "interreligious" ones. Resultant migrant encounters, likewise, are almost always freighted as "cultural" or racial but never religious (see Smith 2018). Brenna Munro, thus reads Aboulela's work as possessing "intercultural possibilities," where Sammar and Rae's encounter in *The Translator* is framed in nationalistic and racial terms, between a Sudanese widow, a white man, and as an "interracial romance" (171).

National and Ethnic Detachments: Ruqiyyah

As I will discuss later in this chapter, a criticism commonly leveled against Aboulela's depiction of Muslim women is that they appear in the most conservative, orthodox, and right-wing Islamist shades to play into the hands of right-wing Salafi or Islamist dogmatism that implicitly mobilizes Western imperialism to bolt to the rescue of the hapless Muslim woman. For now, I focus on the ability of religion to foster *ummah* transgeographically as detached from nationality and race through the figure of Ruqiyyah as a way of addressing the common criticism of Aboulela's characters as victims of hidebound Sunni-Salafi ideologies and Western imperialism. In a recent interview in 2018, Aboulela states that she writes about the "conventional Muslim woman." She eschews polarities between very liberal Muslim women and "very sort of oppressed women" to balance out the two extremes. She says:

> There isn't much portrayal of the majority, who are conventional Muslims. That's where I'm coming from; I'm writing about the conventional Muslim woman, and I don't feel she's often depicted. That's part of what encourages me to write.[5]

A question that must be posed in the context of such portrayals is whether Ruqiyyah would fit the description of a conventional Muslim. Who is a conventional Muslim woman? Can we entertain the possibility that Islam may not be wedded to ethnicity, culture, nationality, or place and be embraced even by someone not ethnically, nationally, or racially Muslim by birth, for example, someone not from historically Muslim-majority (and formerly colonized) societies? More important, can a Western, white, Christian female figure foster *ummah*? What problems does she create or solve for transnational relationships and gender trapped between Western imperialism and Sunni/Salafi quarrels? Through this story, Aboulela produces much in contrast to the critical readings of her work so far in the figure of a white, Western Christian woman who converts to Islam and whose disappointment at her Muslim-born husband's pietistic laxity only reaffirms the critical assumption that Islam is read as tethered to national and ethnic lines, something that Aboulela undoes in this story. In particular, Aboulela reverses many predictable directions here as a rejoinder to the critical reading of her longer work such as *The Translator* that is prominently analyzed as representative of the encounter between two cultures—the Christian North and the Muslim South (colonized Muslim and colonizer Christian)—and the ramified legacies of these fetishized encounters.

"Majed" remains poorly critiqued, perhaps because it troubles the established critical framework of colonial and postcolonial Muslim immigration to the West compared to Aboulela's other short fiction, even though "Majed" is not her only attempt at unhinging religion from nationality, ethnicity, and race. Nor is it her only attempt at exploring mixed marriages. "Something Old, Something New," for instance, maps the romance between a Scottish convert and his Muslim fiancée as the former converts to Islam and journeys eastward for his betrothal and conversion. In fact, in that story, Aboulela baldly alludes to "boundaries and seas" to map both a transnational journey from Edinburgh to Khartoum and a spiritual journey from Christianity to Islam (2001, 125). In *Minaret*, Aboulela briefly presents Wafaa's husband who is also a British convert to Islam to gesture to an Islam that is not meant entirely for Muslim immigrants only. In "Majed," Aboulela gives us Ruqiyyah's conversion and her experience as a Muslim as a means to material and marital security for a woman escaping a failed and abusive marriage. Modeling Muhammad's *ummah* that sunders preexisting modes of social interactions, establishing the primacy of Islam over blood and tribal ties, Ruqiyyah breaks from an old order to embrace a new one. On becoming Muslim, she leaves her old name, life, and world behind (108). Ruqiyyah is not her birth name. We don't learn of her old name or of details of her work as a teller in a bank or that she was also previously married (108). It doesn't matter, for the direction of her individual self and the first community hundreds of years ago has changed. Along with Ruqiyyah, Aboulela also produces the familiar figure of the Muslim migrant, moving from East to West, struggling to escape the void of a hostile and foreign society, although not characteristically turning to religion as a safe haven against racism. Aboulela gives us Hamid, Ruqiyyah's Sudanese-born Muslim husband, a student in Scotland.

That this space of transnationalism in "Majed" is unusual, reversed, and thus respatialized finds its clearest expression in Hamid's inability to decouple religion and culture or nationality, discernible in a minimization of Ruqiyyah's practice. Hamid pales in comparison to Ruqiyyah who pities him for drinking. He attributes her superior piety to her conversion, "she was so good, so strong because she was a convert" (109). As Ruqiyyah gets up at dawn and prays, Hamid attributes "this seriousness that he didn't have" to Scottish culture, "something Scottish she brought with her when she stepped into Islam" (113). He constantly worries not about his Muslim wife, but about his "Scottish wife . . . who was a better Muslim than he was" (110). Hamid, in comparison, is "relaxed about the whole thing" as he had been a Muslim all his life (109). Aboulela takes up each of Hamid's vacuous preoccupations: the pain he feels for his "brothers and sisters suffering in the West Bank" to assuage his guilt for not observing the religion and his belief that Ruqiyyah practices Islam better than him because of her nationally stereotypical discipline as a Scottish convert. He, on the other hand, is Sudanese and therefore culturally naturalized to practice it correctly and rightfully—a proprietorship that Ruqiyyah, as a Scottish national and a former Christian, cannot claim. He can therefore afford to relax spiritually as he has less to prove than his wife who has only recently come into the fold.

Natalie Brierley describes Hamid as "one man, a Muslim student, disavows his cultural inheritance only to find himself envious of his wife, who loyal to her faith, remains 'displaced yet intact.'" (2001). Brierely is referring perhaps to Ruqiyyah's conversion as displacement. Or to Ruqiyyah's surprise as a displaced emotion at Hamid's inability to honor Islam as his "cultural inheritance." Ruqiyyah's displacement, however, is not the same as the feeling of dislocation that migrants from elsewhere feel in Britain. The real displacement here is Aboulela's dislocation of Islam from ethnically and nationally tight affiliations—as cultural patrimony—to the ethnically, racially, and nationally least likely kind of person wishing to embrace it. Nesting in this dislocation is also the imperceptible reversal of direction in the flow of influences and ideas as a white woman embraces Islam. In Ruqiyyah's strong adherence and Hamid's lack of it, Aboulela reimagines the transnational as a space that cannot be overdetermined by lying outside national or ethnic affiliations but as a presence within such unsuspected relationships—mixed marriages—as Ruqiyyah's move toward Islam attests. In other words, if using familiar critical categories to read Aboulela's work—the East versus West analog—we might say that she collapses Western culture within Islam or

Eastern culture through marriage—an intimate zone of meeting, colliding, and merging beyond predictable boundaries and categorizations. It is also in this sense that Ruqiyyah's conversion to Islam rebalances power in such mergers and immersions (marriage). In the shift of direction, as the new *ummah* of Muhammad changed its direction of prayer from Jerusalem to the Kaba, symbolizing its rupture from the impress of its antecedent spiritual counterparts, the direction of influence in Ruqiyyah's case, is mapped in a Christian woman embracing Islam, a dominant culture moving toward the colonized culture.

Ruqiyyah's representation of an adherence to faith is less political and communal than Hamid's association of Islam as cultural inheritance. Nor is her conversion a political act of embracing something new. It suggests stepping into an *ummah* in the same way that the covenant of Medina superseded tribal loyalties in its constitution. This nationless Islam that Ruqiyyah embraces from outside (as a former Christian) presents Islam above any other kind of affiliation. The story thus functions to reverse the theme of "The Ostrich" (1997), also a tale of alienation, immigration, and a longing for Islam. In "The Ostrich," Sumra's husband Majdy makes her feel inadequate and ugly, as Zanchettin points out, "attempting to uphold Western standards" (44). Therefore in "Majed," Hamid's failure to observe Islam underlines the irony of Majdy's desperation to conform to British standards by distancing himself and his wife from Islam and Sudanese culture, within this intimate encounter of two religions (Christianity and Islam) and two cultures (Sudanese and British). While Sumra in "The Ostrich" feels out of place as a Muslim in Scotland, Ruqiyyah, on the other hand, with her light blue eyes, veil, and plain clothes gets her fair share of stares from other women, "at school when Ruqiyyah and Majed went to pick up Robin, no one believed that they were brothers. The other mothers outside the school looked at her oddly, smiled too politely" (111). The awkwardness that Sumra feels for being out of place is squared in the general perception of Ruqiyyah in her hijab. Indeed, it is as strange for the reader to come across Ruqiyyah as it is for the mothers outside Robin's school. I would venture to suggest that it is not simply a matter of interracial or intercultural oddities at the sight of Ruqiyyah's biracial children that shocks others but the interreligious mix—of Ruqiyyah, white and blue-eyed, in her hijab—that supersedes the conflation of mixed-race boys as brothers. It is the Muslim appearance of a white woman that causes more confusion than the mixed races as religions are neatly tied to ethnicity and nationality in the minds of the other mothers outside the school that make it harder to breach perceptual boundaries about the racial and ethnic identities or origins of Muslims.

The second major feature of Aboulela's treatment of the *ummah* is found in focusing on a single person embodying the virtues and qualities of the *ummah* that in fact disrupts the neat metonym of the Third World Muslim woman in need of rescuing. Specifically, the first connotation, alluding to Abraham, relates to good qualities and virtues in Ruqiyyah's character that Aboulela places in Ruqiyyah to unhinge her qualities from (or place Islam above) racial, ethnic, or national identifications. The second meaning refers to human community, that which Denny calls "a universal aspect of ummah . . . [that] "should be understood as standing behind the term in most contexts" (44).[6] When Ruqiyyah reasons to remedy Hamid's weaknesses, she takes on the meaning of *ummah* as the exemplar of religious qualities embodied by Abraham in the Qur'an. Contrary to the idea of expanding a community by joining it as Ruqiyyah converts, her *ummah*-building gesture emerges from steering her guilt-stricken Muslim husband back to the path of Islam as he regrets betraying his faith by drinking (109). Religion here is not presented as the purest form of life but as an aspirational end. Ruqiyyah practices Islam with much devotion, but she can't interpret the Qur'an quite correctly and longs to do so. It isn't the idealistic perfection that Aboulela presents in her but a correction of the misreading of the West as an oasis for Muslims, free from struggles and temptations that they aim to escape through migration. In fact, Ruqiyyah is already Muslim before she marries Hamid. What could she possibly want from him, since it is he who gains everything (including legal status) in Scotland—the reason he marries her in the first place? (110). Aboulela thus flips both tropes of Islam as a quest for spiritual comfort for Muslims and of the Third World woman in need of rescuing from Third World patriarchy by foregrounding a material quest for stability and safety to dull the memories of the rat-infested refuge that Ruqiyyah spent the night in to escape, Gavin, her a physically violent white Scottish husband (111).

A Balm for Colonial Injuries—Gender, *Ummah*, Sufi, Sunni, and Salafi Islam in Critical Scholarship

Ruqiyyah's qualities also overturn the critique that Aboulela often presents religion as an anti-imperialistic salve for Muslims and fails to depict Muslims who resist religion or dissent with it. Notably, Sadia Abbas interprets Aboulela's thematization of Islam in Aboulela's more famous novel, *The Translator*, as an expedient, providential East-West dialectic where only conversion can enable a "halal" romantic marital union (2011, 435, 437). It is useful then to dwell at length here on Abbas's blistering critique of Aboulela's use of religion as a tranquilizer on the bruised sentiments of immigrants in the West. Abbas takes a dim view of Aboulela's expedient packaging of Islam with a romantic plot and the resultant marriage as God's design for a happy ending. She states:

> Religious narrative forms that might be precursors to the novel—stories of conversion, confessions, the providential tale—such as the early modern captivity narrative that interprets the brutality of abduction and the travails of escape as part of God's design. The happy rescue or a fortuitous flight show that God rewards the faithful and punishes the wicked. Of course, conversions and confessions—themselves closely aligned—are usually testaments to Provident reward for their renunciatory patience and devotional labor. Their union is like the divine sleight of (an invisible) hand that replaces Ismail with a lamb because Abraham and Ismail had already consented to the imminent slaughter and accepted it as a duty. Romance, confession, conversion, and providence—neatly wrapped up. (2011, 437, 438)

Speaking of *The Translator*, Abbas presents such fortuitous events of the novel—Sammar's "arc of confession" and Rae's "trajectory of conversion"—as implausible, providential, and unrealistic at best (437). Abbas's main criticism of Aboulela's depiction of Islam, however, centers on the author's offering of a union of East and West to celebrate a "placeless Muslim universalism . . . marriage allows for the conversion that allows for the union of the West and East," writes Abbas, where "protestantism, Salafism and the fantasy of happily consensual ('companionate') marriage can merge" (437, 440; 2014, 80–81).

Abbas's model of critique, however, leaves untouched the ethnic, national, and cultural stereotype of Islam as it reproduces the East-West conflict (Islam-Christianity; immigrants as Muslim [Eastern] and Natives as Christian [European]). Ruqiyyah troubles this model, for she is not subjected to hostility for her poor English or Arab accent. She finds comfort in Islam, not as a happy escape from loneliness in a foreign country—she is on home turf. Abbas also names the pressure of "belonging" in the tensions experienced by immigrant Muslims. Again, this would not apply to Ruqiyyah. In fact, it is in her wanting to belong to Islam (not Eastern culture)—in being a blue-eyed hijabi—that elicits stares and overpolite smiles as she collects her children from school. The stereotype of race (white) embracing Islam (nonwhite) is simply not palatable to other women outside the school. One may ask how Aboulela can imagine Islam as a placeless universal but also as tied to the East ("union of the West and East," as Abbas notes), but the West would not be eligible as a location of Islam in this discussion on culturally rooted Islam as a localized culture? Does this also not project Islam for non-Westerners only? Like Steiner and Zanchettin, Abbas, too, reads Aboulela's work as ethnically tied to Islam and vehicled by domestic immigrant fictions, making it difficult to accommodate the idea of the domestic fiction in "Majed" that illustrates not the longing of an ethnically born Muslim for refuge in Islam but uncharacteristically that of his white convert spouse.

In "localized and customary Islams," as Abbas grudges Aboulela for exceeding their ambit in the lofty deterritorialized space of the novel, Abbas would know that the figure of the female is kept under close control in marriage (2014, 81). Marriage to non-Muslims would be inconceivable for a Muslim woman more so in localized iterations of the religion as Abbas eloquently evokes the metonymization of Muslim women reduced to "Orientalist ciphers" or targets of jihadist violence (159). In *The Translator*, in Sammar's reluctance to marry Rae without conversion, Aboulela does in fact offer a glimpse into a localized and customary form of Islam. Would victimization by jihadist forces on account of an interreligious marriage not be realistically plausible? Or is the issue that it is represented at all means that it plays into the hands of right-wing Salafism? The important question to ask here is why would Aboulela want to present a conversion? Why would she, as Abbas says, make her protagonist cling to "conservatism" in fact provides a clue to the question: can religion be anything other than conservatism? (2011, 441). The response to questions of conversion can balance out these extremes by focusing on female agency in turning down marriage—as Sammar does—from inside this conservatism, raised and bred only for marriage and male guardianship, on the charge that "Muslim women need protective men," as Abbas reads Aboulela's heroines (2014, 88). It is fair to say that if Aboulela presents narrowly focalized fictions that depict women who will their subordination and rehearse what

Abbas recognizes as the oldest trick in the imperial book—of proffering false choices to Muslim women—then it is also true that the broad-brush coding of gendered agency overlooks women's own internalization not of religiously sanctioned subordination but of gender embedded within subordinate systems. Abbas's metonym may not be the only frame of reference to capture Muslim women's experiences. Thus the two tight poles within which Muslim women appear trapped is a critical reading of the observance of right-wing Salafi fundamentalist strains in Islam—the very reading that a Western academic elite appears incapable of shaking off. It is easier, it appears, to dismiss Muslims as trapped between two extreme ends. To deny them internal contradictions, irregularities, imperfect knowledge of religion, inconsistencies, and weaknesses is just as easy as robbing them of their humanity. Why extend human foibles to the classic Other when its easier to dehumanize them?

I do not aim to defend Aboulela from critiques of conservatism such as Abbas's that read the illustrations of gender as pawns in patriarchal and imperial designs. Rather, I want to understand: what kind of Islam is acceptable to academics? What kind of Muslim woman can be represented without ignoring or leaving out other kinds to avoid the trap of a narrow categorization of Muslim women? Any inclusion would create an exclusion—something is always left out. Abbas's criticism of Aboulela's assertion that "faith is properly observed" wherein the writer goes to great lengths to ensure the proper observance of faith, raises more questions (2011, 441). Is it too unrealistic or implausible that Muslims strive for proper observance of faith? Is the issue with conservatism or with the implausibility that Muslims (not all jihadi Salafists) claim conservatism? However, Abbas devotes a great deal of space in her deft analysis to conversion as a telos for the right-wing Islamist/Salafi/Sunni, opposed to the West, attributing it to conservative strands in religion but not to agency that is already anticipated by Abbas as a predictable reason for women willing their own subordination—even the internalization of patriarchy prompting such a stance—in claiming that conservatism (2014, 85). To paraphrase Abbas: conservatism can only be imposed on the woman, since she cannot claim it herself, be misguided by it, or actively promote it. If she does claim conservative agency, then she has bought into orthodoxy that is not representative of Islam. This is because there are many Islams, but the orthodox versions that Aboulela projects are contrived in the space of a novel that allows fantasmic strands of Salafism, Protestantism, and happy marriages to merge. If conservatism is indeed imposed, suggests

Abbas, then the West is vindicated in wanting to rescue the hapless Muslim woman from orthodox impositions not without being reminded of its own complicity in producing and promoting racial and imperialistic oppressions.

So heavily steeped is Abbas's reading in pitting leftism with right-wing Islamism, parsed as they are in neatly categorized domains—Sudanese, Western, imperialistic, Islamism—that she misses the contradictory, imperfectly rational internalizations of affect and instruction on human minds, namely filial connections and environments in which emotions are molded to passively internalize religious truths. These truths are most often merged within the filial fold to inextricably link religion as a filial duty. Therefore, "localized and customary Islams" do not always map onto more rational and formalized versions of Islam (Abbas 2014, 81). As such, Islamic rituals, avid habits, formulations, and instructions are presented to millions of Muslims from an early age as ways of dealing with pressures and stresses in life, not to mention that these "localized and customary Islams" are uncritically imbibed, further layered with contradictions pertaining to emotions of filial and other kinship ties that do not neatly or logically map onto rationally inspired religious practice (2014, 81). Abbas's observation that Aboulela claims to use "Islamic logic" but "does not refer to any specific Muslim thinker on theodicy" fits neatly with her earlier critique of Aboulela's use of providential logic in a world with a "Muslim accent" (438). However, Abbas also quotes from the novel that "marriage was half [a Muslim's] faith," acknowledging Aboulela's reference to their most important Muslim thinker and philosopher—Mohammad—and his exemplary teachings or the logic of the *hadith* (2014, 108). Aboulela uses many such *hadith* to explain her protagonists' actions. Any attempt to resolve a problem using the Qur'an or *hadith*—the two fundamental texts and bases of all logic, laws, and guidance in Islam—would be, to use Abbas's argument, unrealistic, idealistic, and again providential and contrived. Or they would be dismissed as right-wing Islamist thought (in contrast with Sufism). That Aboulela also presents Hamid in "Majed"—a lapsed Muslim who struggles with proper observance, urinates on his child in an inebriated state, consumes alcohol, and grudges his spouse for adhering to their faith—would be, using Abbas's reading practice, more in line with the anticonservative, realistic, and logical Muslim that Abbas would like to see. To re-pose my questions from earlier: where is the leeway in such a tight configuration of Islam and Muslim women? What kind of Islam can we discuss here?

The solution to Salafism, as I see it in Abbas's analysis, is to offer Sufism as a counterclaim, a more sympathetic reading of Nadeem Aslam—who deploys Sufi influences and references via the poetry of Faiz Ahmed Faiz—than of Aboulela, who is dismissed repeatedly as depicting a regressive view of Islam through female characters who willingly play into right-wing Salafism and Western imperial narratives of rescuing the Muslim woman. Aamir Mufti's identification of an upsurge in postsecularism, a "turn to religion"—a staple of the Western global media and scholarship such that the "security expertise that nevertheless merges from time to time in the scholarly discussion itself"—refers not to the sudden importance of Islam in media circles but that a particular brand of Islam has steadily gained salience and can be unproblematically evened out by Sufism (2013, 8). Somehow then, Sufism is more preferable than right-wing Islamism as the latter has a tainted history in imperial politics, something that Sufism does not, owing to its own victimization at the hands of the imperial West and Sunni establishments in such Muslim-majority societies as Pakistan. It is true, as Mufti states, that despite the diverse approaches and disciplines through which Islam is studied, "they tend to view varieties of contemporary political Islam as representative of the (Sunni) Islamic 'tradition' as such" (10). The dialectic for Mufti, as for Abbas, is drawn between Islamic traditions (Sunni, Sufi) and "the modern West" (10). Implicit in this view is the problematic optic that gender is better off in the hands of Sufi Muslims than right-wing Salafis. Hence, for Abbas, Aslam's *Maps for Lost Lovers* elicits a more complex rendition of the psychology of Muslim lives that Aboulela's novels simply cannot. Religious law seems to be at stake in Aslam's novel, but the proscription on a Muslim woman marrying a non-Muslim man simply does not appear to be a matter of law, as Abbas compares the two writers. To truly account for the complexity of Islam and Muslim societies that both Abbas and Mufti propose is to begin by including a broader corpus of such writing that includes not only Muslim-majority societies (to counter the dominant academic attention on the smallest concentration of Muslims that stand in for the rest of the Muslim world, coupled with repeated slippages that produce the use of Arab, Muslim, and Middle East as interchangeable with each other) but also writers who are hardly known outside their linguistic circles. Brenda Cooper's extension of Aboulela's quote on her aim to also depict "the psychology, state of mind and emotions of a person who has faith," urges a recognition of the complexity required to read Muslims and Islam in Aboulela's oeuvre (52). Cooper continues with Aboulela saying that she is "interested in going deep, not just looking at 'Muslim' as a cultural or political identity but something close to the centre" (52). That human psychology is contradictory, even opportunistic (as Abbas rightly reads Sammar's actions) erratic, and difficult to map onto rational choices and answers is somehow inadmissible when read by critics who insist Aboulela's work is neatly symbolic of the politics of West versus the East. I am concerned therefore about a process by which a certain kind of Islam is made to accrue critical purchase to the detriment of a similar theme (interreligious marriages and romance in Aslam's and Aboulela's novels) by a specific writer.

Dating Fiction: The "Mood" about Religion

Nesting within ideological tensions is also the timing of the debates that pit Sunni, Salafi, and Sufi Islams against one another. It is useful to be detained by the question of a datable Islam in the Western academic imaginary or of the rise of the religious novel in the American academic context: this is because doing so also challenges a narrow critical stance on Islam. How broad is this response in its own critical practice? Abbas attributes the turn to religion to a handful of political events—the Rushdie affair, the Gulf War, and 9/11—raising thus the vital question: did characters like Sammar, Rae, and Hamid come into existence only after these events or did Aboulela write about them only after these events? Thus, in response, one may ask: what of a host of Muslim writers—Cheikh Hamidou Kane, Ibrahim Tahir, Ken Bugul, Mariama Ba, Zaynab Alkali—who thematized Muslims and Islam long before the aforementioned watershed moments in Western politics? Common to these writers is that they wrote about Muslims in Africa—a region that has not captured the imagination of Western cultural criticism with regard to Islam as much as the Arab regions and Middle East. Or is it that Islam's salience in academic circles following 9/11 reflected a critical rather than a literary tendency? Mufti raises a similar concern in his study of postsecularism, an analysis that Abbas also references in her robust critique of this "mood" about Islam or the sudden turn to religion (2014, 74). A brief comment on Mufti's influential assessment of Islam in the current academic climate helps frame the critical stance on theory and literature. Common to Mufti's critique in his article (2013) and Abbas's sustained argument in her book (2014) is the dating of a sudden "return of religion" as conservative, orthodox, and majoritarian, among other things (2013, 8). Mufti calls this (re)turn, and his reasons for eschewing postsecularism, in particular, "ethnographic philanthropy," or a neoimperial worldview. This disavowal suggests a complex etiology, among which feature majoritarianism and a destruction of the polyvocality of Islamic institutions (namely the imposing dominance of Sunni Islam) and the resurgence of a politico-religious forms of Islam. He states that

> as a spiritual, intellectual and political culture, Islamism marks a "return" of Islam, either uncontaminated by or having shaken itself free of, the liberal thought and practice of the modern West. (10)

Mufti's anxieties about the treatment of Islam in recent scholarship and his thesis on the global dominance of English, as I discuss later in the book, attribute this sudden turn to Islam as a "return to authenticity" and indigeneity—symptomatic of an attempt in the postcolonial world to recuperate "past social and cultural forms, or a "jargon of authenticity" (10, 11).

The dialectical opposition that Mufti sets up between Sunni and Sufi Islam, in fact, can be approached by underscoring epistemic privilege. Two observations merit attention. First, recognizing that Sufism itself, as scholars would argue, is not a division within Islam but has varyingly aligned itself with and distanced itself from "both popular religion and orthodox expressions of Islamic teachings. It has been both opposed and supported by the state."[7] The second concerns Ayesha Jalal's observation of the well-honed techniques of simplification and provincialization of expansive Islamic concepts to divisions between Muslims and non-Muslims and Islamic and non-Islamic traditions, including vigorous scholarly and academic appropriations of concepts, often overlooking the manipulation by state power of religious concepts to assure temporal control (12).[8] In divisions of a critical, theoretical, and ideological coup, epistemic privilege is symptomatic, as I have maintained throughout the present project, of the process by which only some epistemologies are received within the boundaries of an environment: in this case, the American academic context, then synthesized and disseminated. Such a process will also produce responses that are limited to the kind of knowledge that enters its premises. As I have mentioned earlier and elsewhere, the lopsided production of knowledge on Islam in the American academy that continues to favor

Arab and Middle Eastern regions as producers of knowledge on worldwide Islam, and its steady disaffection for non-Arab Muslim societies such as in sub-Saharan Africa and Southeast Asia, is uppermost in the list of symptoms that delimit the US academy's geographical sphere of interest in Islam. Ayesha Jalal makes a similar case in her study on the critical dynamics pertaining to the topic of jihad, the most controversial and metonymic topic on Islam in Western imagination, second perhaps only to the hijab in academic attempts to make sense of Islam and Muslims. Jalal imputes "the prominence given to the legal and theological writings in modern scholarship" that have reduced the idea of *jihad* to "ideological warfare against the enemies of Islam" (11). Jalal contends that the teachings on jihad by such thinkers as Abul Ala Mawdudi and Syed Qutb, two of the most prominent Muslim theorists in South and West Asia in the early twentieth century, had less to do with opposition to the Western imperium in their lands and more to do with the "internal dynamics of Muslim society than with an outright rejection of modernity under Western colonialism" (18). Jihad, writes Jalal, "has been a more effective instrument of political opposition to the secular modernity promoted by Muslim nation-states than of resistance to Western dominance" (18). On similar lines, Ousmane Kane's (2016) deeply nuanced analysis of the lesser-known and surprising *coexistence* of Sufi and Wahhabi ideologies in contemporary Saudi Arabia enables an understanding of Sufi-Salafi divisions (201–202).[9] For gender, Sufism has not proved to be an elixir, either. A fuller view of the Muslim world itself, one that would include its five hundred million Muslims in Africa (where Sufism thrives and is a formidable socio-spiritual force), easily reveals to scholars, who respond simply to a narrow critique of Islam manufactured in American academic circles, that the problem is not simply of Sunni or Salafi dominance but of the ramifications of unequal power relations in societal structures that sweep over gendered relations.

However, as I mention later as well, the topological examination of Muslims outside the areas of preferred scholarly study—the Middle East and Arab culture—highlight far more incommensurable relations than a simple clash between modernity and a return to authenticity or a relentless focus on only "Muslim-majority societies" (Abbas 2014, 85). It is a little-known story, "Ayesha's Pretty Hate Machine," by the relatively unknown Muslim Filipino writer Arifa Macaqua Jamil that I will analyze in the final chapter: this story spotlights a rare gaze capturing the state of gender in a Muslim-minority society, where gender, both Catholic and

Muslim, is reduced to its value as "womb." The point I want to emphasize at length here is not of right-wing Islamist trends such as the ones Saba Mahmood or Talal Asad study but what the American academic field on Islam has selectively chosen to focus on in the production of this knowledge. Is it the Islamic revivalism that Mahmood analyzes that is problematic or the fact that the circulation and applause of her study contributed to its haloed, near-canonical status in Islamic feminist theorization in American academia? Abbas's and Mufti's own critiques are then simply a response to what they identify as the "mood" without relying on sources other than the ones used by the scholars they critique. What works of fiction other than Aslam's and Monica Ali's (*Brick Lane*) immensely popular and well-received oeuvre can be of interest for theorizing a broader canvas of Islam and Muslims? While the answer to secularism cannot be orthodoxy or an emphasis on it as a response to Western secularism, a renewed focus on literature concerning pre-9/11 Islam may well reshape the perspective on this sudden return of religion in the North American academy.

Finally, how convincing is the dialectical tension between Sufism and Salafism in tackling another well-rehearsed imperial trick of projecting and pitting the "good" Muslim (read Sufi, pacifist, saintly, mystic) against the "bad" Muslim (read Salafi, Sunni, Wahhabi, militant, terrorist).[10] One only needs to look at the systematic evacuation of worldliness, normalcy, and humanity that was denied to Muslims by relegating them to the Sufi category to make sense of the aftermath of 9/11, an event that sent American society and academics into a tailspin by exposing the glaring absence of a substantive body of knowledge and scholarship that could explain such a horrific occurrence. Thus followed "educated" and "tolerant" takes on Muslims with the real (and good) Muslim being the one who denounced jihad and extremism and the "bad" Muslim being the one who resorted to violence. Countless narratives also followed on whether such stances represented the "majority" view of Muslims, not to mention Muslims who felt bewildered at having effectively turned spokespersons overnight for the entire Muslim world. These were, after all, the days when American society felt the birth pangs of Islamophobia, produced, nursed, and sustained in large measure by its own faulty academic approaches. Of course, in such a climate, Aboulela's writing was eagerly welcomed by the American intelligentsia, as Abbas observes. But a novel on Sufi Islam would also have produced equally provincialized perceptions of a topic that the American academic enclave could not epistemologically manage. Along these lines, I am critically skeptical of the near-canonical status of

Mahmood's work and others who have come to define the field of Islamic feminisms in the West. However, I am also concerned about the paucity of a framework that can be more encompassing than the examples and counterexamples that have come to define this field so narrowly. I agree with Mufti about the particular forms of Islam, such as legal and juridical Islam, that have eclipsed everyday forms of the religion under colonial rule in many Muslim societies. However, this has also meant that writers hardly known outside their regional or linguistic domain are rarely or never studied by Western academic circles by scholars who turn endlessly in the gyre of a familiar grammar. As I have argued elsewhere, the mood is not so much for a return to religion as much as it is on the focus on a particular function of religion: namely its political and juridical uses for Muslim women, inseparable from a stentorian foreign policy on the smallest population of Muslims in the world (Edwin 2016). The distant and unmappable voices of practically unknown writers continue to make transnational discussions relevant.

Dating then the current "mood" in tying this "return" of religion solely to 9/11 risks narrowing the field of voices to an overexposed few as part of the academic institutionalization of literature to denounce this mood. Doing so also ignores the broader project on Islam, as Chowdhury efficiently describes this tendency, by stating that it is "analytically dangerous" to imagine that Third World women's stories begin when the West turned its attention to them (2010, xviii). To paraphrase Chowdhury, I ask, when do Muslim women's stories "really become an issue of public concern" for academic criticism and scholarship? (xix). For instance, the controversy over halal meat in France is but one example that points to the origin of the practice among Muslims. On this issue, Kern (2012) states, "Halal meat is also proliferating on menus of schools, hospitals and company cafeterias across France."[11] Did Muslims consume halal food only after it became a matter of recent public debate and scrutiny? What of their habits before this practice entered the public imaginary? Similarly, the often-facile observation that Muslim women began veiling only after 9/11 or that there was a sudden upsurge in the number of women veiling increasingly in a post-9/11 world again begs the question of knowledge of women and girls who have been veiling for centuries. Was it an act of providence that Ramatoulaye in Ba's classic, *So Long a Letter*, does not equate her husband's treachery with her own faith and that she continues to pray dutifully, diligently observing all the austere and strict rituals of Islam? Was Ba also trying to show "faith properly observed" soon after the Iranian revolution in 1979 (as Ba's novel was published soon after in 1980)? Not only has such a connection not yet been made about Ba's iconic novel but more importantly—and to my earlier point about the dating of Islam in critical discourse—the novel was never really received in American academia as an aesthetically or politically relevant work on Islam. Ba's novel continues to enjoy recognition under such artificially constructed disciplines as "African," "postcolonial," or "gender" studies, more occluded than overlapping with each other, but never under "Islamic" studies: that category is critically and academically reserved for "Middle Eastern," "Near Eastern" or "Arab" parts of the world. Abbas's scathing critique of the agency of a Muslim woman—caught between competing pressures of Western imperialist militarization and jihadist violence—holds only insofar as it describes the mood on Islam in Western academic circles. The question to be posed here again is the following: did these characters, like the ones Aboulela illustrates, exist in the literary imagination prior to 9/11? Or is it that the West and Western academics are picking up on them *only now*? The question to be posed is not about a writer's predilection for conservative or liberal Islams but about the timing of the readers' interest in picking up such portrayals and the optics of an entire critical coterie of scholars. Abbas is right about Islamophilia perhaps having made Aboulela popular now, moreso than Ibrahim Tahir who also wrote a similar novel—*The Last Imam* (1984). But in re-posing my question about the timing of critical interest and attention in tracing a thematic itinerary, I ask why Tahir's novel is still not as widely discussed as Ken Bugul's classic novel, *The Abandoned Baobab* (1982)? It is a novel not only about colonial and postcolonial consumption of black women's bodies but intersectionally about Muslim women's bodies in that Ken in the novel is black, Muslim, and a woman?[12]

Gender remains unresolved in the tussle between competing Islamic ideologies and imperialisms that Abbas proffers as a solution out of the metonymic impasse of the traps laid for Muslim women by Western imperialism and Islamic fundamentalisms. Islamophobia (intensified by 9/11) is thus evoked as the context to which Aboulela responds by offering characters conforming to right-wing Islamism, and it is assumed that other writers don't, as Abbas evokes Nadeem Aslam's *Maps for Lost Lovers* (2004) as a point of contrast and to extend her criticism of Aboulela that "faith requires hard work, uncomfortable work, work that Aboulela chooses not to represent" (92). As Abbas observes, Aslam presents the "inner lives of the characters," something that Aboulela can only offer by way of a "psychic representation and realism" (2014, 91). Abbas has already concluded that any turn to religion by Aboulela's heroines in her longer work reinforces the view of women's subordination by right-wing Salafism (2014, 89). Somehow, this cannot be concluded from a reading of Aslam's novel on honor killings, for as Abbas notes, his canvas is much broader than Aboulela's when, in fact, Aslam's main protagonist—Kaukab—is unmistakably an analogue to both Najwa and Sammar, respectively, in Aboulela's novel *Minaret* and *The Translator*. It bears underlining that Kaukab, like Aboulela's heroines, clings obdurately to fundamentalisms that she finds reassuring and soothing in an alien society. Aslam's Sufi antidote to Kaukab's Salafism can be hard work in faith but Najwa's and Sammar's Salafi turn to religion cannot?

Abbas (2014) suggests that using Sufi poetry in his novel on honor killings exposes the fact that "this is first and foremost an internal fight. Muslims have their own historical resources for dealing with such social challenges; Empire does not need to gallop to the rescue." Yet such internal resources as the Qur'an and the *hadith* that Aboulela liberally uses in her work as an explanatory framework for her characters' choices are considered inadmissible as *historical resources* for dealing with challenges internal to Muslims (2014, 91). This is because, as Abbas (2014) has concluded, turning to the *hadith* and the Qur'an smacks of right-wing Islamism where women will their own subordination and play into the hands of sexist Salafis (198). The underlying implication under the pretext of complex layering and psychological depth that Aslam but not Aboulela displays, as Abbas concludes, is that Sufism would not reduce women to will their own subservience or to yearn for male guardianship that Aboulela's right-wing Salafi heroines desire. Kaukab can be read as a right-wing Salafi who inspires sympathy precisely because of the traditional, stereotypical role of a hapless mother drowning in a society she is unable to understand. Which of Aslam's heroines (Suraya, Mah-Jabin, Kiran) then, Islamic or otherwise, exist outside the stereotypical gendered frame? At work here is the contest between a more just version of religious belief—Sufi, Salafi, Sunni. That Aboulela and Aslam topologically explore decolonial solutions for domestic violence, gendered subordination, and sterility by staging their characters in exchanges, dialogues, encounters, and conversations that mobilize community, thereby exposing the processes by which gender is subordinated in both Sufi and Sunni structures, and of patriarchy and its entrenchment, is rarely discussed. It is in keeping with this question that I deploy literary expressions that animate both Muslim and non-Muslim women's relationships to society. A topological study such as the one I attempt in the following two sections on Christian-Muslim relations responds to the academic institutionalization of the limiting optics on Islam.

Marital and Communal Spaces in *Sterile Sky*

If Aboulela's turn to religion appears contrived and providential, then the Nigerian novelist E. E. Sule's solution to communal violence in *Sterile Sky* may also seem unlikely and somewhat unrealistic. The novel unravels lives trapped in religious violence in Kano City in the early 1990s during the Gulf War and the Liberian Civil War. All three violent events—the Gulf War, the Liberian Civil War, and the religious violence in Kano City—are connected transnationally in the novel, not as events across nation-states that influence each other but as present within each other, respatializing cross-national events as an agon of human greed and power. The solution for such barbaric mayhem, I argue, is played out not politically but in intimate, everyday, and informal relations, conspicuous in the motif of interfaith marriage, dialogues, and exchanges.

Murtala, the main protagonist, is a lower-middle-class Christian boy whose father is a policeman. The family lives in a poorer part of Kano—Sabon Gari—but Murtala is bright enough to attend a private school and to prospects of a better life and future that his father is barely able to afford (Sule 2012, 42). His presence in an elite school thus instances Sule's attempt to respatialize geographies, merging class inequalities not as class struggles to dismantle inequalities but as an attempt to blur the space of interlocutors and speakers in such transgeographic relationships. Transnational space is also constructed cross-nationally, as Murtala encounters the world outside Nigeria through headlines in newspapers that his father brings home from work. In particular, Murtala reads *Triumph*, an English-language daily published in Kano, and *The Economist*, and uses a dictionary to help himself with such difficult but recurrent transnational themes that flood his imagination, such as "25 People Killed in Religious Riot in Kano, Normalcy Returns to Kano; Reprisal Killings Erupt in Enugu; Operation Desert Storm Rages; Ten Palestinians Killed in Gaza" (2012, 34). Along with news of Structural Adjustment Programs (SAP), posters merge the violence around Murtala with the wars elsewhere. The city is plastered with "George Bush's screaming mouth facing Saddam Hussein's stony stare. War in their eyes" and another depicting George Bush saying

"In God We Trust," and Saddam Hussein saying, "Insh-Allah, We Shall Win the War" (56). Equally, Murtala learns of "Africa: The Hopeless Continent" from news about Palestine, the Gulf War, and from the war in Liberia as he cuts out a picture of an emaciated Liberian child with the caption, "Child victim of war in Liberia" (35, 188). By devouring these media-driven images, Murtala's lexicon, he tells us, rapidly broadens to include "corruption, infrastructure, government and underdevelopment" (35). Concurrently, this cross-national landscape is inscribed in conversations on unequal material realities between Ola and Murtala, "Why is Iraq taking over Kuwait? . . . Iraq is greedy. Kuwait is an oil-rich country.' 'They want to take what doesn't belong to them?' 'Yes. Bigger countries always bully smaller countries" (57). "I think that's what our social studies master calls imperialism," says Murtala (57). Both boys are able to see that it is about power, greed, and more power, as they conclude that "human beings like using their power to conquer their fellow human beings" (57).

At work here in the immersion of world politics within the violence in Kano is not the use of media to grandstand subjectivities in a space across national borders. Rather, Sule inscribes what Tsitsi Jaji calls the "imaginative possibilities" and "popular lines of affiliations" in cross-national solidarities within more proximal relationships—communal violence in Kano—respatializing thus the elsewhere (the Gulf War, the Liberian War, and the Palestinian struggle) as a distant presence to work out more immediate tensions (2014, 113, 114). This respatialization, as Jaji describes it, unfolded in the fusing of African American consumer capitalism and leisure culture that quietly replaced the nightmare of colonialism through an escapist fantasy or a "consumerist chimera" to overlook class-based and racial inequalities. Jaji coins the term "stereomodern black subjectivity" or the composite space of music, magazines, and popular culture that shaped African women's aspiration of glossy and smooth skin (116). Thus, while revealing the glaring gaps between the sheen of modernity and the corrosive experience of apartheid and colonialism that operated through magazines and music in Africa in the 1960s, Jaji uncovers the antinomical power of interarticulated media literacies that regularly referenced African American styles of film, radio, record, and magazines to construct the chimera or escapism of normalcy. She describes black stereomodernity as follows:

> The interrelated media of film, live musical performance, and popular print culture did much to place the simultaneous consumption of sound and image at the root of a specifically

urban(e) stereomodern black subjectivity that regularly referenced African American music, style, film, and magazines. (116)

In particular, Jaji notes the transformation of the *wall that became a window* of desire to allude specifically to the habit of posting glossy photos of vedettes on walls by black South Africans in the maintenance of stereomodern escapism:

> The case of *Zonk!* reveals how American-style consumer capitalism and leisure culture arguably became as important in Africa as the attenuating ties of colonialism. Just as segregation in the United States made the "American Dream" nightmarish for citizens of color, the racial tensions of not only apartheid but also colonialism in the world of *Zonk!*'s readers brought the limits of capitalist dreams of self-actualization through consumption very close to the surface. Nonetheless, such betrayals also heightened the acute desire for consumerist chimera that might provide imagined respite from the all-too-real consequences of legislated and de facto inequalities. (119)

However, the "interarticulated desires" that Jaji decodes in popular magazines in Africa with other African and African American popular media in the early 1960s uncover the direction of the flow of influences from elsewhere to Africa, positioning African audiences as prolific consumers of such influences. In Sule's novel, on the other hand, the newspapers that Murtala reads are not aspirational paradigms or chimerical respite to emulate glossy modernity but to expose the gaps or disjunctures in his reception of cross-national politics and to suggest possibilities other than cross-nationalism as a dialectical interaction. The flow therefore from the center (Gulf War, the Palestinian conflict or the Liberian War) to Africa is not as seamless as the stereomodern culture of the 1960s that enables Africans to momentarily forget or escape the lived horrors of colonialism or racism.

For Murtala, the newspapers he reads and the cutouts of emaciated children from the Liberian War function as respatialized extensions of war that abet his understanding of greed, violence, and power in Kano to the extent they expose the disjunctures produced by cross-national acts of violence in localized instantiations of greed and power. Conversations by ordinary, poorly educated victims of violence, commenting on the state of affairs in their city and country aptly illustrate this disjuncture: "'My mother said Muslims started the killing.' . . . It's because Christians burnt a mosque in Sabon Gari.' 'They burnt many churches and mosques in Dakata.' 'Did Christians fight in Dakata?' . . . 'Yes Christians killed many Muslims.' 'In Kwana Hudu, it was Muslims that killed many Christians'" (Sule 2013, 42). Such conversations peer deep into the history, the civil war, and the demographics of Nigeria: "Most people from the North are Muslims and most people from the South are Christians" (42). Respatialization of violence does not simply transpose the space of the violence from one location to another. It exposes gaps to show that violent acts are not produced and received in the same manner. Thus, the Gulf War, the violence in Gaza, the Liberian War, the Global North: none of these are referents for the violence in Kano. Nor are these space solutions in the form of escapist chimera, for Murtala discovers a new world within the geography of his own city as he stumbles upon class, flattening out any aspiration of a transnational space in the definitional sense beyond national borders that his newspapers and magazines can conjure. He encounters people unfazed by violence: a part of town untouched by the madness that has wracked his world. He doesn't believe Ola when his friend claims the absence of violence in his place: "Could there be anywhere in Kano City they had not killed people?" (49). Ola lives "close to the governor's house" but living in the upper-class immunized world that is unscathed by riots does not explain or guarantee safety from violence (49). Class protection thus is folded into the larger message of interreligious intercourse through the assertive politics of interfaith marriage within Nigeria. The solution thus is not sought cross-nationally.

Less concerned about conversion to spiritually align the Muslim woman's actions with her marital decision, Sule focuses on a solution that perhaps extends the conversation on class, religious, and ethnic disparities encountered in Adichie's story. In "A Private Experience," Ola's father, like Chika, is Christian and therefore more privileged, better educated, and socially emancipated than his Muslim counterparts. Yet, that privilege and education cannot assure peace without a religious merger such as a transgeographic relationship—marriage. It is executed explicitly to indicate strategies against such problems. Ola tells Murtala, "My father is a Christian and my mother a Muslim" (73). Murtala fails to understand ("How can that be?") because "Christians and Muslims always hate each other" (73). Ola counters, "My dad says it's love. They really love each other" and adds that his siblings are *free* to follow any religion, again underlining the solution in communal contacts (73). Read together, Sule's novel and

Adichie's story offer ways of strategizing against communal violence that emanates from interreligious tensions inside the transgeographic space of disparities within national borders. There are numerous lessons in this motif of marriage and family that Sule wants to foreground. First, Sule merges two rival groups together in a long-term relationship with its attendant challenges of divergent beliefs. He then provides the reason for this long-standing relationship—love—to undermine the hatred and spite around them. Finally, he places the family away from the space of the violence in the city as if to enfold them in a protective circle symbolically shielding them from the gruesome violence that convulses the other parts of town because they are able to overcome differences that others are not. Most of all, the children are not forced to follow any particular faith, removing the last constraint that forces people into paths that provincialize their views of others and themselves. Sule's placement of this relationship within a part of town that is also untouched by the riots and the violence that blazes through Murtala's world functions as a symbol of solutions. Murtala's parents' relationship,is unknown even to other Nigerians squarely spatializes strategies—unconsidered and unexampled. The other world in Murtala's magazines and their conversations, of Africa as a poor and starving continent, are folded into the merger of Ola's parents to be worked out in a space in Nigeria.

Solidarity thus is not only cross-nationally unknown but also transgeographically underarticulated, mooting the important question of relationships fostered cross-nationally that ignore transgeographic relationships both as potential spaces of solutions and as generatively transnational sites that flexibly redraw definitions of the transnational. The class differences between Murtala and Ola then follow from this merger across dissident relations and are not apart from it. Sule twins the description of the mob and the concomitant violence with Adichie's story—"heaps of debris along the road, near the burnt houses . . . burnt flesh, rotten. The odour was heavy in the air . . . burnt vehicles beside the roads" (2009, 48) and blurs religio-ethnic finger pointing in both stories as the Muslim barber saves Murtala's life, evened out in the loss of Murtala's Christian friend Helen's life. Ola's interreligious world presents itself as the oasis of calm away from the madness in Murtala's life as does the shop that serves as the haven for the two women who confront their prejudices. These spaces of tensions and solutions—Ola's home and his parents' marriage; the space of the shop and the barber saving Murtala's life just as the Muslim vendor saves Chika's life and as Helen's death is traced on Nnedi's disappearance—evince a rebalancing as Chika self-revises her opinions, and Murtala witnesses solutions within his own city in unexampled relationships.

Comparatively, Ruqiyyah's conversion to Islam is problematized not in her acceptance of the faith, as she converts much before meeting and marrying Hamid. Rather, it is problematized in Hamid's inability to adhere to the same degree of spirituality that he believes he is nationally and ethnically entitled to fulfill. Aboulela's attempt to delineate such issues of religious identity as tied to race and ethnicity in Hamid's case and religious identity as separate from ethnicity and race, as in Ruqiyyah's case, underscores the respatialization of spaces of contact that are typically read and received cross-nationally. Ola's parents' relationship similarly inverts the solution's space within that of Nigeria, which is unaware of such solutions within its own borders, not least because it is unable to imagine such a relationship in the context of mind-numbing violence and hatred. Moreover, it also inverts the thought that solutions can be found solely in cross-national solidarities. As the Muslim vendor climbs out of the window in Adichie's story, she leaves Chika only with a greeting of goodwill for her people, suspends any pact of solidarity or coalition, and leaves unanswered and unsettled a multitude of questions arising from their brief meeting, backgrounds, and subjectivities. Similarly, Pearlsha Abubakar shifts transnationalism to transgeographic spaces in the trope of a mixed marriage that also suspends any likelihood of solidarity until the nation-space can be recast as a mixed space.

Interfaith Selves, Marriages, Families, and *Ummah*: Pearlsha Abubakar's Fiction

Composer, essayist, filmmaker, photographer, Pearlsha Abubakar writes frequently about religious relations in her native Philippines. Her work has appeared online and in digital venues in *Dagmay, Cha: Asian Literary Journal*, and in a number of documentaries and television series. Abubakar lives in Manila. Transnationalism in Abubakar's short story "Maghrib" (2008) and her essay "Naunu Na Kaw Yan (What's Happening to You?)" (2015) are both boundary-crossing reflections. Both pieces contest the space of the nation as monoreligious. Rooted in the southern Philippines' Muslim-majority islands of Sulu, Mindanao, and Palawan—in a Catholic majority nation of about seventy million people—Abubakar's transnational feminist identity unfurls transgeograpically in relationships of filial ties that ironically culminate in positing ambivalence. Abubakar's identity reflects the sentiments of the Muslim minority community in the Philippines and its relationship with the Catholic majority nation. However, Abubakar's relationship to her Catholic majority country is mediated first through her own identity as an offspring of a mixed marriage between a Muslim father and a Catholic mother.[13] In her introduction to the collection of short stories where "Maghrib" appears, Coeli Barry describes Muslim Filipino identity and community as paradigmatic of these expanding spaces of self, marriage, family, community, and nation: "Muslims are a minority in the predominantly Catholic Philippines and while Muslims' sense of place within the Philippines is mediated by this minority status, it is by no means fully defined by it" (2008, ix). This mediation, I will argue, is also central to the idea of *ummah* as Muslims configure their relationships with each other but are profoundly marked by their presence within a larger community of non-Muslims. As pointed out previously, Muslims are marked by their presence in a non-Muslim nation-state, thus centralizing the idea of community and *ummah* that multiply shapes their self-identities as a fact of dissident relationality. The story illustrates a Christian-Muslim Filipino woman's strategy for clarifying her identity in relation to a respatialized family (mixed marriage, mixed identity), community (Christian-Muslim), nation (multireligious, ethnic, and multilingual), and the *ummah* (Muslims and non-Muslims).

Barry is careful to stress this multispatial engagement as more than a minority's attempt to articulate itself in relation to the nation. As she points out, Muslim writing constitutes *recasting* "Filipino literature" that was "un-problematically modern," and "Muslim literature" that was "confined to the 'traditional'" (xii). For Muslim writers this involved crafting a space where the vernacular languages of Tausug, Meranao, Arabic as well as Tagalog "are never out of listening range," writes Barry (x). Muslim Filipino writers, adds Barry, wrought "fictional landscapes that drew on a world they knew as children or as young adults" as they began writing in English and in a genre—the short story—that was dominated by Christian Filipino writers:

> To the degree that Christianized Filipinos thought about Muslim literary life at all at this time, they likely thought in terms of 'Muslim literature,' a term defined by scholars to include oral narratives, ballads, songs and some written sources. (xi, xii)

Defined this way, continues Barry, "'Muslim-Filipinos' short stories fell beyond the pale of Muslim literature" (xii). Muslim Filipino literature is similar in its impulse to a minor literature, as Deleuze and Guattari famously define it, in that it "doesn't come from a minor language; it is rather that which a minority constructs within a major language." Muslim Filipino literature takes on added significance because of its religious distinction from the Christianized majority, a thematic consciousness that pervades their writing (1986, 16). There are tensions then of language and religion that Muslim Filipino writers balance in crafting their worldview and constructing a literature that can house such a view, thus recasting the canon and not having to fit within it. For women writers, this unruly space takes on yet another meaning as their writing evinces a reversal of the exclusions and separateness that writing, identity, and belonging to their communities and the nation-state meant. This disquieting experience with integration and inclusion permeates Muslim women's writing through a number of techniques borrowing from, as Lilia Quindoza Santiago asserts, the feminist movement—Babaye—in the Philippines, of retracing, retrieving, and recovering the qualities of their foremothers, none other than "poets, artists and cultural leaders," much like Abubakar who retrieves and retraces the meaning of her family within the original *ummah* of Abraham (2018, 110, 111).

Abubakar details a daughter's confusion at her parents' divergent faiths. Maryam's sense of *ummah* or community pushes against a religion she knows through her father, Yusuf, and finally against the nation where Muslims occupy a contested place. This is a place, to evoke Briggs, McCormick, and Way again, where "the nation itself has to be a question" (2008, 628). Abubakar splices the double lens of the heroine's ambivalence toward Islam, owing to Yusuf's long absences due to his political career, with the Filipino Muslim ambivalence to the Catholic-majority nation. Abubakar confronts the monoreligious nation space with the example of Maryam's familial agency—a religiously plural agency. Several kinds of subordination figure in Abubakar's story to be challenged by the aesthetic of *ummah*. The *ummah* is allegorized in the change of direction that models the transformation of the first Muslim community in Medina as it consolidated and matured into, among other existent meanings, Muhammad's *ummah* or community.[14] The narrator, Maryam, is a child of a Catholic mother and a Muslim father. Her mother, Grace, seems to have converted to Islam:

> The twilight prayer. The only prayers her mother Grace never missed, out of respect for her husband. She had regarded it in a practical sense: the time after sunset and before nightfall was the only free time she has, when she had finished with her household chores. (171, 172)

Known as "Balik-Islam" to refer to Catholic converts to Islam, Sajed Ingilan explains the term as "one who is just returning to her nature" as early settlers of the Philippines "were generally or already Muslims before the period of colonialism" (2017, 149). In a country where Muslims are a minority (5 percent Muslim in a population of roughly sixty-seven million), Maryam embraces both faiths and expresses an ambivalence that projects onto her father Yusuf's dichotomous relationship in his private and political lives, onto the broader political identity of Muslims in a Catholic majority country, and as a community or *ummah* in these simultaneous worlds, to borrow Kaplan's words, that push into each other's spaces.

Barry presents the interreligious makeup of the Philippines, "The Muslim communities in the Southern Philippines live with an awareness of non-Muslims and this awareness pervades these stories" (2008, xvi). This awareness of the other is amply symbolized in the story in the resonant trope of the window. Maryam is keenly aware of her absent father, and resents his distance, having grown up without him and knowing him only through paychecks delivered by messengers. Yusuf has stayed away from Grace and Maryam in the southern part of the country due to his involvement in politics (xvi). Abubakar captures this distance and absence in Maryam's life through the window as Maryam peers through it to watch Yusuf pray in the courtyard. This distance metaphorically spatializes the chasm between the Catholic community and the Muslim minority. Both the resentment and distance multiply as she receives no assistance from him to prepare for her mother's end:

> She had done everything by herself—called the ambulance; called her aunt Wilma who lived nearby; called relatives from Cagayan to break the news; got some ice from the ref to rub on her mother's body, hoping for the cold to save her from death. (172)

But Abubakar's aim is to respatialize the public and political interreligious tensions within the realm of the private—the domestic drama of Yusuf's interreligious marriage. His politics is also private. Understandably, Maryam does not relate to her father, to Islam, or to the minority Muslim population in the southern Philippines that he represents publicly and politically. The window has thus served its purpose of separating the courtyard where Yusuf prays and the room in the house from where Maryam watches him. Yet, it is also the window that allows her to glimpse at him, into his life and politics that will draw him closer to her.

Once again, as in Adichie's story, the trope of the window spatializes relationships between communities. Maryam's half-Catholic identity thus separates but also links the spaces of different communities. These overlapping and circular links of Catholicism and Islam in Maryam that spatially and temporally also make up the story delineate the transnational not as spaces distinct from each other but within each other, respacing its boundaries within the individual, the family, the community, and nation-state. This curiosity about the other (the awareness of the other), however, affirms a relationship with one's own land reflected in the Filipino Muslim community's longing for its own literature and voice in a Christian country. Seen from the other side, this longing also affirms a relationship with the other in that Maryam is half Catholic, thus respatializing the dominant center as the distant presence that is not apart from the weaker party (Muslims) but one with it—merged in the space of an interreligious marriage and family. Maryam's transnationalism or relationship across boundaries thus begins with her initiation into Islam through a figure—Yusuf—who embodies the tensions of this multireligious unit onto the multireligious composition of the Filipino nation, folding in the cross-national community of Muslims in the Middle East that endorse Yusuf's cause and is briefly mentioned in the story.[15]

The process of spatializing relationships involves the change in direction of influences and the flow of ideas—as a problem underlying unequal power relations. Maryam's shift from Catholicism to Islam is mediated by her father. Yusuf links these two religious spaces in his marriage and family with his political career in the service of the Filipino Muslim minority. He thus operates a rebalancing of unequal power relations. Maryam is raised in the Catholic tradition but admits that everything "changed" when her father taught them how to pray, thus also "changing" the direction of her faith (Abubakar 2008, 174). The direction, then, of the *ummah* as the direction of prayer facing Mecca, changed with the idea of *ummah*, that Maryam's family embodies as a small community struggling to unite, finding a common voice in prayer. Folding in national politics—Christian and Muslim elections—to two individuals (Christian and Muslim) in the space of a family and marriage, Maryam's identity is immersed in a space where the discrepant hierarchy of the head of the family, the father, is absent but exists through his instruction of Islam as the distant presence. Abubakar thus explains this peculiar change in direction as experienced by Maryam in her habit of praying mediated by her Catholic mother's devotion to Yusuf:

> Maryam would hurriedly wash herself for the ablution, out of respect for her mother more than anything else. First, she would smooth water on the right hand three times, then her left hand three times, so she could feel God, or so her father said: then, in her mouth, three times so she could speak His name; then onto her ears so she could hear His instructions. (172)

This means that even in situations when the relationships do not turn toward a dominant center (Catholics), the hegemony of the discrepant hierarchy is deconstructed, as Yusuf has little influence on Maryam. Yet such a deconstruction is not conclusive in that the father's absence and schizoid mannerisms—the distant presence—that Maryam resents but must accept because of the filial bond is gradually reversed by her own admission that her "fleeting interest in her father" changed on learning how to pray (174). How could an absent force with such tenuous links forge such a bond? The distant transnational—the absent father—now exists as a palpable presence through the titular act of the story—prayer—in Maryam's relationship with a religion that she practices through the space of multiple relationships within her family and interlinked with each other as in Deleuze and Guattari's evocation of Kafka's work as a rhizome or burrow. It matters less where one enters or exits from, as Deleuze and Guattari point out, but more *how* the internal pathways are connected with each other.

Thus, the more well-known meaning of *ummah*—a community of Muslims—is stitched within this family unit of multiple faiths and spaces of relationships and within the private sphere of marriage that the father merges with his politics: this makes it a relationship within the other, mapping onto a broader meaning of *ummah*. Yusuf Zubaira, the father's full name, mobilizes the poorest Muslim fraternities in Sulu, in the southern Philippines. He seeks funding from his contacts in the Middle East to underwrite his campaign among the weakest sections in Sulu (173).

But this cross-national connection is not as rich in meaning as Zubaira's politics invested in "countless interfaith dialogues where he was hailed as the new light of Islam" (173). His reputation as a "man of peace aroused suspicions among certain quarters in the Central government. Disgruntled generals accused him of harboring criminal elements and extremists in the guise of faith" (173). As Barry suggests, "the long years of violence from the 1970s on have left deep divides between the military and local Muslim leaders" (2008, xiv). A man who Maryam dislikes for neglecting his first wife and child (Maryam herself) and who refuses to "even help her hold her mother in a sitting position after she vomited bile out and collapsed," now "clutched his chest, afraid that his heart would crush his ribcage" on learning of his wife's passing (Abubakar 2008, 172, 173).

The idea of an *ummah* then rests on the cognition of this dichotomous relationship through interfaith dialogues, extending Yusuf's personal relationship with a Christian woman. His daughter misunderstands him and resents his absence; and he is derailed by opponents, who are deeply suspicious of his interfaith promotions as a vision for a plural Philippines, flowing from the space of his multireligious family.[16] The ending of the story, however, offers yet more clues to the spaces of transnationalism that Abubakar promotes through the idea of *ummah* as Maryam discerns Yusuf's less-glimpsed side: the indifferent father who spoke "in riddles, in Arabic, in flowery Koranic prose" (174). Ingilan reads the ending of the story as a reinstatement of patriarchal order as the father is "the imam 'leader' in the family, the Khalifah 'bearer of Allah's trust.' Thus, Yusuf is doing his responsibility to observe the teachings of Islam" (2017, 150). I posit that the relationship between Maryam and Yusuf goes beyond the patriarchal imposition of order over a girl unable to assert her will, for he has hardly been present enough for Maryam to respect his authority. Yet the man who refuses to help her hold her mother in a sitting position also humanizes his relationship with his family by explicitly stating his reasons against an autopsy. He explains it cryptically to Maryam by putting "one hand on his wife's cheek. 'It's still soft. She's still alive inside. You want some stranger to cut her up so she could give us peace?'" (175). Maryam bends over to check her dead mother's body: "She's still soft" (175). The cold, emotionless father, in his own mysterious way, discerns life in his dead wife's body. He clings to life in his wife's corpse as he sees beyond her cold exterior and teaches his daughter to feel the warmth or life that cannot be explained scientifically. He closes the distance and the absence between them.

The resentment in Maryam's scream as she insists on the autopsy melts with her father's embrace and tears. These emotions, previously distant or absent, revise the prior relationship: the one in the first part of the story before Maryam learned to pray, before the direction of the family changed from the Catholic tradition to the Muslim one, and most importantly, before Yusuf resets his relationship as a father in a symbolic gesture of moving toward a family united in the faith of the minority. This change enables Maryam to see that her mother still lives ("She is still alive inside") something beyond rational explanation but sufficient to melt the estrangement between father and daughter (175). She is able to discern it only through the mysterious knowledge of her father's Arabic verses, flowery Qur'anic prayers, and riddles, metaphoric of a Christian majority nation unable to accommodate the "cryptic" other. But more importantly, she reconnects with her father, and this reconciliation indicates to Maryam a solution not from afar but something from within translated to her as her father—the absent force—explains his reasons against the autopsy. The filial bond is reforged through inexplicable and cryptic rationality that nevertheless falls short of the emotional pull of relationships. The transnational then lies not in staking a claim for a relationship just with the nation but with many internal relationships as Maryam resolves her confusion vis-à-vis herself and her family.

Abubakar's essay "Naunu Na Kaw Yan? (What's Happening to You?)" presents a similar, if somewhat less metaphoric, view of *ummah* as a transgeographic strategy to solve the Catholic-Muslim impasse in the Philippines. Abubakar understands and explains transnationalism in three tropes: her mixed religious family, the original *ummah* of Abraham, and a handshake. She tasks herself with positing alternatives of community by creating new figurations. As Leela Gandhi has observed:

> There is no dearth of models, we know, for the figuration of community. Yet when confined to the canonical generalization of established affective formations (of family, fraternity, genealogy, filiation), community lapses all too often into a dull, replicative economy, ill-equipped to the task of positing alternatives. (2006, 18, 19)

Abubakar, however, explicitly and emphatically turns to family, filial bonds, and genealogy to creatively claim community. She belongs to the Tausug ethnic group of Muslims from the Philippines, also common to Malaysia and Indonesia, and opens with a transnational line that merges two worlds and faiths in the space of marriage and family, thus preparing the reader for a tolerant optic.[17] She not only naturalizes the multireligious condition but also preempts the peculiarity ascribed to such a condition:

> I find it comforting that in the Tausug worldview, there is no such thing as "what's wrong with you?" Nothing is ever wrong with you; you are a handiwork of Allah and are as perfect as can be. (2015, 5)

This is also how she understands the framework of her own background—an uneasy relationship between two faiths. In a similar nonfictional piece, "No Dowry, No Cry," she recounts the bumps in her courtship and eventual marriage to a non-Muslim. Ironically, in that piece, she describes her conservative father's outlook as he facetiously tells Abubakar's suitor that he's "unlike any Muslim father you'll ever meet, having studied both the Bible and the Koran, having many Catholic friends, having lived in Manila for so long, and having a decadent urbanite like me for a daughter" (2013). He also adds that "back in Sulu, a Muslim woman marrying a non-Muslim was downright unthinkable (2013)" before consenting to the marriage. Ethnic and religious relationships are thus deeply cognizant of the sovereignty of social systems.

In "Naunu Na Kaw Yan? (What's Happening to You?)" Abubakar is fascinated by the leader of the Muslim *ummah*, Muhammad: "'The comforter,' Mohammad truly was a comfort because he was so mortal, so relatable" (2015, 6). At the same time, she is also drawn to "the image of a gaunt-faced man with a bleeding heart . . . Jesus Christ" (6). She balances Mohammad's "contented spirituality" with Christ's "tormented passion" (6). She knows the "Anima Christi song by heart" and models herself on her paternal grandmother Mamsie who she sees as an extension of Mohammed (6). She then goes on to say, "My life has been about reconciling these two different beings and their views within me, without judgment" and likens this reconciliation to sharp edges of a triangle that cause pain, tears, and longing (6). Abubakar's strategy for dealing with the pain is to trace it on the triangulation of her own family (two Catholic mothers and a Muslim father) on the story of Abraham, Sarah, and Hagar, a Qur'anic story and seminal source of inspiration in both religions (9). Merging the *ummah* with family enables Abubakar to tolerate the pain. She describes the respatialization of these parallel worlds:

> These two women of Abraham issued progeny that eventually became bitter rivals. The line of descendants from Sarah the Wife became the Jews, the People of the Book. The line of descendants from Hagar The Concubine became the Arabs. Though they were all descended from just one father, Abraham's many children continue to play out this eons-old rivalry, echoed viscerally in many of the most intractably political issues gripping the world today. (9)

She declares, "We must accept it and know its edges. Love its edges," and respatializes the space of her family with the space of the *ummah* in an effort to make sense of her interreligious and fractured identity.

Abubakar uses yet another strategy, the handshake, a gesture of friendship or a greeting, and extends her *ummah*-building strategy to everyone, "Whenever I am introduced to someone, I shake his or her hand and then do something more. After the handshake, I put my hand to my heart, as though extending the handshake into my soul" (10). It is a way of saying "*you have no escape; you are part of my world now*" (9, emphasis in original). She then concludes her essay, "I hope someday, dear reader, by the grace of Allah, I will get to shake your hand and extend it into my soul" (11). The act of meeting strangers, extending a handshake, and folding in the stranger into her soul, thus extending the *ummah* to everyone. This would mean accepting even the most painful relationship as she confesses the polygamous arrangement that pained her biological mother (and her second mother) as the young Pearlsha imbibes coping mechanisms such as learning music (10). It is furthermore spatialized not always as a relationship between discrete constituents—individuals, faiths, or beliefs—in two or more separate spaces. It can, as in Abubakar's case, exist even within one individual. When this happens, and is out of your control, you build, Abubakar suggests, relationships that respatialize existing bonds and connections. As seen in her declarations above, Abubakar's life is not only about two faiths: it is also about two families—her father married twice, both times Catholic women (8). Like Maryam in "Maghrib," perhaps in Abubakar herself, the transnational is imported in their lives through the politics of the Global North and is then redrawn as a space within Catholic and Muslim intimacies and filial bonds to reimagine the family, the nation, and transnation.

All three writers—Aboulela, Sule, and Abubakar—redefine the transnational through interarticulated examples of mixed marriages and increasingly think of transnationalism as an *ummah* of humanity where some of the most insoluble problems such as communal hatred, marital discord, estrangement, and filial pain are worked out. In "Majed," the transnational/cross-national space is collapsed not by Ruqiyyah's (a Scottish woman) conversion to Islam but by her encounter with Hamid within the contact zone of marriage. Aboulela decouples Islam from the ethnic and national proprietary claims of immigrants in the West. Secondly, in a strained ethnic and religious relationship between Christians and Muslims in Nigeria, Sule's depiction of marital encounters, in the contact zones of cultures, quietly offers a solution in the figure of the Muslim woman married to a Christian man. This relationship is presented as a way to think about the concept of the transnational, which this couple and their family embody against the projections of the civil war in Liberia, the Gulf War, or the conflict in Gaza that Murtala encounters in cross-national and national magazines and newspapers. While it may seem contrived that Ola's parents are peacefully united in a feverishly hateful environment and appear to escape the violence that destroys their city, their example is not the central metaphor of the novel. It appears peripherally, briefly, and blends in with the other frictions that make up the main plot of the novel. It emerges as a brief moment as though Sule himself toys with such a solution, unsure if it can be considered a feasible way out of the mayhem. Likewise, both of Abubakar's pieces illustrate possibilities of transnationalism in figurations of mixed marriages and identities. Both national and transnational politics, however, are deeply modified by multi-religious and mixed identities and relationships in the contact zone of the family by Yusuf's vision of the Philippines and Maryam's self-correction of her understanding of this vision. Abubakar lays out these simultaneous worlds, folded into tropes of intimate relationships that mobilize dissident relationalities and friendships—knowing the other—in such contact zones as selves, marriages, and families. The mounting tensions in Nigeria or the Philippines between Christians and Muslims are not isolated or rare. Nor are they disconnected from broader conjunctures involving Islamophobia and long-standing suspicions of others. However, the idea of Islamophobia as a Western-centric phenomenon, keeping the space of the West as the primary interlocutor, is fundamentally challenged by these three writers who share an understanding of relationships respatialized in visions of transnationalisms. Aboulela, Sule, and Abubakar correct such notions by modifying the nation space through depictions of relationships—marriages and mixed identities—that are fraught with dissidence.

Chapter 4

The Sterile Womb

Nation Space, Domestic Violence, Polygamous Relationships, and *Ummah*

> The model of motherhood is absolutely natural because if anything binds women together in collective experience, it is childbearing and the mothering of children."
>
> —Oyeronke Oyewumi, "Abiyamo: Theorizing African Motherhood."

This chapter focuses on women's unusual, unconventional, and oftentimes paradoxical strategies against the naturalization of women as biological producers and the concordant tropes of domesticity. While theorizations of motherhood emphasize the fusing of motherhood and nation in national struggles and the enshrinement of gender in the domestic space, they do not account for the (in)ability itself to bear children—sterility and barrenness—as paradoxically fertile spaces of a new conception of self and nation. Sterility not only breaks the bond between gender and nationalism but also questions the single narrative of national culture. This chapter also examines a selection of short stories largely unmapped beyond their regional and philological boundaries that highlight the relationship of gender to the nation-state in the overlooked idea of barrenness and sterility, mobilized by *ummah*-building strategies of dialogue, encounter, and exchange. These include Anna Dao's short story "A Perfect Wife," Pearlsha Abubakar's "Ayesha's Pretty Hate Machine," Arifa Macaqua Jamil's "Sakeenah," Abidah el Khalieqy's "Road to Heaven" (translated from Bahasa Indonesia by John McGlynn), and Jemila Abdulai's short story "#Yennenga."

The least fashionable of all literary forms, as Daniel Halpern describes it, short fiction functions as "documents of our condition" (1999, xiii). All five stories take an unusual approach to contest the coding of national construction in the figure of the woman as mother by creatively giving purpose to the supposed handicap associated with motherhood—sterility, silence over physical abuse, and marital negligence—through transgeographic connections to redefine the nation itself and in the process also redefine the *ummah* as a transgeographic network of connections. In other words, the redefined self—gender as barren and sterile—also recasts the nation as a plural ideal via tropes of encounters, exchanges, and dialogues.

My main argument in this chapter thus rests on the type of self—a multireligious one—in relation to the nation constructed on the basis of the type of marriage and then the type of family, influencing the self and in turn the community and nation. These levels of influence on the self, as explained by Niara Sudarkasa, means that motherhood is contingent on the type and structure of family itself.[1] This is not to say, as Nzegwu has pointed out, that motherhood cannot be defined (2003, 2). Rather, it is to draw attention to the *structure of the family* itself that determines the constraints and elasticity of the role of motherhood, leading Sudarkasa to assert, "mothering is encased in culturally variable rules, regulations, expectations, and patterns of behavior." Encasing, explains Sudarkasa, involves a variety of meanings of "motherhood," ranging from the marital status of the mother to the act of childbirth or "a set of behaviors, expectations and responsibilities that constitute culturally defined kinship roles," as she puts it. This point of "family structure or kinship grouping" (Sudarkasa 2004) refocuses attention not only on such spaces of relationships as marriage and then family but also on the *nature of relationships* across various spaces. It holds, I believe, key clues to rethinking motherhood, its relationship to the nation, and the definitions of nation and transnation as well. To mention just two examples briefly, a theorization of gender in relation to the nation overlooks the complex family structure of extended families, as Sudarkasa points out. Indeed, the concept of extended families developed within the discipline of sociology in the West only from African societies. Second, the theorization of gender and nation also overlooks multireligious relationships starting from a multireligious self, marriage, family, and likewise a religiously plural community, nation, and by extension a transnation. Thus, the writers I study contest gendered sterility by taking on the cultural sterility of the nation to reimagine transnationalism as a community unmediated by national boundaries or as *ummah*.

To this end, I shift the passive construction of gender in the nation—"excluded from direct actions as national citizens" per McClintock—to an active reconstruction that charges the equity and inclusivity inherent in plurality in reimagining transnationalism as transgeography (1997, 90). The genesis of such a redefinition emerges not merely in the deployment of the dialectical obverse of fertility and motherhood (i.e., sterility) to wrest the nation space from the ideologies that it set up as a unitary voice on gender, womanhood, and sexuality. It emerges also in the contestation of the overdetermination of motherhood in a space that lacks religious, ethnic, sexual, and linguistic plurality. The South African writer Rayda Jacobs, for instance, uses "variety as a community reality" as a gambit in her novels, which often explore religious and racial tensions in Cape Town. Her novel *My Father's Orchid* (2006) maps the splintered self as microcosmic of a religiously split marriage, family, community, and nation of Muslims and Christians in South Africa.[2] As Hui Yew-Fong asserts, "Religion, whether institutionalized or otherwise, has an uncanny tendency to intervene in the political life of nation-states from time to time" (2013, 3). This religion, one that is not always institutionalized, formalized, and legislated in policy pronouncements, serves as the conduit to redefine the fetishization of motherhood in tropes of gender and the nation.

Similarly, Simon Gikandi calls the active reconstruction that contests dominant narratives, a "third discourse" of strategies and expressive agencies by women writers who don't simply reverse the dialectical relationship of voice and silence. Instead, they activate a process of interleaving the nation space with minoritized religious, ethnic, and linguistic strategies to counter gendered problems (1992, 199). As such, the subversive "third discourse" is not to be found in a simple reversal of motherhood as barrenness but in a revamped definition of the nation accomplished by despoiling the trope of nationalism and motherhood. In his reading of works by Caribbean women writers' revisions of the "mother figure" and their contestation of the location of the mother in the "signifying systems of the colony and the new nation," Gikandi observes Caribbean male writers as twinning the national narrative with the familiar figure of the woman as mother, where the "mother represents the utopian space of the nation, of home and belonging" albeit silent and subordinate to the male's quest for identity (1992, 197–198).

This contestation by female writers, as read by their male counterparts, rides on the precondition of absence and voicelessness or the dialectic of presence and absence as "women writers strive to underscore the converse process—the absence of the female subject and its silencing in the master/slave dialectic" (199). However, this voicelessness and absence meant that a particular form of culture in the Caribbean—oral culture—had not been restored to the extent that women (its custodians) remained muted, marginalized, and largely invisible in national narratives (202). In other words, Caribbean culture is viewed as open ended and incomplete without women's voices. But in this context of voicelessness as more than a simple reversal of the master-slave or presence-absence dialectic (or the restoration of the absent female voice) Gikandi sights a "third discourse," or strategies by which female writers manage to subjectify their female characters in a male-dominated world of female degradation (200). Thus they "deflate "the make-believe value system" of the colonizer" in history, and recenter themselves "as custodians of an oral culture," *inserting* themselves within both the male and colonial discourse of writing, and confronting their "material objectification in the language of the colonizer" (201). The ensemble of strategies that constitute this "third discourse" is, avers Gikandi, a "precondition for subjectivity" and not an awkward burden to be tarried in the process of self-determination (201). Gikandi thus enumerates such strategies as the folklorization of language, the use of "patois" and popular culture to underscore the uniqueness of the challenge to both colonial and male-centered discourses of nationalism (200). Quoting Michelle Cliff, Gikandi states, female writers despoiled "the master's soup"—"*mixing in* the forms taught us by the oppressor, undermining his language and co-opting his style, and turning it to our purpose" (1992, 203, emphasis added). The revisionist impulse of a third discourse that Gikandi reads as exceeding the "Manichean relationship between self and other" can be seen in a number of texts analyzed in this book. But this third discourse can be found more prominently in the five stories under analysis in this chapter in that they foreground a granular narrative of social, emotional, gendered constraints, as well as power in women's lives when dealing with the figure of the woman as mother and its concordant tropes of domestic violence, sterility, and polygyny (202).

The mixing-in strategy of the third discourse can also be discerned in the relationship of literary expression with other such expressive forms of knowledge as histories and ideologies. Ato Quayson observes the third discourse in the context of literature and urban society that variant histories—nonliterary discourses, government policies, documents, media representations, opinions from everyday life, the colonial and historical archive, as well as many discourses of orality—may or may not intersect with literary expression (213). Quayson (2014) suggests that these variant histories constitute

> discursive ensembles in which different fragments "speak" to each other across a nexus of knowledge, ideology and power, . . . [and] the task in this instance is to understand the asymmetrical nature of the relationship between variant histories that may or may not intersect with the literary domain. (214)

Similarly, Mukoma wa Ngugi proposes a way to rethink writing as a relationship between literary and nonliterary sources to enable a redefinition of African literatures provincially constructed and canonized in relation to European literatures. Ngugi notes writers such as Aminata Forna, of Scottish and Sierra Leonian parentage, who wrote the novel *The Hired Man*, set in Croatia during the Serbian-Croatian war. Her novel would not be by any "plot-stretch" of imagination, states Ngugi, an African novel. Yet, Forna's shape-shifting work draws from the Sierra Leonian war, raising questions about the resonant sources that "empower" subjects to write (2018, 14). None of the five writers analyzed in this chapter is well established or known beyond their regional audiences, at least not in Western academic circles. Their work is variant at best. This book's labor is therefore directed at asking how variant voices on knowledge and ideology map onto broader sites of knowledge dissemination. These writers may not be canonical or representative of discursive trends in African and Southeast Asian writing. However, the writers in this chapter appeal in various ways to the idea of womanhood and symbolic of motherhood. These authors also express diverse ideas on motherhood mostly through short fiction and sometimes in just a handful of short stories, as opposed to more sustained narratives such as novels, essays, or a more substantial oeuvre. Most of all, their strategies to solve gendered problems of sterility, domestic violence, and polygyny appear improvisational, irrational, unusual, and even counterintuitive to accepted theorizations of gender in society. They are variant and asymmetrical fragments at best. Yet variant history, ideology, and knowledge, if mapped equitably, constitute resonant (if asymmetrical) intersections to redefine gender's relation to the nation (and consequently to the transnation). I begin my reading by focusing on the motif of sterility to demonstrate the active contestation of gendered symbols in the construction of the nation as culturally sterile. But first, I elaborate on the discursive techniques, tropes, and patterns of motherhood and its naturalization in national narratives.

Nationhood, Motherhood, and Mixed Selves

The governing symbol of gender in the nation, as Yuval-Davis and Anthias specify, is of women as "as biological reproducers of the members of national collectivities" (1989, 7). The relationship between gender and nation in African literature is expressed similarly where even the most classical narratives fail to complicate the relationship of gender to the nation through ethnic, religious, or linguistic variations. In other words, the contestations of this gendered fixation with motherhood almost always unfurl on a monocultural scale. Theoretically, too, as I discuss in this section, analyses focus on the dissonance between symbolism (mother as exalted and revered) and reality (subordinate sociopolitical roles) in monocultural frameworks. Most notably and memorably in literature, Buchi Emecheta's classic *The Joys of Motherhood* (1979) depicts sterility as a taboo and a curse, a sign of failure for a woman. The two opening chapters of the novel are tellingly titled "The Mother" and "The Mother's Mother," encapsulating the socially and psychologically entrenched preoccupation of gender and motherhood in Nigerian society. At one point, Emecheta situates motherhood as the line between sanity and insanity, rational and irrational behavior, and gendered success and failure. Proving fertility to the world therefore is vital to a woman's social success, self-worth, and sanity: "She is not made after all. . . . She has only just lost a child that tells the world that she is not barren," and "they all agreed that a woman without a child for her husband was a failed woman" (62). More recently, Lola Shoneyin's novel *Baba Segi's Wives* (2013) also touches on the curse of sterility within a Nigerian Muslim family. Similarly, Yvonne Vera thematizes the concept of motherhood and its multilayered significance for women in her novel *Butterfly Burning* (2000) particularly, and in much of her work to undermine the fetishized identity of woman as mother and nation. As previously noted, McClintock traces this nexus of gendered roles and nation in expanding scales in the metaphor of the nation as family, extending into the world as a family of nations (transnations) that was contingent on "the prior naturalizing of the social subordination of women and children within the domestic sphere" (1997, 91). Elleke Boehmer also affirms this insistent conflation of maternal symbols and national feeling, stating that "often set in relation to the figure of her nationalist son, her ample, childbearing, fully representative maternal form typically takes on the status of metaphor" (2005, 28). In addition, Boehmer explains that

> it is virtually a literary and socio-political given that mother symbols cement national feeling, and that, worldwide, the cognate-metaphors of soil, earth, home and family buttress the process of making national claims, or invoking the modern nation into being. (26)

Like McClintock, Boehmer traces the morphing of nation and gender as naturalized functions and feelings that fuse the identification of the mother with the beloved earth, the national territory and the first-spoken language, and the national tongue.

However, this naturalization of womanhood, enshrined in the space of domesticity and functions of motherhood, dichotomously dovetails with both reverence for the mother/nation and oppression of other gendered roles of woman/lover/wife (Ray 2000, 39).[3] It also widens the gap between nation space and minority identity in the self-emergent nation. Speaking of Igbo society, the "exalted category" of motherhood, states Nzegwu, is of social ascension from the subordinated position of wife (2003). Although cast as originator or progenitress, a role authorized by her national sons, she herself is positioned outside the central script of national self-emergence. Thus, "the woman—and usually the mother figure—stands for the national territory and for certain national values: symbolically she is ranged above the men; in reality she is kept below them," writes Nzigwu (2003, 28–29). As for minorities, writes Haleh Afshar, although the "function of womanhood" was particularly amplified as producers of "future martyrs" of the nation in the context of the Iran-Iraq war, it entailed the paradoxical suppression of minorities and local versions of Islam in Iran as the state sought to repress diversity in Islam—local cults—for the sake of a unitary national vision (1989, 110). This suppression ran counter to the Islamic concept of *ummah* that is transcendental to national and international boundaries. Afshar states that

> local cults can easily be accommodated by the flexibility of Islamic ideology. But the religious establishment has always resisted such fragmentation of its central authority and the *ulama* have usually supported policies that imposed and

maintained a sense of national unity. This is surprising since, in essence, nationhood is a relatively unimportant concept in Islam. The whole Muslim community, *Ummat*, is seen as one people guided by total submission to the rule of Islam, which, by its nature, transcends national and international boundaries. (112)

It is in challenging this specific dichotomy between the vision of the state and its appropriation of *ummah* as centralized spaces of unity and unitary identities that Muslim women remobilize boundaries of community and gendered roles. The writers examined in this chapter intervene in the symbolism of woman as mother as the concept of *ummah*—community—produced in dialogues, exchanges, and community-building gestures enables them to remediate their gendered roles as women by recuperating a mixed space.

Sterile Selves and Fertile Spaces: Redefining Self and Nation

I begin with the Filipino writer Arifa Macaqua Jamil's "Sakeenah," written in 2010.[4] The story showcases different levels of identity through relationships of language, ethnicity, and religion. In the preface to the collection in which Jamil's story is reprinted in 2015 as *Rays of the Invisible Light: Collected Works by Young Moro Writers*, the editor, Gutierriez Mangasakan II, attributes the renewed impetus behind anthologizing the voices of Moro writers who had been writing in diverse venues until then, not only as a physical compilation of Moro voices in one anthology but as a symbolic collectivization of their voices in the island nation. Mangasakan evokes the infamous "Mamasapano Incident that has jeopardized the future of the Bangsamoro Basic Law that will hopefully pave the way for greater liberty for our people."[5] Jamil's voice reappearing in the anthology serves as a reminder of a "noble jihad" roused from "silence and passivity to defend our right and honor with the best weapon we can muster—our writing," claims Mangasakan. Ultimately, the personhood of the Moro Muslim, emotionally tied to the political recognition (visibility) of Muslims in the Philippines, through such legislations as the Bangsamoro Basic law that Mangasakan references, rests on informal and improvisational negotiations of a deeply double and mixed identity as Jamil's writing maps the everyday encounters and exchanges between Filipino Muslims and Christians. Incidentally, Pearlsha Abubakar's essay "Naunu Na Kaw Yan? (What's Happening to You?)" analyzed in the previous chapter, is also anthologized by Mangasakan in the same collection as a voice that upholds a vision for an inherently plural Philippines.

Jamil opens her story with Meranao words, embedded in the description of marriage rituals to situate her Meranao identity as gendered by marriage. Meranao thus holds the key to the narrator Sakeenah's role as a wife. She reflects on her gendered identity through the stations of marriage, beginning with her engagement or "dialaga," and the "sayat" or the customary gifts offered to the bride on the wedding day; and finally the "let a igaan" or the customary gifts given to the bride on the night of the wedding (2015, 12). She states that she is allowed to keep these bridal gifts that are lawfully hers, but it is not material security or the "glitter of the stones" that she seeks, "the gold mocks the absence of my husband" (13). This pride in the language and therefore ethnicity and religion (Meranao-Islam) through its repeated insertion in the English-language story is inextricably linked to the pride of wifehood. This strong emotional identification with marriage and culture sinks deeper as the story also turns into a stream of consciousness—an internal monologue of a heartbroken divorcee separated from her husband for the perceived inability to conceive. So deeply internalized are her role and identity as a Meranao woman and wife that she is unable to come to terms with the reality of her sterility. She attributes her impending divorce to "katao" (or sorcery) and "maratabat" (or pride), locating once again her womanhood within Meranao words, desperate to understand the "intertwined reasons" for her situation (12). She settles on "hormonal imbalance" and "hormonal lapses" (15). Sakeenah's muddled thinking and emotions thus emanate from the internalized merging of culture that reifies gendered roles and a language that freights these gendered roles.

To grieve this void and find clarity in this confused state of separation awaiting divorce, denominated by the internalization of motherhood as an ideal of gendered completeness, the narrator moves out of her husband's house and also away from her own family. She thus operates what Quayson (2014) terms, in the context of urban space, a "spatial traversal" or movement from one location to another (214). For Sakeenah, this traversal is also symbolic of the space of the woman—marriage, homestead—as she migrates across several "ethical domains" (215). Space, as Quayson asserts, is not foreshortened or abbreviated, percolating through the character's consciousness (214). Rather, it triggers, as in Sakeenah's case, "an ethical impasse that raises implications either for the protagonist's sense of identity or about their hitherto unexamined understanding of the basis of social order and organization" (215). Sakeenah will examine both her incomplete identity as a divorcée, along with the social order predicated on the absence of other voices. Admittedly, she relocates to Manila and rents a room for two months. She fervently hopes that her husband will change his mind and turns to religion, her "pashbi," bargaining feverishly with God for her sanity to return as she is unable to cope with the "abnormality" of barrenness (14). Against the burden of her lost marriage, as well as the gendered role of mother that she yearns to fulfill even on relocating to Manila (not having heeded her family's advice of marrying a relative, for a relative "values family"), Sakeenah begins a hitherto unexamined understanding of the basis of social order and organization through her relationship with her Catholic landlady and her lover (14).

Sakeenah's reversal of the internalization of her gendered functions as mother begins with the "Buddha in bronze smiling at Mary dressed in purple. The holy trinity is artistically crocheted and framed, hanged [sic] on the wall opposite a mini bar. This is not a sinful place" (15). The sin here is the sexual deviance of lesbianism and also of Sakeenah's own deviance from the naturalized role of motherhood, for Sakeenah's mother calls the place "sinful" and perceives her daughter's spatial traversal as an act of desperation. But the sentence can also imply the latent potential of a nation space as plural that enables Sakeenah to see beyond the narrow limits of fetishized roles, intimately vehicled in her language and culture. The landlady's lover thus puts in perspective for Sakeenah their tabooed relationship. She speaks in defense to console Sakeenah and suggests to her, "Jesus does not like us to be sad" (15). It is also the same woman who reveals to Sakeenah that she divorced her husband abroad when she was younger as an act of sexual self-determination (15). This interfaith encounter is not sentimentally presented to Sakeenah as a blind embrace of differences. It is an unconsidered space of community unmediated by the boundary of the nation-state where the landlady apologizes for the "offensive smell of pork," and informs Sakeenah that "the chicken is halal" so her Muslim tenant may consume it (15). Nor is it offered as a Band-Aid to instantly heal Sakeenah in that even toward the end of the story she sinks back into the despondent cycle of hoping to reconcile with her husband as she reminisces about her wedding gown on viewing the calendar that reminds her of the time she was still married (16).

If women are "bearers of national culture," as Boehmer states or "biological reproducers as members of national collectivities," as observed by Davis and Anthias, to code the relationship of gender with the nation in the trope of motherhood, barrenness operates also on twin levels: it serves as a blow not only to the national culture and tradition—in that their symbols fail in their fertile duty to produce sons—but also a blow to the nation's ability to produce a space for its minority communities (Boehmer 2005, 4; Davis and Anthias 1989, 7). Ironically, barrenness spurs Sakeenah to overturn despair into a productive trope of connections through conversations with her Catholic lesbian landlady and her partner, metaphorizing thus interreligious relationships as generative of solutions to the impasse of gendered and national sterility and a heteronormative and monoreligious nation.[6] In conversations with her landlady, Sakeenah respatializes the sterile nation transgeographically to generative, if subversive, spaces of its strained communities—Muslims and homosexuals. By contesting the nation's ability to interact with its minorities, Sakeenah inventively upends the flaw of coding the nation as naturalized through motherhood on the grounds that the space of the nation—a heteronormative Catholic majority—remains narrow in its conception until it expands to include marginalized and minoritized voices.

The story functions as a possibility of viewing the self and the nation through spaces of relationships previously unexplored. Jamil explores the internalized burdens of gendered roles and identities, vehicled in practices and language, more recently in the short story "Amirah," where the title character refuses a match for marriage from a man born of mixed parentage (and not of "pure Meranao blood")—a Muslim father and a Catholic mother.[7] I find in this metaphoric connection with the other an *ummah*-building strategy that Jamil interpellates in the story to deal most especially with internalizations of gendered stigmas of sterility, for what worries Sakeenah the most is the taboo of being sterile or "bitowanen," "the term sounds slightly close to bitoon. A star. A bitowanen has no sparkle to invite a new relationship" (15). Less concerning than lesbianism for Sakeenah is the "stigma" of "bitowanen" or being separated. She explains that it is not the marital separation itself that worries her. It is the fear of not being able to have another relationship that allows her to procreate. The impulse of a new relationship is common to both states—sterility and *ummah*. The way out of the sterility of culture then is to embrace its plurality and its plural sexuality as Jamil also illustrates in the figures of Buddha, Mary, and Jesus as a way out of the muddled thinking that Sakeenah has internalized as a Meranao bride.

The Malian writer Anna Dao's short story "A Perfect Wife" (1999) also deals with sterility, female self-sacrifice, and the gendered tropes of wife and mother as symbolic of tradition, culture, and community, even nation. Dao sets her transgeographic relationships in the context of two kinds of spatializations, namely family structures in Mali and the colonial wars, to connect gender to the idea of a nation yearning for self-emergence. Dao overturns the metonymy of mother as nation by conveying the idea in the title of the story "A Perfect Wife" but not through the dutiful character of Sira, who is only twelve when she marries a man whose first wife is sterile. Dao reserves her title for Sira's senior co-wife, the barren Astou, to counter the gendered idiom of mother as nation rooted in biology. The reader discovers this twist in Dao's revelations of a transgeographically multirelational and multispatial structure of marital and familial relations in Malian society rife with possibilities for redefining gendered roles, set in motion by an interaction with patrilineal and colonial sociopolitical structures. Whereas the narrator in "Sakeenah" does not yet confront the fear or shame of a second spouse despite being faintly suspicious, Dao's story not only reifies this fear and insecurity but twists it deeper in, to the point that Astou, the barren senior wife, importunes her husband to remarry for an heir, reinforcing the symbolism of woman as biological producer and the internalization of this gendered trope by a woman herself. But on the other hand, such a decision also mobilizes the differences in the social fabric of communities in that the story unravels in an unusually intimate framework. Dao's story pivots on three points. First, it delves into a transgeographic relationship in dissident relationality or friendship that the two co-wives develop—their exchanges, dialogues, and encounters—that moves the idea of community and state in a different direction, that of female *ummah* through a rupture in the gendered expectation of their role as mothers. The main point of this relationality is that Astou's social status is not beholden to her motherly status. This is the first subversion of the motherly trope. Secondly, and as previously mentioned, it is Astou who suggests Idrissa take another wife, ostensibly willing her own marginalization. Finally, in this narrative on progeny and the continuity of a community through heirs, it is the barren Astou whose name lives on in the name of the baby that Sira eventually births on remarrying Idrissa's brother when her first husband dies. The reader discovers the remediation of the symbolism of wifehood and motherhood through community principles, a "third discourse," that neutralizes both patriarchal and colonial signatures over gendered roles.

First, I examine dissident relationality that emerges from the space of family structures in traditional, colonial Malian society. The co-wife, Sira, is "chosen" by Astou (1999, 160). To this end, Astou tasks the griot Sekouba Kouyate to find her a co-spouse, a young girl who would "share her space in Idrissa's bed" but also "know how to set aside Astou's 'due share of water,'" implying the braiding of the self, marriage, and family within a transgeographic space of multiply stratified relationships—gendered (male-female), class-based (differences in wealth and material comforts), familial (family structures and units) and political (governance based on precolonial and colonial Malian societies) (160–161). Admittedly, the male national narrative reinforced here is of gendered subordination in the marital domain through polygyny. However, the family structure in the colonial context in Malian villages bears the imprint more of a space for the self, marriage, community, and nation than of a simple sidelining of a sterile spouse; of a resentment at being marginalized; or that of the subsumption of gendered societal structures within the Western colonial imperium. This structure also accedes to an alternative for the nationalized or communal symbol of motherhood in the relationally dissident community of the two co-wives. The feminist cause of uniting around common feminist issues for solidarity in the transnational sense is worked out in this case through a relationship that is transgeographic across status (sterile versus fertile) and positions (senior versus junior wife) within families. An early pointer to this way of spatializing relationships that I am suggesting registers in Sekouba's mistake in asking for Sira's hand from Oumar Keïta, her uncle. Sekouba learns that Sira is Oumar's younger brother's daughter, and "that because he was not Sira's only father, he needed time to think and also consult with others" (162). Dao explains this filial spatialization in a footnote:

> In Malian tradition, the natural parents of children are consulted in private by other family members but have no right to take an active or visible part in organizing their offspring's wedding ceremony. They neither accept nor share the cola nuts or dowry. *The child's paternal uncle and maternal aunts are the ones considered as his or her parents, with all the parental rights and duties.* They are the ones who organize the wedding. In

Malian society, a child doesn't belong to the one who brought him into the world but rather to the entire community. (162, emphasis added)

The self, family, community, and their myriad relations are much more interarticulated than is first evident.

Second, Astou's status in the family is not contingent on her ability to bear children. Dao accomplishes this by tracing the gendered national narrative as sterile on the grammar of dominance in the colonial wars forced upon Mali. Dao's use of a gendered title for her story is not accidental as she underscores the double narrative of gendered symbolism in both colonization and patriarchy. Thus, she twins the subordination of colonization with gendered symbolism in her illustration of the colonized nation as "the lady love," a gendered object of control to be possessed:

> The colonizer, who was afraid of the same fate he had once inflicted, now demanded 'their' assistance to help drive away and keep out a new intruder who was threatening to invade and take away his homeland, his history, and his lady love. (163–164)

Astou and Sira's husband, Idrissa Keïta, is sent to fight this war of the "temporary master of their lands." This points to the temporary hold of patriarchal control over Astou and Sira that is lifted with their beloved husband Idrissa's departure (164). As the male members of society steel themselves for possibly the end of life, the female sphere is also barren, boding no future or outlet for the family, community, or nation and stilling motherhood in a patriarchal family, community, and nation. Idrissa is the head, and in his absence, as he is "confiscated" by the colonizer, his brother Lamine takes charge of his family as "the acting head of the family; the one to make all the decisions and ensure that the family needs were met" (166). Male privilege, however—both indigenous (patriarchal) and foreign (colonial)—is tokenized first by its temporary hold over others, then by Idrissa's absence, and finally by the colonizer's fear of losing their own dominion in Europe. As Idrissa departs in the service of the "temporary master," life continues as the two women develop a profound bond of friendship. Sira, for instance, learns about Idrissa and comes to love him "through her co-spouse's words" (170). This absence is made permanent with Idrissa's death. Dao neutralizes the relationship of subservience to the male order through Astou's perfection in sterility. It takes many miscarriages before Sira can conceive. Finally, a girl is born, all symbolizing the break from patriarchal norms of male control, male presence, and male progeny. To seal this rupture from patriarchy and male order, the girl is named Astou in honor of a barren woman.

This remediation of gender to the nation through the trope of sterility is also the theme of the Filipino writer Pearlsha Abubakar's story "Ayesha's Pretty Hate Machine" (2008), which humorously frames the anguish of a sterile woman. Reminiscent in many ways of Mariama Ba's iconic *So Long a Letter* in narrating the pain of emotional abandonment in polygamy, this short story captures a woman's feelings of humiliation in a polygamous triangle. Narrated in the first person, the story maps Ayesha's heartbreaking experience of being unable to bear children. Unlike Astou, the eponymous heroine Ayesha in Abubakar's story is appalled when her husband is persuaded to remarry. No more than a "womb" to her in-laws, Ayesha's husband Sayid takes another wife—a Christian woman who converts and is renamed Khadija, after Muhammad's first wife, also as a mark of respect that burns Ayesha as she never received such recognition from her husband as his wife. She describes her experience as being pushed aside by her husband's family after twenty years of marriage to welcome the new wife (2008, 165). Ayesha traces polygamous practice to the prophet's practice of polygamy. She recognizes its basis in Islam. Yet she wrestles with that code and her weaknesses of envy, betrayal, and abandonment. It is through these emotions and her turmoil that Ayesha revises her situation in this marital impasse where she is nothing more than a "womb" and the act of bearing children a "duty" (166).

Ironically, her soon-to-be co-wife, Connie, a Catholic convert, charges Ayesha to record the wedding ceremony. With the camera in her hands, Ayesha's gaze is on herself as she re-views her situation and worth as a "womb" through a "hate machine," punning on the pronunciation of the "Hi-8 camera" that Connie, a broadcast journalist and Ayesha's new co-wife brings with her (165). When Ayesha gets behind the (Hi-8) hate machine, her gaze changes in three ways. First, while everyone admires Ayesha's dexterity with the camera as she films the wedding they "don't see the tears that fall from the eye that is glued to the eyepiece" (168). Ayesha learns to distance the social perception of her—the flowing admiration for her technical bravura—from her own feelings, the tears at the betrayal she records. Next, while Ayesha peers through the lens to witness her present downfall (Sayid's wedding), she also gazes at a life that awaits Connie.

Finally, this morphing of two spaces in the lens of the camera—the viewer and the viewed—operates the change in Ayesha's own vision of herself, gazing at a life from which she gradually recoils while clearing the way for a new start. She realizes, "I'm coming alive through the machine. What a pretty machine, goes on and stops with one click of a red button. I wish my heart was like that" (168).

Ayesha moves on with her life. She divorces Sayid and marries Ahmed. She regenerates from her barrenness. According to Susan Sontag, a photograph, more than a picture or any other mimetic object, has a more "innocent" and therefore "more accurate relation to visible reality" (1973, 4). But more important, per Sontag, photography is a way of "certifying experience," so commonplace that it is used as a "defense against anxiety" (6, 8). Our "sense of situation," says Sontag, is articulated by photography (10). We understand our situations through the pictures we take. We plan our situations through pictures. But unlike nonintervention through photography, which allows a photographer to continue recording and capture an event so it may last longer, as Sontag suggests, Ayesha's dilettante photographer gaze provokes a dissonance within the situation precisely because she would like to intervene and stop the wedding. Her desire to intervene is amplified only by amateurish peering through the camera, revealing tears, disapproval, and an intense desire to stop the wedding she is charged with filming. It is only after peering through the lens for a considerable length of time does she see that photographing is not a defense against anxiety or a way of distancing from pain, for it is the camera that proximates her to the fate that awaits Connie. Thus in Ayesha's case, the camera functions as a defense against the internalization of herself as just a "womb." As such, photography enables her to distance herself from the plight of her new co-wife that she has just discerned as the compendium of the twenty years of her marriage unravels before her eyes through the camera's lens. In this sense, the photograph may be said to validate Sontag's view of having a more accurate relation to visible reality.

Whereas for Jamil the trope of sterility expands from a woman's inability to bear children to the nation's ability to accommodate its minorities, in this story it is not so much the minority Muslim community that aspires for integration but Connie's conversion that is symbolic of the erasure of the dominant Catholic community—a respatialization of the majority community into the space of the Muslim minority community. Connie is of use to the Muslims because of her gendered identity as a biological producer, but she must first embrace their beliefs. This topological relation balances the focus on religion, not to compare the relative merits of one over the other. Rather, it serves to show that Connie's position, even from the dominant community in the Catholic majority nation, is of no more value than her ability to produce heirs. It is on viewing this reality that Ayesha decides to divorce Sayid and reveal a consciousness that rejects the gendered subordination to both community and nation—Muslim and Catholic. Instead, she carves out a space where both communities are accountable to gendered agency. Nor is this visible reality of both Connie and Ayesha as gendered subalterns an opportunity, for solidarity as Ayesha turns Connie out of her new home when her former co-wife visits her and encounters Ayesha's new husband, Ahmed. The new space of the nation, as Ayesha rebuilds her life with Ahmed, thus rests in a disavowal of both communities' expectation of gender as a "womb." It also dismisses any hope for solidarity between Connie and Ayesha despite their common feminine condition as biological producers.

Such unconventional turns in strategies to deal with polygyny and sterility also constitute the theme of Abidah el-Khalieqy's short story "Road to Heaven" and its stance on domestic violence. El-Khalieqy is both a poet and a prose writer in addition to being an activist, having worked for several NGOs and political organizations for women. Known as the "Nawal el-Sadaawi of Indonesia," as Diah Arimbi calls her, el-Khalieqy's activism unmistakably feeds her fiction writing by noting that she was an active member of YKF or *Yayasan Kesejaheteraan Fatayat* (Fatayat Welfare Foundation) and continues to work for other organizations to advance the cause of reproductive justice and female education (2010, 95, 152).[8] Her fiction often takes up the themes of her activist work in NGOs, namely on such issues as abortion, polygamy, sexuality, and community or Muslim women's *ummah*-building strategies as in her novels *Perempuan Berkalung Sorban* (2001) and *Geni Jora* (2004). The latter has been translated into English and German. A tireless critic of patriarchy and deeply engaged in developing *fiqh perempuan* or "Islamic jurisprudence from women's perspectives," in "Road to Heaven," el-Khalieqy offers thus an unusual story, uncharacteristic of the tangible gains accrued from her unflagging activism. She offers an example of what she might term as "Bahasa perempuan" or female language that decolonizes masculine hegemony through women's experiences (Arimbi 2010, 97). "Road to Heaven" deals with extreme violence leading to death. The story is narrated through the technique of a supernatural flashback in which the mother talks to her daughter even after she is dead and "tells" of the first day of her marriage when the insanely jealous husband (and the narrator's father) pummels the mother for having prayed at the mosque. The story's solutions lie in different strategies that turn away from formal techniques such as petitions and policymaking.

El-Khalieqy presents an emotionally and physically abused woman's life as a silent victim of marital violence at the hands of her sadistic husband ("a man of property") consumed by the power to control everything. The psychopathic husband can brook no threat to his authority—not even divine authority. Thus the wife is brutalized when she steps out of her house on the day of her wedding to pray in the neighboring mosque. In a fit of rage, the husband mercilessly beats her: he resents the wife's autonomy in leaving home without his permission to seek out submission to God that defines religious identity as a Muslim. While correcting the aim of his foot to land a blow, he tells her that

> starting today, I am your husband. I have more right over you than anyone. And as for you, you will obey my orders above anyone else's. Your loyalty must be unconditional and reserved for me alone. (el-Khalieqy 2009)

So begins a marriage of terror that the wife suffers in silence as a "model victim." Indeed, the mother exemplifies the vulnerable victim and the father, wealth, fame, and male power. Nevertheless, el-Khalieqy countermands formal strategies of defiance in the mother's postmortem smile, where death functions not customarily as erasure of the weaker sex, for at this supernatural, unconventional, and logic-defying moment, the one person who cannot decipher the smile is her antagonist husband. The wife is unrecognizable as a corpse, but not because she is bruised or scarred from the violence that was her fate during twenty years of marriage. She tells her daughter, "I am your father's sacrificial victim; they think I died for him." She is unrecognizable even to her own sister because as a corpse, to everyone's astonishment, she wears "the smile of an angel on her lips," a smile she never had when alive. The story opens thus with the dead woman's only daughter announcing, "When my mother died, her face changed." Not even the doctors and nurses who cared for the mother in her last moments believe their eyes. In a reversal of sorts, she comes alive as a corpse having lived her marital existence like one. Thus also begins the supernatural conversation as the mother whispers to the daughter, also the narrator of the story. "This is my true face," she says, and recounts the nightmarish abuse at the hands of her socially powerful husband.

El-Khalieqy's metaphorical nuance conveyed in the corpse's triumphant smile over her perpetrator extends beyond the simple action of formal measures. It also unearths the granular narrative of emotions, restrictions, and inabilities that obstruct women seeking help, positing Amrita Basu's observation that women inexplicably negotiate filial ties and considerations despite the benefits offered by legislative and policy protections (1995, 14–15). In telling contrast to the figure awakening to political consciousness and organizing for political upliftment, el-Khalieqy's protagonist finds liberation in death—only ostensibly self-erasure, self-negation, and the desired result of the male order in muting women's voices. Yet, the mother explains her victory: "It was only when he suddenly saw me smiling like this that he realized that my smile was the same one I had on my face when returning from the mosque twenty years ago, before he began to beat me." The happiness that eluded the mother now paradoxically suffuses her body in death. More important, it disturbs the father, thereby raising questions about the mother's inability to counter his violence. If death or erasure of agency was the desired goal of the father, then why does he look shocked? Surely, not to mourn the loss of his wife. What does the mother's defiance tell us? Perhaps el-Khalieqy's strategy is to foreground what Rachel Rinaldo, following Ann Tickamyer and Siti Kusurjiati, recognizes as a "gender paradox" or "discrepancy in perception and interpretation," "a conundrum" in Indonesia, the fourth largest country in the world, and the most populous Muslim country in the world.[9]

In their comparative analysis of two Javanese rural sites in the special province of Yogyakarta, Tickamyer and Kusurjiati investigate the "conundrum" that

> the vigorous participation of women in economic life and village affairs, a long-standing staple of Indonesian society, is matched by a combination of state, cultural and religious prescriptions that promote domesticity and denigrate women's agency. (2012, 18)

Tickamyer and Kusurjiati appear somewhat skeptical of women's public presence, property ownership, and control by attributing such visibility to "state-reinforced patriarchal gender ideology that limits women's autonomy and mobilizes their labor for particular political ends." (2012, 16) Yet Rinaldo's interpretation of this uneasy coexistence of expectations of womanhood—grounded in self-sacrifice and submissiveness, with the daily reality of women's education and work outside the home in Javanese society—underscores precisely the *underarticulated inapplicability* of state-reinforced expectations of womanhood (2013, 35):

> Contemporary Javanese gender ideology, which is influential throughout the country, idealizes submissive, self-sacrificing women, *even though such notions coexist uneasily with a daily reality* in which many women are educated and work outside the home. Indonesian Islam has often emphasized women's domestic roles and exalted motherhood, but it has rarely prohibited women from taking on public roles. (emphasis mine)

The "gender paradox," as Rinaldo calls it, foregrounds the spaces where women create their own strategies to engage with patriarchal gender ideologies. El-Khalieqy's story serves as a response to such aporia where women celebrate victories in tragedies, resort to such irrational methods as willful death and abuse to prevail. What el-Khalieqy uncovers are the sort of inexplicable situations Koshy describes as lying beneath the threshold of rational consciousness—memories, anxieties, and dispositions (2008, 1545). Notably, the mother's struggle—and in fact, martyrdom, as she suffers abuse for submitting to God (being Muslim is submission to God)—is the irrational disconnect between practicality, reality, and materiality that the mother shuns. Placing the example of the mother as a victim of domestic violence against a template for women's legislations and policies on domestic violence amplifies the gaps between everyday complexities of emotions, restrictions, and policy victories for women as, ultimately, the father remains legally unpunished for his crime. From this story emerge chasms that need to be filled with more effective strategies for taking up feminist causes. If the story is read as a metaphor of gendered erasure in abuse and death at the hands of a powerful male elite, it bears asking why el-Khalieqy chooses to allow a corpse to smile. And moreover, why does that smile unsettle the father? Where is the victory for feminist praxis? Can the corpse's smile be considered triumphalist?

Just as this conundrum may not have a straightforward answer, we may need to revisit el-Khalieqy's vision of the "global woman" to reanalyze boundaries of feminist transnationalism (Arimbi 2010, 153). As Arimbi

(2010) rightly notes, el-Khalieqy's activism springs from a contestation of the gendered injustices in pesantren culture, a subculture of Islamic lifestyle rooted in the tradition of learning centers that impart Islamic education in parts of rural Southeast Asia, particularly in Malaysia, Thailand, the Philippines, and Indonesia. According to Federspiel (2020), "Madarasah is the generic name for such schools throughout the Islamic world." The defining features of the pesantren lie in their historic value and their continuance of a long tradition of a particular style of religious learning to the faithful or *santri*. Pesantren schools are often defined in contrast with nonreligious (and therefore modern) centers of learning. The curriculum in pesantren schools comprises the *kitab kuning* (or "old books"), a collective term for literature based on the Sha'fi school of thought, comprising subjects ranging from Arabic grammar to ethics. El-Khalieqy considers herself a *santri* (or Muslim faithful) who inhabits the unique, exclusive world of the pesantren and revises the pesantren culture from her subject position of a *santri*. The pesantren world, notes Arimbi (2010), is a closed universe with glaring differences between itself and the "world outside" or the urban, city-dwelling, modernist landscape. Thus el-Khalieqy reveals the wide gulfs in Indonesia between geographies of lifestyles based on religious views; geographies of spaces, rural or pesantren, and urban or modern cities; geographies of religious ideologies, religious or Islamic; and nonreligious or unbothered by Islam. In her novel *Perempuan Berkalung Sorban* (2001), el-Khalieqy indicts pesantren ideology of child marriage and domestic violence by contrasting the world of difference between rural (pesantren) and urban (Yogyakarta) divides. Traversing this transgeography of pesantren and nonpesantren spaces within Indonesia is a hallmark of el-Khalieqy's work. Her novel *Geni Jora*'s locational impetus then, outside of Indonesia in the Middle East (as Arimbi reads the thematic of a global *ummah* or a global Muslim woman), is mediated by women schooled in pesantren culture aspiring for greater gendered justice—rights to education, access to reproductive justice, freedom from domestic and polygynous abuse, among other issues (2010, 153).

I would read this claim for the "global Muslim woman" as issue driven and less about fostering a transnational connection across these nation-states and more about finding a space (education, autonomy from male control, self-emergence) that offsets the risk of cultural implosion from the lack of reform. The trope of transnational travel from Indonesia to Algeria, Morocco, and Mecca—and then to Jordan and Syria—functions as a release from a stifling environment that places more emphasis, as Arimbi correctly notes, on the *kitab kuning* than on the fundamental sources of Islamic knowledge, the Qur'an and *hadith* (98). The global Muslim woman then, as Arimbi reads el-Khalieqy's portrayal of the main character, Jora, may be the one who seeks autonomy from the burden of pesantren culture, making the transnational outing no more than a station in the quest for autonomy. That the landscape of el-Khalieqy's activism is more transgeographically tuned within Indonesia can also be discerned in Arimbi's reading of Ratna Indraswari Ibrahim's novel *Lemah Tanjung* (2003), which explores the "in-betweenness" of cultural and religious geographies in Indonesia, where ethnic and racial differences divide Indonesian Muslims (135). A point to raise in the context then of global solidarity and the Muslim *ummah*, as frequently illustrated in Southeast Asian literature—as Indonesian writer Helvy Tiana Rosa's war and conflict short stories instantiate—is to probe the awareness of the suffering of other Muslims (Rosa's stories delineate the plight of Palestinians at the hands of Israel, which she depicts as a settler-colonial state). How do such narratives develop into transnational measures to fight injustice? Indeed, the "resistance literature" that these writers—el-Khalieqy, Ibrahim, and Rosa—produce often thematizes global concerns of oppression, suffering, and discrimination. However, the bulk of their work, as Arimbi's study thoroughly examines, focuses on these issues transgeographically across racial, ethnic, and religious relations within the same nation-space rather than cross-nationally.

The Ghanaian writer Jemila Abdulai's short story "#Yennenga" also takes an unusual look at sterility in that it is not directly tied to the biological functions of motherhood or childbirth or of women as biological producers of the national narrative. It deals with the circulation and production of gender justice via the transnational network of media. This network, however, that emerges in Abdullai's story is in the trope of woman not as a producer but as a destroyer of life—a murderer. Just as sterility is the obverse of fertility, murder is the opposite of life. Abdullai thus recasts the nation space by revamping the symbol of womanhood in the act of murder by her main protagonist, the titular Yennenga. Moreover, this trope of female as murderer, the destroyer of life, is developed not transnationally—not across two or more nation-states (even in its allusion to Twitter in the titular hashtag)—but transgeographically, across class divisions, intersected by gender as a social category, and across and rural and urban spaces within Ghana. The story centers on Yennenga, an extremely successful celebrity on trial for murder, taking away life, racasting thus the definition of womanhood as motherhood on both national and transnational levels. It disrupts thus the symbol of woman as producer of life in that Yennenga takes a life. Most of all, Yennenga is a Muslim woman. This aspect of her identity affects the reaction to her crime: "The 29-year-old Muslim woman is just too dangerous" (2015, 98). Furthermore, the victim is a minister, a male, and representative of the patriarchal politics of the state and society. Transnationally then, Yennenga's crime circulates through Twitter, newsfeeds, national radio, and television channels. She becomes news, on the "hashtag universe" or "#Yennenga," bringing to the surface a slew of transgeographic and subnational ramifications of class, religion, and language within Ghana (101). As a gendered symbol of poverty, subordination, and religious discrimination, Yennenga traces the space of her journey from her village to the capital Accra and not outside Ghana. I thus retrace Yennenga's trajectory from her village to Accra in an effort to map the transgeographic connections that influence women's relationships in geographies of class and religion.

Yennenga is brought to Accra for schooling as her poverty-stricken family cannot care for her (103). She rises quickly through media and political circles by befriending powerful ministers, prostituting herself and living a dissolute life, and exemplifying the dissolution of all the values of her lackluster origins. As such, the responses that Yennenga's arrest and imprisonment generate are ambivalent, veering from "#DeathToYennenga" to "FreeYennenga—@CTVGhana" and "Yennenga Ntenga saved me, my children, five years ago. She's a hero not a murderer!" (108). Yennenga's arrest becomes part of a "TheDigiRealityPact" that even the US president endorses (108). And to shield herself from the uncomprehending world outside, Yennenga recedes to her cocoon of prayer, "the most excellent worship is dua," she tells herself (109). Yennenga thus maintains this paradoxical duality—the "virgin prostitute," she calls herself on her Twitter account to open up the wound of a nation unable to account for its gendered minorities (111). The female criminal (or the morally sterile woman), as in the previous stories, does not disrupt the national narrative by simply overturning its symbolism but by shifting the nation space itself through everyday communities in unusual ways. Yennenga's community is her Twitter account and rural space that she wants to protect even at the cost of murdering her lover, the influential minister of trade. She finally divulges the reason for the murder:

> I knew exactly what needed to be done when I discovered Adil's impending deal with China's corporation: the deal that would strip bare the savannah grasslands of the northern plains, displace my people, despoil our country, shatter the one place where I'd known little suffering, exchange generations of heritage for ships full of junk. Like that black-assed man who had ravaged a four-year old girl to satisfy his lust and pacify his ego, Adil's deal would have ripped out our nation's very hope, Its very soul. (116)

The "dangerous" Muslim woman claims her space in the nation, which protects its interests as a mother protects her own by resorting not to the expected role of producer but that of murderer. It is a tricky move, as solicitude for her land places her within the stereotype of benevolent mother of the nation. Yet, her trial, her isolation, and incarceration for the danger she poses to the nation on account of her religious identity by the ungrateful land cast a shadow on its extension of this trope of benevolent mother to all women regardless of their religious affiliation. So while she is on trial legally, Yennenga's cause cannot be mapped onto the formal landscape of the nation-state that erases the agency of gender and Muslims. This dual mapping of legal proceedings and informal media exposure recasts gender and its relationship with nation and transnation transgeographically as it respatializes Yennenga's journey through class struggle (poverty), gender struggle (sexual exploitation), and religious struggle (spiritual peace amid worldly chaos and religious discrimination).

The main aim of this chapter has been to analyze women's unusual and unconventional strategies for dealing with such gendered issues as polygyny, sterility, and domestic violence by recasting the space of the nation-state onto unconsidered spaces. Expressed via a relatively unrecognized and underappreciated literary genre, the short stories in this chapter document variant histories—media representations and opinions from everyday life as seen in "#Yennenga" and colonial archives as illustrated in "A Perfect Wife"—alongside the third discourse that mixes its variations in the master's soup or the official versions of stories as seen in the prose of Abubakar, Jamil, and el-Khalieqy. All five stories engage with the trope of woman as biological producer to subvert this gendered expectation and conjure new ways of articulating feminist causes. Each produces a disparate strategy for engaging with the symbolic of motherhood. If not directly dealing with the trope of childbirth or biological producer, the stories tangentially allude to the idea of woman as symbolic of lifegiver through tropes of murder or the denial of life. This is idea is conveyed via unconventional means of triumphing over patriarchy (i.e., death itself) that on the one hand frees the woman from abuse but also exposes, on the other, new venues of weakening patriarchy. They also allude to the paradoxical symbolism of motherhood in sterility or the inability to fulfill the desired gendered expectation, shifting the space of the nation to its transgeographic spaces, as Yennenga eschews the cross-national gain to save her rural space. Common nevertheless to all five stories is the shaping of community for feminist causes through a transgeographic dialogue or exchange across religions, classes, filial status, or recourse to nonpolitical strategies to overcome patriarchal state-based control. These two strategies—subverting the trope of women as biological producers and everyday activisms of dealing with gendered problems such as polygyny and domestic abuse—rewire both the relationship of gender to the nation-state and the nation-state itself as more than a unified and univocal space.

Epilogue

To redefine the transnational warrants a retracing of its definition that shifts its space to other such geographies as religions, languages, ethnicities, and communities. Working backward, the widely accepted formulation that the nation-state itself is a contested space and no longer a homogenous territorialized terrain means that the genealogies that produce the unitary narrative of the nation space are inherently fractured, multiple, and mixed. The claim of such genealogies then to reshape the nation space also modifies the transnational as unfolding primarily in spaces beyond the national level. In particular, gender as a category of identity and its potential to pluralize the space of the nation-state has gained much urgency in plural societies, particularly in Africa and Southeast Asia, which are under consideration in this book as the two regions that have the largest concentration of Muslims in the world. Equally, religious identity is another powerful category of identity, as in many societies within these regions, Muslims occupy minority positions, prompting questions about the approach to Islam in academic venues that have culpably focused only on Muslim-majority regions and have abetted the configuration of Islam and Muslims in the narrowest geographic, ethnic, and linguistic terms. Such scholarship is often incapable of distinguishing between ethnic (Arab), regional (Middle Eastern), and religious (Islam) lines of identity and ironically focuses almost exclusively on those regions in the Muslim world inhabited by the smallest proportions of Muslims. Thus, these two regions—sub-Saharan Africa and Southeast Asia—and numerous Muslim-majority and Muslim-minority countries and societies within them exemplify a disparate range of Islamic practices of scant interest to the academic circle that has produced and codified knowledge about Islam and Muslims for an international audience from the perspective of a language and a foreign policy that have substantial influence but not an all-encompassing global circulation. These gaps, therefore, of what is not picked up by the American academic enclave raise questions on the effectiveness of transnationalism and on its improvement over global or international feminisms.

Literature as a site to discuss transnational feminist organizing importantly highlights the voids, gaps, and disjunctures. Translation posits unmappability, of knowing, as a way to rethink transnational solidarity. While I focused on the unmappability of linguistic expressions onto a global landscape to point to the incommensurable challenges facing transnational feminist organizing, I want to acknowledge here Mufti's nuanced argument on Global English to clarify my own stance on languages other than English. In his stunning inquiry on the genealogy of English and the processes by which the language rose to global dominance (and continues to consolidate its global reach), Mufti's counterclaim rests on the "ghostly presence" of vernaculars "within the discourse of the Anglophone novel" (2016, 160). It is easy to miss the nuance here as Mufti bases his counterclaim on the vernacular's lack of immunity from "the broader colonial (and postcolonial) process and the assimilative powers of the English cultural system" (2016, 159). The vernacular for Mufti and its positioning against English is grounded in the former's claim to "authentic" and "indigenous" or "uncontaminated" such that vernacular writing is ultimately and predictably subsumed/trapped into the European cultural system (2016, 156). Mufti is right in also pointing out that it is not the straightforward process of simply reading or receiving the foreign mode through translation. For the postcolonial subject, it is a fact of "double translation," or a double estrangement of reading their own language in translation, serviced, in other words, for the world literary system (156). I want to clarify my position by stating that the problem of indigeneity and a claim to authenticity is satisfying in the contextual framework of a genealogy of literary expression and circulation. Beyond that, and as I have tried to explore in this book, the relationship of communication and conversations between different philologies cannot be solved by claiming contamination, not even in the postmodern sense of the irrevocable intertwinement of the local and global. It is not about a claim to authenticity or indigeneity here that confronts transnational feminism or transnational communication and conversation: it is one of conceiving a framework that solves the persistent problem of material, historical, and linguistic inequalities. It is the stumbling block of unmappability that brings invocations of transnationalism to a grinding halt, as well as the reality of the various modes of expression that cannot be practically or realistically traced onto a global landscape. As a result, there is a need to explore alternatives. As I have demonstrated, the possibility that there is another interlocutor, another venue of exchange in the very idea that experiences are voiced in modes other than the dominant currencies of thought and expression also nudges possibilities on sites of knowledge production and ways of mapping such historically different modes of expression to eventually remake the complexion of nationalism and transnationalism.

Turning to other possibilities has also meant exploring such frameworks as the *ummah* or forms of community other than the Europeanized and Westernized paradigm of the nation-state. Such reversals occur in the unnoticed energies of everyday activisms, exchanges, and encounters and not perforce in such formal venues as legislative and policy gains. In his illuminating study of the long underserved intellectual history of Muslim West Africa, Ousmane Kane briefly alludes to the persistence of unmappability by sharing details from his early life in colonial Senegal. In particular, Kane emphasizes the unique ability of Islamic education to coexist with Western/colonial schooling as was the case with Kane and his siblings. At the same time, this ability to coexist also exposed Kane to the reality of the dissonance between official and informal and of a "different story of ethnic and racial politics than does the dominant academic discourse of an ethnically and racially fragmented West Africa" (2016, 5). Recollecting his early encounter with West African cosmopolitanism witnessed on a daily basis at his family home—on account of the charismatic stature of his grandfather, the legendary Ibrahim Niasse—Kane writes the following:

> On the one hand, this meant that I grew up navigating easily between ethnic, racial, cultural, and epistemological boundaries. On the other hand, I heard time and again in school or read in books the narrative of Arabs enslaving and looking down upon blacks, of Africa being torn by ethnic warfare, and of the civilizing impact of Western colonialism, which introduced literacy to hitherto exclusively oral societies. The colonial narrative contrasted with what I experienced in everyday life. (5)

Kane goes on to track the disjunctures in perceiving epistemologies between Africans such as himself—simultaneously committed to two systems of education—who were exposed to a society in everyday life that did not match with the world of his Western-educated schoolmates, schooled exclusively in the colonial system. Kane's is but one of many accounts of such struggles to map traditions without which the history of knowledge production in West Africa, as Kane claims, will remain incomplete (18).

I want to stress here again Deleuze and Guattari's thesis on the cramped space of the minority in which other stories are nested. The individual, family, and community gain salience because of "other stories vibrating within" them. The family then seeps into other circles—economic, political, and bureaucratic. These stories within stories reshape the nation (and transnation) space. The *ummah*, as it supersedes narrow ethnic, national, and other limitations and yet remains bounded by these fragmentations—instances in Muslim women's encounters, exchanges, and dialogues that reframe transnationalism from transnationalism to transgeography—allows for a framework where inequitable relations even in such spaces of contacts, connections, and exchanges. I forwarded this idea of the *ummah* as a new way of imagining transnationalism, a way that is not grounded in Western concepts of community, such as nation-state, Enlightenment, or Reformation but a way to consider epistemic alternatives. This way of imagining the transnational also redefined the *ummah* itself by emphasizing some of its unnoticed iterations as a community deeply cognizant of other faiths, identities, and affiliations. In particular, scholars find clause twenty-five of the foundational Constitution of Medina or the treaty of Medina, truly baffling. The clause states, "The Jews of Banū 'Awf are a community (*ummah*) along with the believers. To the Jews their religion (*dīn*) and to the Muslims their religion." The question frequently posed is: how can a theocracy confirm and allow the practice of other faiths?[1] And it is in this visionary feature of community or *ummah* that we must recognize a template for interreligious relationships and explore undertheorized solutions for contemporary interreligious interactions pertaining to peace, security, and governance in plural societies. The *ummatic* model of community as encapsulated in Muhammad's vision and practice of interreligious cohabitation reifies Islam's ability to serve as a "contact zone"—a social space—to evoke Mary Louise Pratt again, "where cultures meet, clash, and grapple with each other, often in contexts of highly asymmetrical power" (1991, 34). Making plural communities, I argued, is the spiritual ideal that Muslims share and is also the aspiration of an *ummah* as troped in the document of Medina and in numerous instances of Prophetic practice attributed to Muhammad.[2] This shared goal does not presume stability or coherence, unity or uniformity.[3] Rather, it is underpinned by the shared conviction of the well-being of humankind toward which peoples of various communities strive. Muslim cosmopolitanism and its community-building ideals are like Islam—plural in space and time.

Gender, of course, as Boehmer, Ray, and McClintock have amply shown, finds a solid presence in national narratives through tropes of tradition, culture, and gendered roles: mother, wife, and homemaker.[4] McClintock (1997) has suggested that the nation is identified with the needs, aspirations, and frustrations of men, constructed and naturalized essentially on *"gender* difference" (89). The nation shaped itself on the "single historical genesis narrative," writes McClintock, for organizing national history around the subordination of women. This genesis, as I argued in the introduction of the book, is premised on a male-female difference, presupposing a stability in the religious constitution of male and female selves. By extension, then, the gendered difference of self is mapped onto marriage, family, community, nation, and transnation, as mentioned in earlier chapters. But if the genesis of the narrative of the self is mixed, plural, and multireligious, as in the case of the fiction I have read, the "single" in the historical genesis narrative is now troubled. Furthermore, if the genesis of the narrative reveals improvisational, unconventional, and tangential conversations across borders of class, religion, ethnicity, or race in solving such problems as domestic and communal violence, sterility, minoritized citizenships, and polygyny as these stories illustrate, then the space of the nation can no longer be determined by the geographies of its borders nationally but by the geographies of the borders across which dialogues and exchanges unfold. As such, the idea of pluralism has gained much ground around the world, particularly in such Muslim-minority societies as India through a number of initiatives that seek to reshape the nation-state. Initiatives such as SNAP; Chalchitra Abhiyaan; Open a Door in India; De Colores Collective in the United States, and the Kayamandi participatory video project in South Africa, all posit a groundswell in rerouting the relationship of gender via the lens of minorities in geographies other than the boundaries of the nation-state.[5] In particular, overturning the gendered narratives of nationalism has also meant a contestation of the space of the nation-state itself, not to accommodate gender alone but to factor in a minoritized population across multiple differences. My analyses thus join the impetus of such initiatives as SNAP, *Chalchitra Abhiyaan*, participatory video projects, and many others around the world to rearticulate the space of the nation-state and transnation through neglected sites of knowledge production in the theorization of a more equitable and inclusive transnationalism.⁶ My reading of African and Southeast Asian fiction has considered the transnational not as a discrete space beyond two or more national spheres as such a space reinstantiates the same power that transnationalism was meant to disclaim in Global Northern feminist agendas and international feminisms focused on nation-states. Rather, it has emphasized the transnational as transgeographic in tropes of aleatory dialogues, exchanges, and interfaith relationships, using the framework of community or *ummah* from the founding moments of the earliest Muslim community in 622 AD. The written document (kitāb, as ibn Isḥāq terms it) or the Constitution of Medina serves precisely as a template for *ummah*-building strategies that women actively mobilize against gendered problems without positing cross-national spaces as the privileged interlocutors of a transnational relationship.⁷ As such, my reading has redrawn the lines of transnational feminist relationships within more proximal (transgeographic) boundaries to retain the decolonial and anti-imperial character of the idea of the transnational as counteracting exclusions and inequalities.

Notes

Introduction

1. See "In Indonesia, Interfaith Marriage is Legal but with Many Obstacles," accessed November 16, 2019, https://www.voanews.com/east-asia-pacific/indonesia-interfaith-marriage-legal-many-obstacles.

2. See also Basu (1995) and Desai (1992, 15–32, 30–31). Desai succinctly enumerates the growing challenges to transnational solidarities posed by a reproduction of existing inequalities between Global North and Global South; the reliance on funding and donors from the Global North; the complex face of NGOs where some NGOs, points out Desai, may be "fronts for the government and others"; and finally, Desai notes the elitism and exclusivism of transnational solidarity politics "guided by experts with special skills shaping international gender policy." In "Globalization and Feminism: Opportunities and Obstacles for Activism in the Global Arena," Myra Marx Ferree expresses some of the same concerns about transnational feminism as it becomes "a more fragmented field of special interest groups . . . How can inequality of resources around the world be used to create constructive flows of support?" (See Ferree and Tripp 2006, 16). In the same collection, see also Aili Marie Tripp's "Challenges in Transnational Feminist Mobilization."

3. This question is influenced by Gayatri Spivak's well-known statement that perhaps "the subject's itinerary has not been left traced so as to offer an object of seduction to the representing intellectual" (32). Spivak is pointing to the politics of prioritization that ails all forms of cultural and intellectual critique. In the Muslim context, in particular, Sadia Abbas has called such a tendency "discursive preferences," which are preferences elevated to broader levels of culture and the field of feminist studies itself on Islam (2014, 69).

4. A quick look at the titles of books that have won prestigious prizes in recent years in women's and gender studies in the United States reveals the focus of methodologies and disciplines—social sciences—that are rewarded for furthering knowledge production on women and gender. See the website of the

flagship association for women's studies in the United States, the National Women's Studies Association (NWSA), under the "past recipients" link of the "Awards and Prizes" section, accessed May 26, 2020, https://www.nwsa.org/page/bookprizes.

    5. See Halliday (2002, 20–41) and Halliday (2003).

    6. See Badran (2010).

    7. See al-Ahsan (2007, 611) and Arjomand (2009). Al-Ahsan describes the *ummah* Muhammadiyyah or *ummah* of Muhammad by focusing on the events that led to its formation. He states, "The 'Constitution of Madinah,' signed by the inhabitants of Madinah and the new immigrants to the city, named Muhammad as the chief officer of Madinah. At the outset, it declared itself to be "a document from Muhammad, the Prophet, and the believers and Muslims of Quraish (the tribe of the Prophet and most other immigrants) and Yathrib, and those who followed them, joined them and lived with them. They constituted one single ummah (*ummatan wahidatan*) to the exclusion of all (other) people (*min dun an-nas*)." However, Al-Ahsan argues that the Constitution of Madinah recognizes Islamic identity as topological—awareness of other affiliation and affiliates. He states, "This document recognized that an individual may have more than one identity. It declared the formation of one ummah for Muslims, but allowed for the tribal identities of those who accepted the faith of Islam. It also permitted the Jewish inhabitants of Madinah to retain their religious and tribal identities. The document's recognition of multiple identities has sometimes created confusion among historians concerning the nature of the Muslim ummah" (611–612).

    8. See Al-Ahsan (2007).

    9. See Afsaruddin (2010, 48) for a critique on the recuperation of female voices in Islamic history and particularly of the female *Sahabiyyat* or Companions of Muhammad in the infancy of the Muslim *ummah*.

    10. Appadurai's model of the global cultural economy, based on a flow of ideas, people, and commodities, mobilizes questions on interactions within and beyond national boundaries that I examine throughout this project. Appadurai's invitation to view difference not as taxonomies but as interactions and refractions illustrates that interactions are not decided by givenness but by dynamic relationships. However, Appadurai's argument, too, takes off from the basic premise of the national as situated within nation-state boundaries and the transnational as beyond the control of such boundaries, something that I aim to redefine in this book.

    11. For in-depth studies on these terms, see Hannerz (1996) and Mandaville (1999).

    12. Jean-Luc Nancy, Homi Bhabha, Edouard Glissant, among numerous other postcolonial scholars, have advanced our understanding of spaces where cultures meet, clash, and converse to counter a single story or history, symbolic of power (alluding to the imposition of history by the West through colonization). They accomplish this by foregrounding a cross-fertilization of histories and

by "repossessing a true sense of one's time and identity," as Glissant puts it in *Caribbean Discourse*, with the aim of revaluating power (93).

13. If not engaging spaces beyond the nation-state, as Nagar and Swarr explain, transnational feminism is defined more accurately as an "intersectional set of understandings, tools, and practices," one that grapples with a select set of themes in contradistinction to international (nation-states) and global (mostly Global North) feminisms, "racialized, classed, masculinized, and heteronormative logics and practices of globalization and capitalistic patriarchies, . . . of domination and subordination" (4, 5).

14. Boehmer defines the transnational as bypassing the nation, as distinct from the national, encompassing migrancy, nomadism, cross-border activities while its converse, namely the home and belonging, are seen as stable and rooted. This identification is enabled precisely when the geographic boundary of the nation-state is taken as a chief marker of such spatial categories as local, national, international, global, and transnational. It is in this context of identifying the transnational as distinct from and beyond discrete national border spaces that Boehmer makes the important observation of "centers of power remain concentrated, as they do, in the western metropole" (187).

15. In the chapter on global English, Mufti (2016) sharply analyzes the paradox of global dominance by uncovering the continued dominance of English. Despite the claim to "World Englishes" and the various forms of its vernacular, Mufti writes, the "language continues to be conceived of as a single organism, with its origins on a little island in the North Sea, whose subsequent history in the world can be charted as a continuous evolution or unfolding" (149).

16. James Clifford (1997, 29, 30). In a similar analysis of the shift away from the focus of "advanced," "late capitalist" societies to study cultures and experiences in a "nonteleological" sense of working together in cultural studies, Clifford argues in favor of broadening the disciplinary implications and orientation of the broad field of anthropology as its various subdisciplines and methdologies, ethnography, travel writing, and participant interviews, shift focus from the concerns of the metropole (elite institutions in the West) to a genuinely wide domain of experiences that are comparative, bifocal and prioritize multiple paths to "modernity."

17. See Lim (2010).

18. "Indonesia History—Sultanate of Mataram—1586-1755" https://www.globalsecurity.org/military/world/indonesia/history-sultanate-mataram.htm. Accessed July 28, 2021.

19. Mohanty and Alexander suggest "shifting the unit of analysis from local, regional and national culture to relations and processes *across* cultures" (emphasis added, 1996, xix).

20. Boehmer's study of Roy and Dangarembga is placed under the chapter "Transnational Feminism," which justifies the title and its consensual definition, as the two writers are of different national origins and affiliations.

21. With respect to the minority question, Mufti sees nationalism not as a "unifying project" but as a "great *disrupter* of social and cultural relations." He uses the term "minority" in the sense of "exile" that actualizes the "threat inherent to the condition of minority," as a minoritized people disrupt the distinction between memory and history in the establishment of "disruptive forms of remembering," and recasting thus the nation each time it appears settled (13).

22. Werbner cites Friedman (1997, 84–85).

23. The authors quote Anna Lowenhaupt Tsing's ethnography where she opines that global capitalism transforms the world into "a single imperial system" (625).

24. Mohanty and Alexander (1996, xvi) also make a similar observation in tracing the provenance of current feminist theorizations to the emergence of gender as a category of analysis and the "social demographic, and class composition of those who actually theorized gender in the U.S. academy."

25. I am influenced here by Achille Mbembe's essay (2002) on African modes of self-writing where Mbembe argues for the shifts in self, polis, and cosmopolis in African modes of being. Critiquing the short-term approach to understanding Africa, Mbembe says, "African criticism, dominated by political economy and by the nativist impulse, has from the outset inscribed the quest for political identity within a purely instrumental and short-term temporality" (262).

26. Moghadam describes in detail the important transnational work of such organizations as DAWN (Diaspora African Women's Network), WLUML (Women Living Under Muslim Laws), WIDE (Women in Development Europe), Code Pink, MADRE, and WLP (Women's Leadership Partnership).

27. See Bohemer (2005). The literature on the socialized identities of gender is copious. See, for instance, the milestone study by Barlow (1997, 173–196). See also two seminal texts: Yuval-Davis (1997) and Jayawardene (1986).

28. Ray quotes Sarkar's reading of Rabindranath Tagore's vision of India as grounded in the Hindu religion: "The bond of unity with the country is being sought explicitly now through the Hindu religion and samaj—'Will not Hinduism be able to bring everyone of us day by day into the bonds of affinity and devotion to this *Bharatvarsha* of ours—the abode of our gods, the hermitage of our rishis, the land of our forefathers?'" (94).

29. Ramat Yakubu's work is part of the wildly popular feminist literary movement in Africa called (in Hausa) the *Littatfan Soyayya* (books of love), a genre of romance fiction encompassing topics ranging from teenage love and marriage to parental authority. Novels are written in Hausa and rarely translated into English or other languages. They reach an audience of roughly fifty million Hausa speakers in parts of Niger, Nigeria, Ghana, and the Ivory Coast. *Alhaki Kuykeyo Ne* sold about two hundred thousand copies in Hausa, cementing Ramat Yakubu's place in the Hausa literary canon. It was then spotted by a publisher in Chennai who

believed that the themes—women and marriage, virtuosity, family values, and filial duties—would be well received by a similarly conservative Indian audience.

30. McCain highlights the dissonance in the global reception of Hausa women's voices and their localized resonance in that Hausa women read, write, and speak widely in Nigeria, thus delving into the multivalence of "exposure"—of Hausa writers abroad and of Muslim women within Africa. McCain calls this gap the "double dimensioned" idea of home and exposure where the private space of the home that Hausa women write about also becomes a space of exposure. These writers mobilize topics that should remain private but are exposed in the spirit of revealing the abuse and corruption of the domestic sphere by "womanizing patriarchs" who hide their bad behavior in the privacy of their homes (137, 139).

31. In the novel, Ramat Yakubu functionalizes the practice of gift giving to restore financial security to a destitute family. Gift giving in Hausa society, often misused to exploit families and extract dowries during weddings, in this novel serves to balance the economic destitution of a woman and her children deserted by a negligent husband.

32. Email correspondence with author in March 2018.

33. See Mukoma wa Ngugi's extensive discussion on the topic of translation and the challenges facing African languages in circulating/conversing more widely with other languages. Ngugi lists structures of literature—writing, mentoring, reviewing, critiquing, publishing for literatures in African languages. By contrast, Ngugi identifies the depth and sophistication of such structures in other parts of the world, particularly in the United States, that facilitate writing and make it a feasible process (67–69).

34. The practice of "gift giving" during weddings in Africa is a multilayered practice that is variously known as "bride price," "bridewealth," or even "bride compensation" and commonly also referred to as "dot" in French, deriving also from the Islamic practice of *mahr* to ensure the woman's material rights. Not only religiously significant and necessary (especially in Muslim societies), the term *dowry* has acquired many nuanced social, financial, and gendered meanings, making it more than a mere exchange of material gifts. See, for instance, Masquelier (2005), an insightful study of Muslim women in Dogondoutchi, Niger, and Asha (1997).

35. In Lionnet and Shih's model of minor transnational transnationalism, relationships are articulated between binary units (major or minor) even if the direction of these relationships (vertical or lateral) changes. When Fanon traveled, as Lionnet and Shih evoke the example of his travels from one minor location to another (the Caribbean to Algeria), the relationship between major and minor shifted to two minor locations, but the minor continued to be defined as such in relation to the major. Another way of posing the question is this: what are the Caribbean and Algeria minor in relation to? Fanon's travel simply respatialized the relationship by circumventing the center or the major but without troubling its power.

36. Such unions, argues Gandhi, underpin Saidian contrapuntality and Bhabha's concepts of "hybridity," "in-between," and "interstitiality" that instance an osmosis between colonizer and colonized, writes Gandhi, to expose the "leakiness of imperial boundaries" and antagonize the imperial project not just of civilizational quarantine but of the idea of its authorization of colonial culture and of the propagation of the "Western Sign" (3, 5). See also Bhabha (1993, 1994).

37. Patterson has suggested the presence of worlds within each other through capitalism on regional levels; immigration from Third to First Worlds and expanded military, cultural, and political occupations and interventions to the extent that the center is now incapable of defending its own borders (1987, 260).

38. https://referenceworks.brillonline.com/entries/encyclopaedia-of-islam-2/umma-COM_1291. See also Dallal, Sikand, and Moten (2019).

39. Watt undertakes a detailed analysis of the term *ummah* in the context of the Constitution of Medina to delve into what he terms as "the character of the Islamic State." Watt focuses on the development of the term *ummah* by mapping its religious, kinship-based, and even territorial or spatial dimensions. He also clarifies that it is the religious dimension of community that supersedes all other meanings, particularly kinship or tribal loyalties and bases this statement on the implied and assumed idea that when the *Anṣār* or helpers in Yathrib (Medina) accepted Muhammad as a messenger from God, "then there must be a message; and a message in turn implies that God is giving directions to the ummah in the practical affairs of life. In many matters of principle Muhammad does not act of his own accord, but merely announces what God commands. This God is the head and director of the *ummah*" (239).

40. "Quran Tafsir Ibn Kathir": the *Tafsir* of Ibn Kathir comments on this verse to affirm the diversity among Muslims and non-Muslims across nations, regions, and communities (tribes). "It was also said that 'nations' refers to non-Arabs, while 'tribes' refers to Arabs. Various statements about this were collected in an individual introduction from the book, Al-Inbah, by Abu Amr Ibn ʿAbdul-Barr, and from the book, *Al-Qasad wal-Amam fi Maʿrifah Ansab Al-Arab wal-Ajam*. Therefore, all people are the descendants of Adam and Hawwa' and share this honor equally. The only difference between them is in the religion that revolves around their obedience to Allah the Exalted and their following of His Messenger." Accessed March 2019, http://www.qtafsir.com/index.php?option=com_content&task=view&id=1751&Itemid=105.

41. Al-Ahsan deconstructs the articles of the constitution of Medina to explain the nature of the *ummah* of Muhammad that was distinguished along lines of religious beliefs but also allowed to share the space of the city with nonbelievers/others: the Jews of Banu Awf, in particular. The main concern of the newly established *ummah* of Muhammad, as al-Ahsan notes, "is plainly the security of Madinah" (612).

Chapter 1

1. Gupta, Ong, and Grewal (1999); Kaplan (1994); and Lionnet and Shih (2005). In *Scattered Hegemonies*, Grewal and Kaplan use the term "constructed opposition" in the sense of directions that define transnationalism. They recognize the "historicized particularity" of feminized exploitation by patriarchies. But they also break the "constructed opposition" of such exploitation to only one particular kind of historical patriarchy by linking and cutting across patriarchies historically and spatially in an effort to link transnational feminist practices beyond constructed opposition, found in such spaces as global-local or center-periphery. They define the transnational as lines cutting across such constructed oppositions (15, 17).

2. Basu (2010), 1; Mohanty and Alexander (1996), xv.

3. Basu (2010); Baksh and Harcourt (2015).

4. A number of feminist theorists foreground the idea of transnationalism a inherently "asymmetrical" as it engages with uneven processes and relationships in globalizing capitalism (Nagar and Swarr 2010, 3). Grewal and Kaplan (2002) state that "there is no such thing as a feminism free of asymmetrical power relations" (73). Transnationalism, they argue, involves alliances, subversion, and complicity within which asymmetries can be critiqued (73). Thus, they recommend an understanding of the transnational as a network of "uneven and dissimilar circuits of culture and capital" to reveal linkages rather than comparisons between "patriarchies, colonialisms, racisms, and feminisms" (73).

5. Nagar and Swarr note that international feminisms were too rigidly tied to nation-state borders and do not always account for the effects of globalization. On the other hand, global feminisms were mostly articulations of the priorities of northern feminist agendas and perspectives and for homogenizing women's struggles for sociopolitical justice (4).

6. Briggs, McCormick, and Way trace a history of the main dimensions of transnationalism that leans on an analogy with the intellectual work of feminism in thinking about gender. They point out that in the well-known problems with presuming the homogeneity of the Third World that many leading scholars and thinkers pointed out in European models of history and epistemologies. They mention Spivak, Chakravathy, Guha, Said, and Wallerstein, as well as Diane Nelson, Gloria Anzaldúa, among others, who "underscored the 'back and forth' movements of people and ideas within spaces that challenged our notions of discrete domains" (633) and who pointed out the problems of conceiving of nationalism or the nation as a unit of analysis that elides local intersections of gender with race, class, and imperialism. Transnationalism thus emerged as a fluid and migrant idea of people moving across categories even within a "world economy" (633).

7. In the thirty-odd chapters of their handbook on movements, the authors cover every aspect of feminist praxis and epistemology as a goal for transnational

movements, ranging from "collective identity" to the formation of a "global civil society" (6).

8. On the other hand, the theorization of transnational feminism itself holds many challenges within it as Basu differentiates between transnational networks and movements. The former, explains Basu, are loosely affiliated constituents, more decentralized and loosely affiliated bodies that tend to disband more quickly—sustenance is an issue (6). Basu maintains that it is difficult to organize transnationalism in regions with enormous cultural diversity (11). But movements often engage the state and shift their agendas and are often contained within borders and seldom mobilize beyond borders because of difficulties of trust and practical reasons. Coupled then with problems of reproducing power disparities and deepening divisions between historically and materially unequal sites such as local-global, center-periphery, the challenge remains of equating global activities—the growth of transnational networks, advocacy groups, and international funding for NGOs and international conferences—with equity between and within transnational movements.

9. A number of highly influential works including Leila Ahmed's *Women and Gender in Islam*; Ziba Mir Hosseini's *Islam and Gender: The Religious Debate in Contemporary Iran*; Valentine Moghadam's *Toward Gender Equality in the Arab/Middle East Region: Islam, Culture and Feminist Activism*; Margot Badran's *Feminism Beyond East and West: New Gender Talk and Practice in Global Islam*; and Amina Wadud's *Qur'an and Woman: Rereading the Sacred Text from a Woman's Perspective*, centralize activism and legal reform in Islamic feminism to claim a rereading of the Qur'an or "gendered works of exegesis" (Badran, viii) and reinstate gender equality. Badran defines these scholar-activists as "women who have defined themselves in overtly religious terms and are producers of Islamic feminist discourse" (vii).

10. Mama mentions organizations such as the Tanzanian Women's Media Association, the Women and Law in Southern Africa network, and Women in Nigeria. See also Vatuk (2008). I focus on Rachel Rinaldo's work on Muslim women in Indonesia, Vatuk's research on Muslim women in India, and Mama's work on activism by Muslim women in Nigeria to underscore the striking similarity between the work of influential theorists in the American academic context and in other parts of the Islamic world.

11. Schroter traces the birth of WLUML as an organization started in 1984 by nine women from Algeria, Bangladesh, Iran, Mauritius, Morocco, Tanzania, Sudan, and Pakistan to promote the struggle for women's rights in countries with Muslim majorities and in those with Muslim minorities. They launch campaigns to fight death by stoning and to promote awareness of LGBTI rights. Its agenda is organized along the lines of the Universal Declaration of Human Rights (127).

12. In Edwin (2016), I focus primarily on the twin marginalization of African Muslim women and the apolitical kinds of engagements with Islam that remain

relatively underarticulated in studies of Muslim women. I contend that shifting the weight of scholarship from one geographic area to another understudied one is not as effective in promoting an understanding of Islam and Muslim women. Thus, a conceptual shift from collective, organized, and movement-based feminist activity to a more private, individual, and personal engagement with the religion, broadens the approach to understanding Muslim women's engagement with the religion.

13. Al-Faruqi refers to some of the most radical and conservative reformers of Islamic history such as Hasan al Banna, Muhammad Idris Sanusi, and Muhammad ibn Abd al Wahhab. Using *ummah* and Islamic state interchangeably, Al-Faruqi states that it was bound to include not only Christians and Jews but all of mankind interacting with mutual respect and in peace (188).

14. Elmadmad details a number of diverse and contradictory aspects about Muslim women, including age—a woman in one place can be considered a child in another as there is no clear definition of women in international refugee organizations. Elmadmad draws up the plight of Muslim women in general as refugees and not along lines of race, class, or ethnicity.

15. One of the deftest critiques of Mahmood's evacuation of Western pressures on Muslim women beyond the stereotypical perception of them as oppressed and voiceless is nevertheless by Sadia Abbas (2014), who shows that Mahmood's comparison of gender is based on the constructed oppositions of culture as stable and different—West and East—"erasing the Egyptian drag queen completely" by positioning Muslim women from Egypt against non-Muslim women from the West, instead of choosing to compare Muslim women in Egypt with non-Muslims in Egypt itself (63). Abbas notes, "Mahmood has chosen to talk about drag queens in the West versus Islamist women and not drag queens in Egypt" (63). Abbas furthermore notes Mahmood's oversight of the Islamist right and gender injustice to craft a critique against imperialism, pointing again to the concomitant and concurrent influences that produce gender and not religion alone (222).

16. B. Venkat Mani's engrossing study on "bibliomigrancy" and the world as a library (or vice versa) plumbs the topic of world literature and the accessibility of books. This world of migrancy, argues Mani, is endowed with a sense of accessibility or inaccessibility to worlds. Thus such epics as Sunjata, Gilgamesh, or the *Ramayana*, states Mani, traveled from one part of the world to another. Mani's takes a rather optimistic view of the ability of books to travel and in the process to code, recode, locate, and relocate worlds (or parts of those worlds). This leads Mani to ultimately conclude on the note that world literature itself cannot be considered a "definitive literary catalog of the world" precisely because books travel endlessly and become accessible in far corners of the earth, but in the process they also undergo coding, recoding, and changes (11–12). Such migrancy or fluidity is undergirded by translation/accessibility, and it also troubles the definitive sense of the category of world literature. What of books left untranslated because of the politics that Mani rightly identifies between the world of books

and the rather narrow domain of academic scholarship where books are key to the production of knowledge? (15).

17. Aljunied studies such marketplaces as Tanah Abang in Jakarta, the Geylang Serai in Singapore, and the Siti Khadijah market in Kelantan, Malaysia, as a site of fluid interactions that he terms "cosmopolitan" (8).

Chapter 2

1. See Adichie (2009).

2. Kalliney focuses on the narrative uniqueness of African fiction in its vying for a place in the global canon. He extends Marx's theory of commodities and objects to study African fiction where objects do not function merely as commodities but as "narrative labor" that is different from socially determined and alienated labor (413). Objects then—trinkets, mementos, heirlooms, and keepsakes—structure the narrative itself, argues Kalliney. Such narrative objects exceed Marxist theorizations of labor and objects, thus allowing African fiction to insert itself in allusive and intertextual ways that tie it inextricably to global literature.

3. Achebe's essays "The Role of the Writer in the New Nation" (1964) and "The Novelist as Teacher" (1975) highlight writing as a duty of writers. Several critics quoted in this essay—Eisenberg, Emenyonu, Sackeyfio, and others—share the opinion on Adichie as Achebe's literary successor. As such, they read some of Adichie's fiction as responding to or continuing Achebe's literary legacy of the writer's role as educator, intellectual, and entertainer. See also Doherty (2014).

4. See Adichie (2010).

5. Li's illuminating study unearths the emerging transnational links and new paradigms that "limn the contours of fresh encounters with blackness in America" between Africans and Americans, especially black Americans, in the conjunctural and disjunctural dimensions of race. Li's reading of the rich depths of Pan-African American writers such as NoViolet Bulawayo, Helon Habila, and established writers like Adichie amplifies the "bridging of Afropolitan concerns with American realities." It would be a mistake, writes Li, to "identify Bulawayo as solely an Afropolitan or African American writer" (24).

6. Ochonu argues for rethinking the idea of indirect rule as the paradigmatic form of governance in colonial history and for understanding the deeper politics of contemporary ethno-religious strife in the middle-belt region of Nigeria. He states that indirect rule was not applied uniformly, and the colonizer sometimes chose foreign insiders; or alien insiders as agents and sometimes did not. Furthermore, these communities chosen for such purposes also invented their own ways of governance and interactions that predated European colonial rule and politics. This agency, asserts Ochonu, is vital to understanding contemporary interreligious relationships (5).

7. https://www.aclu-wa.org/pages/timeline-muslim-ban. Accessed June 2019.

8. See also articles on the terrorist group's activities in the *Guardian*, accessed March 31, 2019, https://www.theguardian.com/world/boko-haram.

9. Carmen McCain argues that the story mirrors the "public discourse" in Nigeria about Muslims and Muslim women. McCain thus states, "While Adichie was obviously attempting to explore the way that an encounter with an "Other" complicates Chika's assumptions, her portrayal of the nameless Hausa woman, in fact, reinforces the stereotype of the northern woman as seen in public discourse in Nigeria—the ultimate subaltern, married young, uneducated, unable to speak" (2014, 109).

10. Akpome quotes Petersen and Rutherford and Twagilimanna to delineate the double pressures facing gendered agency in African women writers' works. Critics often analyze Adichie's work in relation to her literary forebears—Ba, Emecheta, and Dangaremba—and her peers, Bulawayo and Atta. In the latter comparison the theme of migration is particularly resonant with the idea of competing claims on female agency. When Adichie's protagonists, like Bulawayo's and Atta's, travel abroad, they face a number of challenges in addition to the stifling cultural, religious, and economic practices at home.

11. Written in the context of the US war on Afghanistan and the rhetoric of saving Muslim women from the Taliban, Abu Lughod's article is still resonant as Adichie illustrates similar resultant problems of Islamophobia and violent ethnic conflicts that are mounted on religious discourses of intolerance.

12. See Appiah (1997).

13. Eisenberg contrasts Adichie's longer works with her short stories in terms of what the length allows Adichie to do. Her shorter work, suggests Eisenberg, exculpates Adichie from "offering solutions" and "resist[s] the very call to literary-political activism about which they speculate." I propose that the absence of closure in the short stories can be construed, particularly in this short story, as an absence of solidarity.

14. See for instance, notable analyses on Ba's small but significant oeuvre by Mildred Mortimer, Omofolabi Ajayi-Soyinka, Uzoama Ada Azodo, and Obioma Nnaemeka, among others.

Chapter 3

1. Abubakar's story appears as "unpublished" in the collection edited by Barry. I am referring to the date of its publication in Barry's 2008 volume. Abubakar's essay "Naunu Na Kaw Yan? (What's Happening to You?)" appears in Abubakar (2015).

2. Azizah Y. Al-Hibri and Hadia Mubarak explain the dual nature of marriage in Islam as pertaining to *ibadat* (worship), *muamlat* (worldy contractual

matters), and legal agreements. They state that the Qur'anic view of marriage and divorce can be summed up as "staying together on equitable terms or separating with kindness." The Qur'an also describes the marriage contract as *mithaqan ghalithan* (a solemn covenant). . . . Many jurists noted that God placed the marriage contract within the category of 'ibādat (which relate to God's worship), and not within the category of mu'āmalāt, where contracts are usually placed. From the days of the Prophet, the marriage contract was used to articulate the rights and stipulations prospective wives required from their husbands, and hence offered a unique vehicle for the protection of women. This vehicle was part of an elaborate structure based on the Qur'an, the Prophet's *sunnah* (sayings and example), and subsequent juristic interpretations. See http://oxfordislamicstudies.com/article/opr/t236/e0507, accessed March 2019.

3. In their definition of a minor literature, Deleuze and Guattari suggest that it is composed of three main characteristics, "deterritorialization of language, the connection of the individual to a political immediacy, and the collective assemblage of enunciation" (3).

4. See Arifa Akbar, "Elsewhere, Home, A Review," accessed April 7, 2019, https://www.theguardian.com/books/2018/jul/09/elsewhere-home-leila-aboulela-review.

5. See Smith (2018). Smith reads Aboulela's work as grappling with "cultural identities."

6. See Denny (1975). Denny, like Al-Ahsan, enumerates the various meanings and contexts of the term as it appears in the Qur'an, undertaking a deeper analysis of the word through its etymological changes and details. Both undertake a study of the word by dividing the verses into the two major periods of the revelation of the verses—Meccan and Medinan—to show that it was in the latter sense that the term acquired a more specific salience as "the genuine Muslim community." Moving from general to specific where the term specifically means "Muslim community," Denny groups the motifs and themes that appear in the context of the word in the Qur'an into six main categories. He lists "oneness," "messengers and other agents of God connected with ummahs," "each ummah has its appointed term," which Al-Ahsan refers to as the "time period" or "life of a particular community or civilization" (608), "ummahs that have perished or will do so," "ummah meaning 'religion,'" and "ummah as ahl al-kitab (or godly peoples)."

7. "Sufism," Oxford Islamic Studies Online, accessed July 10, 2019, http://www.oxfordislamicstudies.com/article/opr/t125/e2260.

8. See Jalal's pointed highlighting of the internal refractions in Muslim communities, particularly in South and West Asia that rarely feature in Western/Orientalist "expert" accounts of Muslims. She cites the classic slippage and misconstrual of Syed Qutb's and Abul Ala Mawdudi's approaches to *jihad*, as examples of two of the most frequently cited thinkers behind the radicalization of the Asian region, having to do more with struggling against "faithless and unethical Muslims" than with organizing anti-imperial resistance among Muslims (18).

9. Kane refutes the popular perception both outside and within academia of the covert dissemination of Wahhabi ideology by Saudi Arabia that pours billions of dollars into educational institutions in the West and other parts of the world. He points, in particular, to what he calls an "open secret" that the first president of Ghana, Kwame Nkrumah (a Christian) consulted the legendary Ibrahim Niasse, Kane's maternal grandfather, and sought his spiritual protection to continue the long tradition of West African political elites consulting spiritual guides. Although in the context of tracing a broader history of intellectual learning in West Africa, Kane's observations affirm the coexistence and community of a number of diverse influences and ideologies that West African Muslims regarded as part of their worldview.

10. See, for instance, a relatively unknown study (because it deals with the figure of the West African and not Arab Muslim) on Islam in the West African novel by Sheikh Ahmed Bangura that systematically analyzes the long colonial and neoimperial genealogy of the current ignorance about Muslims in general that consistently isolated the African Muslim from the larger Muslim world as someone who was intellectually capable of practicing only a diluted and syncretic version of Islam. See also Bangura's reading of the figure of the cleric in a number of West African novels, correcting the familiar stereotype of the "good" and "bad" Muslim in the popular imaginary. See Bangura (2000, 33).

11. See also Chrisafis (2015). This article explores the issue of secularism or *laïcité* that is being exploited for political gain when, in fact, as this article posits, the same cafeterias had been serving nonpork options to Muslim and Jewish children for decades. See https://www.theguardian.com/world/2015/oct/13/pork-school-dinners-france-secularism-children-religious-intolerance, accessed July 12, 2019.

12. See my analysis that foregrounds Ken's Muslim identity that she clearly and explicitly claims in the novel but one that remains critically understudied in favor of the black and racial politics of colonization and postcolonization: this is the more preferred framework for studying African experiences, even in transnational theorizations of Africans.

13. Abubakar's writing has been featured in a number of literary venues, including *Cha* magazine, where her story "Hegira" appears. See https://www.asiancha.com/content/view/3211/677/, accessed June 30, 2019. Abubakar has also written essays in addition to the one analyzed here where she discusses interreligious encounters. See "No Dowry, No Cry" (2013) in *Dagmay,* accessed June 30, 2019, https://dagmay.com/2013/05/27/no-dowry-no-cry/#more-2495.

14. Denny calls this moment the time when the meaning of the *ummah* reached its most mature stage and also took on a certain clarity as "Muslim community" (1975, 54).

15. Chowdhury (2011, 157) notes a similar transnational influence in Bangladesh as a consequence of increased labor migration to the Middle East.

The sudden presence of the "purist" strain of religious ideology pressures labor migrants to return to their homelands and preach a rigid form of religious values that contrast with a historically more plural and syncretic form of Islam practiced in Bangladesh.

16. Although not directly related to the theme of gendered self-determination, it is important to note that Abubakar facilitates the idea of community or *ummah* in the story via the plural and multireligious example of al *Isra wal Miraj* or the story of Isra and Miraj in Islamic tradition. She does so by alluding to Buraq in the story. The events known as Isra and Miraj refer to Muhammad's night journey when he rode Buraq, a winged horselike creature, to travel from Mecca to Jerusalem and then up the seven heavens. It is during this journey that the Islamic obligation to pray five times was commanded by God. However, the original commandment, it is believed, was to pray one hundred times. Muhammad descended the heavens with this order but was counseled on the way by the prophets who preceded him in the Judeo-Christian tradition—Moses, Abraham, Jesus, David, and others. These prophets explained to Muhammad that it was impractical and impossible to pray one hundred times. Muhammad ascended the heavens again and received a fresh commandment, this time reduced to pray fifty times a day. As such, Muhammad traveled up and down the heavens several times before the order was settled on the obligation to pray five times a day. This story reaffirms the continuity and the acknowledgment of the role of the other two Abrahamic faiths in shaping Islam and Islam's spirit of recognizing the contributions of the themes and ideas of the other two monotheistic faith traditions. This spirit also animates the idea of community in Islam that recognizes the rights and duties of non-Muslims. In Abubakar's story, Yusuf Zubaira dreams of Buraq and uses the dream as a sign to embark on his political mission to emancipate his disenfranchised community by entering into a dialogue with the Catholic majority.

17. The Tausug people are mostly Muslim and inhabit the islands of southern Philippines—Sulu, Mindanao, and Palawan. The Tausugs are also called "Moro." See Haskins (1982).

Chapter 4

1. In her conceptual essay on the typology of motherhood in African societies, Sudarkasa studies four categories of motherhood prevalent in African cultures. She organizes types of motherhood on the basis of household compositions and postmarital residence, power and influence of mothers, and definitional variations of "real" mothers and "half siblings," among other variables shaping kinship structures in African societies. In so doing, she unravels a range of complex roles and images that women as mothers play in diverse family structures including spaces of residence, power, and influence as wives as well as mothers,

relationships between "real" mothers and half siblings, and the relationship between marital and family stability. Each of these spheres is demarcated and not necessarily mutually inclusive or imbricated. This means that the family unit's stability may take precedence over marital stability in an extended family.

2. https://en.qantara.de/content/muslim-authors-at-the-first-south-african-book-fair-variety-as-a-community-reality. Accessed May 15, 2019.

3. Ray reads Chatterjee's iconic *Anandmath* to posit the ways in which women breach gendered codes of socialized behavior through cross-dressing and male behavior. Shanti for instance disrupts male organization in an ascetic group by disguising herself as a man to join them. She sheds her given name and adopts a male name—Navinanda—with "navin" meaning "new" to assume a new (male) identity (46–47).

4. The story first appeared in the literary journal *Dagmay* online in 2010. See https://dagmay.com/2010/09/19/sakeenah/, accessed June 30, 2019. Jamil is also the author of several short pieces, such as "Initiation," "Aesthetics," "Mukna" (appearing in Barry's collection *The Many Ways of Being Muslim*) and more recently of the short stories "Sukran," (2008) and "Amirah" (2016), among others, both appearing in *Dagmay*. See https://dagmay.com/2008/10/19/sukran/ and https://dagmay.com/2016/10/09/amirah/, accessed June 30, 2019.

5. For a complete timeline and coverage of the events described as the Mamasapanao incident in 2015, see https://www.rappler.com/nation/81883-pnp-saf-maguindanao-terrorists, accessed June 30, 2019. And see Villareal (2016). See also the official document on the Bangasmoro Basic Law signed by the Philippine president Rodrigo Duterte and ratified by the Philippine Congress in 2018, accessed June 30, 2019, https://web.archive.org/web/20150924025414/http://www.hdcentre.org/uploads/tx_news/Primer-on-the-proposed-Bangsamoro-Basic-Law.pdf.

6. See McKenna (1998).

7. See "Amirah," accessed June 30, 2019, https://dagmay.com/2016/10/09/amirah/.

8. For a detailed study of el-Khalieqy's work, see Arimbi's layered and thorough critique of el-Khalieqy's place in Indonesian letters. From a host of important intersectional angles, Arimbi delves into el-Khalieqy's contributions to gendered activism in contemporary Indonesia along with a comparative study of other important Indonesian writers, Titis Basino and Helvy Tiana Rose.

9. See Rinaldo (2013) and Tickamyer and Kusurjiati (2012).

Epilogue

1. Michael Lecker's extensive study on just this written document (or kitāb as the Islamic scholar ibn Isḥāq calls it) provides a well-rounded explanation of the many meanings and scholarly interpretations of the term ummah in 622 AD

when the document was drafted. One observation that Lecker makes in his study is that in the early days of the Muslim community in Medina, Muhammad sought to unite heterogenous elements—Jews, heathens, idolators—and even Muslims into a united community. Lecker underscores the idea that the term ummah, as implied in the Constitution of Medina, included the citizens of Medina and its surrounding area, even those who had not heeded Muhammad's appeal to accept Islam and his prophethood (49). As such, ummah included even non-Muslims.

2. Muhammad spent much of his life in dialogue with coreligionists, unbelievers, atheists, and idolators. Studying his numerous dialogues either oral or textual therefore offers a rich canvas of techniques and tools to craft interfaith relations based on mutual respect and recognition in contemporary society. For instance, W. Montgomery Watt (1956) reproduces the text of the letter that Muhammad sent to the bishop of B. al-Hārith b. Ka'b and the bishops of Najrān, extending his protection to the minority community of Christians and affirming their faith. The letter states: "For all their priests and those who followed them and their monks, that for all their churches, services and monastic practices, few or many, they had the protection (jiwar) of God and His messenger. No bishop will be moved from his episcopate, no monk from his monastic state, no priest from his priesthood. There will be no alteration of any right or authority or circumstance, so long as they are loyal and perform their obligations well, they not being burdened (suffered?) and not doing wrong. Written by al-Mughirah" (359).

3. See Ibn Isḥāq's biography of Muhammad, Sirat Rasoul Allah, that recognizes the early struggle in uniting disparate communities in the period following the hegira or migration of the first Muslims from Mecca to Medina. In his account, Ibn Isḥāq clearly states the different motivations, ranging from political opportunism to political security offered by a victorious confederacy to a genuine acceptance of Muhammad's prophethood, behind allying with Muhammad in Medina in the early days following the migration from Mecca to Medina (44–46).

4. See McClintock (1997).

5. https://www.dallasobserver.com/arts/oak-cliffs-de-colores-collective-giving-marginalized-communities-a-voice-9533185. Accessed July 8, 2019; https://pdfs.semanticscholar.org/6f7b/a92b7784e0dc83ec1bbe9f7b770663e539bc.pdf. Accessed July 8, 2019. See also http://www.youthfx.org/.

6. https://www.chalchitraabhiyaan.com/. Accessed May 23, 2019.

7. See Watt (1956, 221) and Ibn Isḥāq, Sirat Rasoul Allah (48).

Bibliography

Abbas, Sadia. *At Freedom's Limit: Islam and the Postcolonial Predicament.* New York: Fordham University Press, 2014.

———. "Religion, and the Challenge of the Novel." *Contemporary Literature* 52, no. 3 (2011): 430–461.

Abdulai, Jemila. "#Yennenga." In *Lusaka Punk and Other Stories: The Caine Prize for African Writing 2015*, edited by Lizzie Attree, 97–118. Northampton, MA: Interlink.

Aboulela, Leila. "Barbie in the Mosque." In *Being Scottish: Personal Reflections on Scottish Identity Today*, edited by Tom Devine and Paddy Logue, 1–3. Edinburgh: Polygon, 2002.

———. *Coloured Lights.* London: Polygon, 2001.

———. *Minaret.* New York: Black Cat, 2004.

———. *The Translator.* London: Polygon, 1999.

Abu Lughod, Lila. "Do Muslim Women Really Need Saving? Anthropological Reflections on Cultural Relativism and Its Others." *American Anthropologist* 104, no. 3 (2002): 783–790.

Abubakar, Pearlsha. "Ayesha's Pretty Hate Machine." In *The Many Ways of Being Muslim: Fiction by Muslim Filipinos*, edited by Coeli Barry, 165–170. Ithaca, NY: Cornell University Press, 2008.

———. "Hegira" *Cha: As Asian Literary Journal.* 40 (2018). https://www.asiancha.com/content/view/3212/673/. Accessed on July 1, 2019.

———. "Maghrib." In *The Many Ways of Being Muslim: Fiction by Muslim Filipinos*, edited by Coeli Barry, 165–170. Ithaca, NY: Cornell University Press, 2008.

———. "'Naunu Na Kaun Yan?' (What's happening to you?)." In *Rays of the Invisible Light: Collected Works by Young Moro Writers*, edited by. Gutierrez Mangansakan II, 11—15—General Santos City: Bidadali, 2015.

———. "No Dowry, No Cry." *Dagmay.* https://dagmay.com/2013/05/27/no-dowry-no-cry/. Accessed July 1, 2019.

Adejunmobi, Moradewun. "Major and Minor Discourses of the Vernacular: Discrepant African Histories." In *Minor Transnationalism*, edited by Françoise

Lionnet and Shu Mei Shih, 179–197. Durham, NC: Duke University Press, 2008.

Adichie, Chimamanda Ngozi. "The Scarf." *Wasafiri* 17, no. 37 (2002): 26–30.

———. "A Private Experience." In *The Thing Around Your Neck*, 43–56. New York: Anchor, 2009.

Adichie, C. N. "The Role of Literature in Modern Africa," *New African*, November 8, 2010.

Afsarudin, Asma. "Early Women Exemplars and the Construction of Gendered Space: (Re): Defining Feminine Moral Excellence." In *Harem Histories: Envisioning Places and Living Spaces*, edited by Marilyn Booth, 23–48. Durham, NC: Duke University Press, 2010.

Afshar, Haleh. "Women and Reproduction in Iran." In *Woman-Nation-State*, edited by Nira Yuval Davis and Floya Anthias, 110–125. New York: Palgrave, 1989.

Ahmed, Leila. *Women and Gender in Islam: Historical Roots of a Modern Debate*. New Haven, CT: Yale University Press, 1992.

Ahmed, Sara. *Living a Feminist Life*. Durham, NC: Duke University Press, 2017.

al-Ahsan, Abdullah. "The Quranic Concept of Ummah." *Institute of Muslim Minority Affairs. Journal* 7, no. 2 (2007): 606–616.

Ajayi-Soyinka, Omofolabo. "Negritude Feminism and the Quest for Identity: Re-reading Mariama Ba's So Long a Letter." In *Emerging Perspectives on Mariama Ba: Postcolonialism, feminism and postmodernism*, edited by Uzoamaka Ada Azodo, 153–174. Trenton, NJ: Africa World, 2003.

Akpome, Aghogho. "Cultural Criticism and Feminist Literary Activism in the Works of Chimamanda Ngozi Adichie." *Gender and Behavior* 15, no. 4 (2017): 9847–9871.

Akram, Ejaz. "Muslim Ummah and its Link with Transnational Muslim Politics." *Islamic Studies* 46, no. 3 (2007): 381–415.

Alexander, M. Jacqui. *Pedagogies of Crossing: Meditations on Feminism, Sexual Politics, Memory, and the Sacred*. Durham, NC: Duke University Press, 2005.

Al-Faruqi, Ismail Raji. *Al-Tawhid: Its Implications for Thought and Life*. Herndon: IIIT, 1982, 2000.

Ali, Abdullah Yusuf. *The Translation of the Meanings of the Noble Qur'an*. Beltsville, MD: Amana, 2006.

Ali, Monica. *Brick Lane*. London: Scribner, 2003.

Alidou, Ousseina. *Engaging Modernity Muslim Women and the Politics of Agency in Postcolonial Niger*. Madison: University of Wisconsin Press, 2005.

Aljunied, Khairudin. *Muslim Cosmopolitanism: Southeast Asian Islam in Comparative Perspective*. Edinburgh: Edinburgh University Press, 2016.

Angeles, Vivienne. "The Middle East and the Philippines: Transnational Linkages, Labor Migration and the Remaking of Philippine Islam" *Comparative Islamic Studies* 7, nos. 1–2 (2011): 157–181.

Appadurai, Arjun. *Modernity at Large: The Cultural Dimensions of Globalization.* Minneapolis: University of Minnesota Press, 1996.

Appiah. Kwame Anthony. "Cosmopolitan Patriots." *Critical Inquiry* 23, no. 3 (1997): 617–639.

Apter, Emily. *Against World Literature: On the Politics of Untranslatability.* London: Verso, 2003.

———. "Untranslatability and the Geopolitics of Reading," *PMLA* 134, no. 1 (2019): 194–200.

Arjomand, Said Amir. "The Constitution of Medina: A Sociolegal Interpretation of Muhammad's Acts of Foundation of the *Umma*." *International Journal of Middle Eastern Studies* 41 (2009): 555–575.

Arimbi, Diah Ariani. *Reading Contemporary Indonesian Muslim Women Writers: Representation, Identity and Religion of Muslim Women in Indonesian Fiction.* Amsterdam: Amsterdam University Press, 2010.

Asha, Ghassan. *Mariage, polygamie et répudiation en Islam: justification des auteurs arabo-musulmans contemporains.* Paris. L'Harmattan, 1997.

Azodo, Uzoamaka Ada, ed. *Emerging Perspectives on Mariama Ba: Postcolonialism, Feminism and Postmodernism.* Trenton, NJ: Africa World, 2003.

Ba, Mariama. *So Long a Letter.* Translated by Modupe Bodé-Thomas. Portsmouth, NH: Heinemann, 1981.

———. *Scarlet Song.* Translated by Dorothy S. Blair. London: Longman, 1986.

Badran, Margot. *Feminism Beyond East and West: New Gender Talk and Practice in Global Islam.* London: Global Media, 2007.

———. *Feminism in Islam: Secular and Religious Convergences.* Oxford: Oneworld, 2009.

———. "Re/placing Islamic Feminism." *Critique Internationale* 46, no. 1 (2010): 25–44. https://www.cairn-int.info/article-E_CRII_046_0025--re-placing-islamic-feminism.htm. Accessed February 11, 2019.

Baksh, Rawwida, and Wendy Harcourt. "Introduction" Rethinking Knowledge, Power, and Social Change." In *The Oxford Handbook of Transnational Feminist Movements*, edited by Wendy Harcourt and Rawwida Baksh, 1–45. Oxford: Oxford University Press, 2015.

Bangura, Ahmed. *Islam in the West African Novel: The Politics of Representation.* Boulder, CO: Lynne Rienner, 2000.

Barlow, Tani. "Theorizing Woman: Funu, Guojia, Jiating (Chinese Women, Chinese State, Chinese Family)." In *Scattered Hegemonies: Postmodernity and Transnational Feminist Practices*, edited by Inderpal Grewal and Karen Caplan, 173–196. Minneapolis: University of Minnesota Press, 1997.

Barry, Coeli, ed. *The Many Ways of Being Muslim.: Fiction by Muslim Filipinos.* Ithaca, NY: Cornell University Press, 2008.

Basu, Amrita. *The Challenge Of Local Feminisms: Women's Movements in Global Perspective.* Boulder, CO: Westview, 1995.

———. *Women's Movements in the Global Era: The Power of Local Feminisms*. Boulder: Westview, 2010.

Bhabha, Homi. *Edward Said, Culture and Imperialism*. London: Chatto and Windus, 1993.

———. *The Location of Culture*. London: Routledge, 1994.

Boehmer, Elleke. *Stories of Women: Gender and Narrative in the Postcolonial Nation*. Manchester, UK: Manchester University Press, 2005.

Brierely, Natalie. "*Coloured Lights*." Review of *Coloured Lights*, by Leila Aboulela. *New Statesman*, July 30, 2001.

Briggs, Laura, Gladys McCormick, and J.T. Way, "Transnationalism: A Category of Analysis." *American Quarterly* 60, no. 3 (2008): 625–648.

Campbell, John, and Asch Harwood, "Boko Haram's Deadly Impact." August 20, 2018. *Council on Foreign Relations*.

Chatterjee, Piya. "Transforming Pedagogies: Imagining Internationalist/Feminist/Antiracist Legacies." In *Activist Scholarship: Antiracism, Feminism and Social Change*, edited by Julia Sudbury and Margo Ozakawa-Ray, 131–148. Boulder, CO: Paradigm, 2009.

Chowdhury, Elora. *Transnationalism Reversed: Women Organizing against Gendered Violence in Bangladesh*. Albany: State University of New York Press, 2010.

———. "The Space Between Us: Reading Umrigar and Sangari in the Quest for Female Friendship." In *Dissident Friendships*, edited by Elora Chowdhury and Liz Philipose, 160–181. Urbana: University of Illinois Press, 2016.

Chrisafis, Angelique. "Pork or Nothing: How School Dinners are Dividing France." *Guardian*, October 13, 2015. https://www.theguardian.com/world/2015/oct/13/pork-school-dinners-france-secularism-children-religious-intolerance. Accessed July 12, 2019.

Clifford, James. *Routes: Travel and Translation in the Late Twentieth Century*. Cambridge: Harvard University Press, 1997.

Cooper, Brenda. *A New Generation of African Writers: Migration, Material Culture and Language*. Oxford: James Currey; Pietermaritzburg: University of KwaZulu-Natal Press, 2008.

Cousins, Helen. "Nothing Like Motherhood: Barrenness, Abortion, and Infanticide in Yvonne Vera's Fiction." In *Rites of Passage in Postcolonial Women's Writing*, edited by Pauline Dodgson-Katiyo and Gina Wisker, 21–40. Rodopi; 2010.

Dallal, Ahmad S, Yoginder Sikand, and Abdul Rashid Moten. "Ummah." In *The Oxford Encyclopedia of the Islamic World*. Oxford Islamic Studies Online, http://www.oxfordislamicstudies.com/article/opr/t236/e0818. Accessed March 27, 2019.

Dao, Anna. "A Perfect Wife." In *Opening Spaces: An Anthology of Contemporary African Women's Writing*, edited by Yvonne Vera, 159–177. Portsmouth, NH: Heinemann; Harare: Baobab, 1999.

Davies, Carole Boyce. *Black Women, Writing and Identity: Migrations of the Subject.* New York: Routledge, 1994.
Davis, Yuval Nira, and Floya Anthias. "Introduction." In *Woman-Nation-State*, edited by Nira Yuval Davis and Floya Anthias, 1–15. New York: Palgrave, 1989.
Davis, Nira Yuval. *Gender and Nation.* London: SAGE, 1997.
Deleuze, Gilles, Felix Guattari, and Dana Polan. *Kafka:Toward a Minor Literature.* Minneapolis: University of Minnesota Press, 1986.
Denny, Frederick Matthewson. *An Introduction to Islam.* New York: Routledge, 2016.
———. "The Meaning of "Ummah" in the Qur'an." *History of Religions* 15, no. 1 (1975): 34–70.
Denkyi-Manieson, Gladys Agyiewaa. "Purple Hibiscus, Half of a Yellow Sun and the Thing around Your Neck by Chimamanda Ngozi Adichie: A Thematic Study." *Africology: The Journal of Pan African Studies* 11, no. 1 (2017): 52–65.
Desai, Manisha. "Transnational Solidarity: Women's Agency, Structural Adjustment, and Globalization." In *Women's Activism and Globalization: Linking Local Struggles and Global Politics*, edited by Manisha Desai and Nancy Naples, 15–32. London: Routledge, 1992.
Dimock, Wai Chee. *Through other Continents: American Literature across Deep Time.* Princeton, NJ: Princeton University Press, 2006.
Diouf, Sylviane. *Servants of Allah: African Muslims Enslaved in the Americas.* New York: New York University Press, 2013.
Dirlik, Arif. "The Postcolonial Aura: Third World Criticism in the Age of Global Capitalism." In *Dangerous Liaisons: Gender, Nation and Postcolonial Perspectives*, edited by Anne McClintock, Aamir Mufti, and Ella Shohat, 501–528. Minneapolis: University of Minnesota Press, 1997.
Doherty, Brian. "Chimamanda Ngozi Adichie's 'The Headstrong Historian' as a Response to Chinua Achebe's Things Fall Apart," in *Tradition and Change in Contemporary West and East African Fiction*, ed. Ogaga Okuyade (Amsterdam: Rodopi, 2014), 187–201.
Dowd, Robert. *Christianity, Islam, and Liberal Democracy: Lessons from Sub-Saharan Africa.* Oxford: Oxford University Press, 2015.
Edwin, Shirin. "African Muslim Communities in Diaspora: The Quest for a Muslim Space in Ken Bugul's "Le baobab fou." *Research in African Literatures* 35, no. 4 (2004): 75–90.
———. "Geopolitical and Global (Ex) Changes: African Muslim Women and Interfaith Dialogues and Anxieties about Africa's Global Place." In *Handbook of African Literature*, edited by Moradewun Adejunmobi and Carli Coetzee. London: Routledge, 2019. 261–275.
———. *Privately Empowered: Expressing Feminism in Islam in Northern Nigerian Fiction.* Evanston, IL: Northwestern University Press, 2016.

———. "(Un)Holy Alliances: Marriage, Faith, and Politics in Leila Aboulela's The Translator." *Journal of Middle East Women's Studies* 9, no. 2 (Spring 2013): 58–79.

Eisenberg, Eve. "Real Africa/Which Africa? The Critique of Mimetic Realism in Chimamanda Ngozi Adichie's Short Fiction." In *ALT 31 Writing Africa in the Short Story: African Literature Today*, edited by Ernest Emenyonu, 8–24. Boydell and Brewer, 2013.

El-Khalieqy, Abidah. "Road to Heaven." *Words without Borders*. January 2009. Translated by John H. McGlynn. https://www.wordswithoutborders.org/article/road-to-heaven Accessed March 10, 2018.

———. *Geni Jora and Other Texts*. Translated by Joan Suyenaga and Heike Reissig. Jakarta: Lontar, 2015.

Elmadmad, Khadija. "The Human Rights of Refugees with Special Reference to Muslim Refugee Women." In *Engendering Forced Migration: Theory and Practice*, edited by Doreen Indra, 261–266. New York: Berghahn, 1999.

Emecheta, Buchi. *The Joys of Motherhood*. New York: George Braziller, 1979.

Emenyonu, Ernest. "Introduction." In *A Companion to Chimamanda Ngozi Adichie*, edited by Ernest Emenyonu, 1–13. London: James Currey, 2017.

———. "Once Upon a Time Begins a Story," Editorial. In *ALT 31 Writing Africa in the Short Story: African Literature Today*, edited by Ernest N. Emenyonu, 1–7. London: James Currey, 2013.

Federspiel, Howard M. "Pesantren." In *The Oxford Encyclopedia of the Islamic World*. Oxford Islamic Studies Online. March 14, 2020. http://www.oxfordislamicstudies.com/article/opr/t236/e0632.

Ferguson, James. *Global Shadows: Africa in the Neoliberal World Order*. Durham: Duke University Press, 2006.

Ferree, Myra Marx. "Globalization and Feminism: Opportunities and Obstacles for Activism in the Global Arena." In *Global Feminism: Transnational Women's Activism, Organizing and Human Rights*, edited by Myra Marx Ferree and Aili Mari Tripp, 3–23. New York: New York University Press, 2006.

Finbarr, Barry Flood. *The Great Mosque of Damascus: Studies on the Makings of a Great Umayyad Visual Culture*. Leiden, The Netherlands: Brill, 2001.

Fong, Hui Yew. "Introduction—Encountering Islam." In *Encountering Islam: The Politics of Religious Identities in Southeast Asia*, edited by Hui Yew-Fong. 3–16. Singapore: Institute of Southeast Asian Studies, 2013.

Friedman, Jonathan. "Global Crises, the Struggle for Cultural Identity and Intellectual Porkbarrelling: Cosmopolitans versus Locals, Ethnics and Nationals in an Era of De-hegemonisation." In *Debating Cultural Hybridity: Multicultural Identities and the Politics of Anti-racism*, edited by Pnina Werbner and Tariq Modood, 84–85. London: Zed, 1997.

Friedman, Susan Stanford. *Mappings: Feminism and the Cultural Geographies of Encounter*. Trenton, NJ: Princeton University Press, 1998.

———. *Planetary Modernisms: Provocations on Modernity Across Time*. New York: Columbia University Press, 2015.
Gandhi, Leela. *Affective Communities: Anticolonial Thought, Fin-de-Siècle Radicalism, and the Politics of Friendship*. Durham, NC: Duke University Press, 2006.
García-Peña, Lorgia. *Borders of Dominicanidad: Race, Nation and Archives of Contradiction*. Durham, NC: Duke University Press, 2016.
Ghazoul, Ferial. "Halal Fiction." *Al-Ahram Weekly Online* 542, July 12–18 2001.
Gikandi, Simon. "Contested Grammars: Comparative Literature, Translation, and the Challenge of Locality." *A Companion to Comparative Literature*, edited by Ali Behdad and Dominic Thomas, 254–272. London: Blackwell, 2011.
———. *Writing in Limbo: Modernism and Caribbean Literature*. Ithaca: Cornell University Press, 1992.
Gilroy, Paul. "A New Cosmopolitanism," *Interventions* 7, no. 3 (2005): 287–292.
Gimba, Abubakar. *Sacred Apples*. New York: Vantage, 1997. US Edition is entitled *Golden Apples*.
Glissant, Edouard. *Caribbean Discourse*. Charlottesville: University of Virginia Press, 1999.
Grewal, Inderpal, and Caren Kaplan. "Introduction: Transnational Feminist Practices and Questions of Postmodernity." In *Scattered Hegemonies: Postmodernity and Transnational Feminist Practices*, edited by Inderpal Grewal and Caren Kaplan, 1–33. Minneapolis: University of Minnesota Press, 1994.
———."Transnational Practices and Interdisciplinary Feminist Scholarship: Refiguring Women's and Gender Studies." In *Women's Studies on its own*, edited by Robyn Wiegman, 66–81. Durham, NC: Duke University Press, 2002.
Gunning, Dave. *Race and Antiracism in Black British and British Asian Literature* Liverpool: Liverpool University Press, 2010.
Gupta, Akhil, Aihwa Ong, and Inderpal Grewal. "Asian Transnationalities: Guest Editors' Introduction." *Positions* 7, no. 3 (Winter 1999): 653–666.
Halliday, Fred. "The Politics of the Umma: States and Community in Islamic Movements." *Mediterranean Politics*, 7, no. 3 (2002): 2041. See also "The Problem of the Umma." *Economist*. https://www.economist.com/special-report/2003/09/11/the-problem-of-the-umma. Accessed April 15, 2019.
Halpern, Daniel. Preface to *The Art of the Story*, xi–xiii. New York: Penguin, 1999.
Hannerz, Ulf. *Transnational Connections: Culture, People, Places*. London: Routledge, 1996.
Haskins, Jim. *The Filipino Nation*. New York: Grolier, 1982.
Hassan, Waïl. "Leila Aboulela and the Ideology of Muslim Immigrant Fiction." *Novel: A Forum on Fiction* 41, no. 2–3 (2008): 298–319.
Hosseini, Ziba Mir. *Islam and Gender: The Religious Debate in Contemporary Iran*. Princeton, NJ: Princeton University Press, 1999.
Ingilan, Sajed. "Unveiling the Muslimah: A Feminist Stylistic Analysis of the Image of the Female Filipino Muslims in Short Stories." *JATI* 22 (2017): 139–157.

Isḥāq, Ibn. *Sirat Rasoul Allah*. Translated by Edward Rehatsek. London: The Folio Society, 1964.

Jacobs, Rayda. *My Father's Orchid*. Cape Town: Umuzi, 2006.

Jaji, Tsitsi. *Africa in Stereo: Modernism, Music, and Pan-African Solidarity*. Oxford: Oxford University Press, 2014.

Jalal, Ayesha. *Partisans of Allah: Jihad in South Asia*. Cambridge, MA: Harvard University Press, 2008.

Jamil, Arifa Macaqua. "Amirah," *Dagmay: Literary Journal of the Davao Writers Guild* (2016) https://dagmay.online/2016/10/09/amirah/ Accessed on July 1, 2019.

———. "Sakeenah." In *Rays of the Invisible Light: Collected Works by Young Moro Writers*, edited by Gutierrez Mangansakan II, 12–16. General Santos City: Bidadali, 2015.

———. "Sukran" *Dagmay: Literary Journal of the Davao Writers Guild* (2008) https://dagmay.com/2008/10/19/sukran/ Accessed on July 1, 2019.

Jayawardene, Kumari. *Gender and Nationalism in the Third World*. New Delhi: Kali for Women, 1986.

Kalliney, Peter. "African Fiction in a Global Context." In *The Oxford History of the Novel in English: The Novel in Africa and the Caribbean since 1950*, edited by Simon Gikandi, 411–426. Oxford: Oxford University Press, 2016.

Kalu, Anthonia. "The African Short Story." In *The Novel in Africa and the Caribbean since 1950*, edited by Simon Gikandi, 375–392. Oxford: Oxford University Press, 2016.

Kane, Ousmane. *Beyond Timbuktu: An Intellectual History of Muslim West Africa*. Cambridge, MA: Harvard University Press, 2016.

Kaplan, Caren. "The Politics of Location as Transnational Feminist Critical Practice." In *Scattered Hegemonies: Postmodernity and Transnational Feminist Practices*, edited by Inderpal Grewal and Caren Kaplan, 137–152. Minneapolis: University of Minnesota Press, 1994.

Karim, Jamillah. *American Muslim Women: Negotiating Race, Class, and Gender within the Ummah*. New York: New York University Press, 2008.

Kern, Soeren. "France Goes Halal," Gatestone Institute International Policy Council February 28, 2012. https://www.gatestoneinstitute.org/2886/france-halal. Accessed July 12, 2019.

El-Khalieqy, Abidah. "Road to Heaven." Translated by John H. McGlynn. https://www.wordswithoutborders.org/article/road-to-heaven. Accessed January 23 2018.

Koshy, Susan. "Why the Humanities Matter for Race Studies Today." *PMLA*, 123, no. 5 (2008): 1542–1549.

Krishnaswamy, Revathi. "Postcolonial and Globalization Studies: Connections, Conflicts, Complicities." In *The Postcolonial and the Global*, edited by Revathi Krishnaswamy and John C. Hawley, 2–21. Minneapolis: University of Minnesota Press, 2008.

Laffan, Michael. "Islam in Southeast Asia," https://asiasociety.org/education/islam-southeast-asia. Accessed October 2018.
Lecker, Michael. *The "Constitution of Medina": Muhammad's First Legal Document.* Princeton: Darwin, 2004.
Li, Stephanie. *Pan African-American Literature: Signifying Immigrants in the Twenty-First Century.* New Brunswick, NJ: Rutgers University Press, 2018.
Lim, Mendry Ann. "The Dilemmas of Muslim Feminism in a non-Muslim Country: The Case of Nisa-Ul Haqq Fi Bangsamoro in the Philippines." MA thesis, Brandeis University, 2010.
Lionnet, Françoise, and Shu Mei Shih. "Introduction: Thinking about the Minor, Transnationally." In *Minor Transnationalism*, edited by Françoise Lionnet and Shu Mei Shih, 1–26. Durham, NC: Duke University Press, 2005.
Loimeier, Roman. "Boko Haram: The Development of a Militant Religious Movement in Nigeria." *Africa Spectrum* 23 (2012): 137–155.
Mack, Beverly, and Jean Boyd. *One Woman's Jihad: Nana Asma'u, Scholar and Scribe* Bloomington: Indiana University Press, 2000.
Mahmood, Saba. *Politics of Piety: Islamic Revival and the Feminist Subject.* Princeton, NJ: Princeton University Press, 2005.
Mama, Amina. "Sheroes and Villains: Conceptualizing Colonial and Contemporary Violence Against Women in Africa." In *Feminist Genealogies, Colonial Legacies, Democratic Futures*, edited by Chandra Mohanty and M. Jacqui Alexander, 46–62. London: Routledge, 1997.
Mandaville, Peter. *Transnational Muslim Politics: Reimagining the Umma.* New York: Routledge, 2002.
———. "Territory and Translocality: Discrepant Idioms of Political Identity." *Millennium: A Journal of International Studies* 28, no. 3 (1999): 653–73.
Mangasakan, Gutierrez, ed. *Rays of the Invisible Light: Collected Works by Young Moro Writers.* General Santos City: Bidadali, 2015.
Mani, Lata. *Contentious Traditions: The Debate on Sati in Colonial India.* Oakland: University of California Press, 1998.
Mani, B. Venkat. *Recoding World Literature: Libraries, Print Culture, and Germany's Pact with Books.* New York: Fordham University Press, 2017.
Martin, Dahlia. "Gender, Malayness and the *Ummah*: Cultural Consumption and Malay-Muslim Identity." *Asian Studies Review* 38, no. 3 (2014): 403–421.
Masquelier, Adeline. *Women and Islamic Revival in a West African Town.* Bloomington: Indiana University Press, 2005.
Mbembe, Achille. "African Modes of Self-Writing." Translated by Steven Rendall. *Public Culture* 14, no. 1 (2002): 239–273.
McCain, Carmen. "The Politics of Exposure: Contested Cosmopolitanisms, Revelation of secrets, and Intermedial Reflexivity in Hausa Popular Expression." PhD diss., University of Wisconsin, 2014.

McClintock, Anne. "Family Feuds: Gender, Nationalisms and Family." *Feminist Review* 44 (1993): 61-80.

———."No Longer in a Future Heaven: Gender, Race and Nationalism." In *Dangerous Liaisons: Gender Nation and Postcolonial Perspectives*, edited by Anne McClintock, Aamir Mufti, and Ella Shohat, 89-112. Minneapolis: University of Minnesota Press, 1997.

McKenna, Thomas. *Muslim Rulers and Rebels: Everyday Politics and Armed Separatism in the Southern Philippines*. Oakland: University of California Press, 1998.

Menon, Jisha. *The Performance of Nationalism: India, Pakistan, and the Memory of Partition*. Cambridge: Cambridge University Press, 2013.

Miller, Jack. "Religion in the Philippines." https://asiasociety.org/education/religion-philippines. Accessed on July 28, 2021.

Misra, Maitreyi, and Manish Shrivastava. "Dislocation, Cultural Memory & Transcultural Identity in Select Stories from *The Thing Around Your Neck*." In *A Companion to Chimamanda Ngozi Adichie*, edited by Ernest Emenyonu, 185-197. London: James Currey, 2017.

Moghadam, Valentine. *Globalizing Women: Transnational Feminist Networks*. Baltimore: Johns Hopkins University Press, 2005.

———. "Islamic Feminism and Its Discontents: Toward a Resolution of the Debate." *Signs: Journal of Women in Culture and Society* 27, no. 4 (2002): 1135-1171.

———. "Transnational Feminist Activism and Movement Building." In *The Oxford Handbook of Transnational Feminist Movements*, edited by Wendy Harcourt and Rawwida Baksh, 53-81. Oxford: Oxford University Press, 2015.

Mohanty, Chandra Talpade, and M. Jacqui Alexander, eds. *Feminist Genealogies, Colonial Legacies, Democratic Futures*. London: Routledge, 1996.

Mohanty, Chandra Talpade, and M. Jacqui Alexander. "Cartographies of Knowledge and Power: Transnational Feminism as Radical Praxis." In *Critical Transnational Feminist Praxis*, edited by Amanda Lock Swarr and Richa Nagar, 23-45. Albany: State University of New York Press, 2010.

Mohanty, Chandra, and Linda Carty, "Mapping Transnational Feminist Engagements: Neoliberalism and the Politics of Solidarity," *The Oxford Handbook of Transnational Feminist Movements*, edited by Wendy Harcourt and Rawwida Baksh, 82-115. Oxford: Oxford University Press, 2015.

Morey, Peter. *Islamophobia and the Novel*. New York: Columbia University Press, 2018.

Mortimer, Mildred. "Enclosure/Disclosure in Mariama Ba's *Une si longue lettre*." *The French Review* 64, no. 1 (1990): 69-78.

Mount, Ferdinand. *The Subversive Family: An Alternative History of Love and Marriage*. New York: The Free Press, 1982.

Mufti, Aamir. *Enlightenment in the Colony: The Jewish Question and the Crisis of Postcolonial Culture*. Princeton, NJ: Princeton University Press, 2007.

———. *Forget English: Orientalisms and World Literatures*. Cambridge, MA: Harvard University Press, 2016.

———. "Why I Am Not a Postsecularist." *boundary 2* 40, no. 1 (2013): 7–20.

Mukhopadhyay, Maitrayee. "Gendered Citizenship in the Postcolony: The Challenge for Transnational Feminist Politics." In *The Oxford Handbook of Transnational Feminist Movements*, edited by Wendy Harcourt and Rawwida Baksh, 607–627. Oxford: Oxford University Press, 2015.

Munro, Brenna. "Gender and Sexuality and Africa Fiction" in *The Oxford History of the Novel in English The Novel in Africa and the Caribbean since 1950*, edited by Simon Gikandi, 161–180. Oxford: Oxford University Press, 2016.

Nasr, Seyyed Hossein. *The Heart of Islam*. San Francisco: Harper, 2002.

Nayel, Amina Alrasheed. *Alternative Performativity of Muslimness: The Intersection of Race, Gender, Religion, and Migration*. London: Palgrave, 2017.

Ng, Andrew Hock Soon. *Intimating the Sacred: Religion in English Language Malaysian Fiction*. Aberdeen: Hong Kong University Press, 2011.

———. "Islam and Modernity in the Works of Two Contemporary Malay Anglophone Writers: Che Husna Azhari's 'Mariah' and Karim Raslan's 'Neighbors.'" *Journal of Commonwealth Literature* 44, no. 3 (2009): 127–141.

Ngugi, Mukoma wa. *The Rise of the African Novel: Politics of Identity, Language and Ownership*. Ann Arbor: University of Michigan Press, 2018.

Nnaemeka, Obioma. "Mariama Ba: Parallels, Convergence and Interior Space." *Feminist Issues* 10, no. 1 (1990): 13–35.

Nolte, Insa, Olukoya Ogen, and Rebecca Jones, eds. *Beyond Religious Tolerance: Muslim, Christian and Traditionalist Encounters in an African Town*. London: James Currey, 2017.

Nzegwu, Nkiru. "Cultural Epistemologies of Motherhood: Refining the Concept of 'Mothers.'" *JENdA: A Journal of Culture and African Women Studies*. 4, no. 1 (2003). https://www.africaknowledgeproject.org/index.php/jenda/article/view/92. Accessed May 2, 2019.

Ochonu, Moses. *Colonialism by Proxy: Hausa Imperial Agents and Middle Belt Consciousness in Nigeria*. Bloomington: Indiana University Press, 2014.

Omar, Noritah. "Paradoxes of Malaysian Literature and "Collective Individuality." In Theorising National Identity." *Pertanika Journal of Social Sciences and Humanities*. 22 (2014): 131–145.

Özcan, Ezra. "Who is a Muslim Woman?: Questioning Knowledge Production on 'Muslim Woman.'" In *Introduction to Women's, Gender and Sexuality Studies: Interdisciplinary and Intersectional Approaches*, edited by L. Ayu Saraswati, Barbara L. Shaw, and Patricia Rellihan. 327–331. Oxford: Oxford University Press, 2018.

Oyewumi, Oyeronke. "Abiyamo: Theorizing African Motherhood." *JENdA: A Journal of Culture and African Women Studies* 4, no. 1 (2003). https://

www.africaknowledgeproject.org/index.php/jenda/article/view/79. Accessed April 28, 2019.

———. *African Women and Feminism: Reflecting on the Politics of Sisterhood.* Trenton, NJ: Africa World, 2003.

Padilla, Yajaira M. *Changing Women, Changing Nation: Female Agency, Nationhood, and Identity in Trans-Salvadoran Narratives.* Albany: State University of New York Press, 2012.

Patterson, Orlando. "The Emerging West Atlantic System: Migration, Culture, and Underdevelopment in the United States and the Circum-Caribbean Region." In *Population in an Interacting World*, edited by William Alonso, 227–260. Cambridge, MA: Harvard University Press, 1987.

Pratt, Mary Louise. "Arts of the Contact Zone," *Profession*, 1991, 33–40.

Quayson, Ato. *Oxford Street, Accra: City Life and the Itineraries of Transnationalism.* Durham, NC: Duke University Press, 2014.

Rajan, Rajeswari Sunder. *Real and Imagined Women: Gender, Culture and Postcolonialism.* London: Routledge, 1993.

Ray, Sangeeta. *En-Gendering India: Woman and Nation in Colonial and Postcolonial Narratives.* Durham, NC: Duke University Press, 2000.

Riesz, János. Translated by Richard Bjornson. "Mariama Bâ's *Une si longue lettre*: An Erziehungsroman." *Research in African Literatures* 22, no. 1 (1991): 27–42.

Rinaldo, Rachel. *Mobilizing Piety: Islam and Feminism in Indonesia.* Oxford: Oxford University Press, 2013.

Sackeyfio, Rose. "New Spaces of the Self: Diaspora Identities in Short Fiction by Chimamanda Ngozi Adichie and Sefi Atta." In *ALT 31 Writing Africa in the Short Story: African Literature Today*, edited by Ernest Emenyonu, 102–114. London: James Currey, 2013.

Sangari, Kumkum, and Sudesh Vaid. "Recasting Women: An Introduction." In *Recasting Women: Essays in Colonial History*, edited by Kumkum Sangari and Sudesh Vaid, 1–26. New Brunswick, NJ: Rutgers University Press, 1990.

Sanneh, Lamin. *Beyond Jihad: The Pacifist Tradition in West African Islam.* Oxford: Oxford University Press, 2016.

Santiago, Lilia Quindoza. "Rebirthing Babaye: The Women's Movement in the Philippines." In *The Challenge of Local Feminisms: Feminisms in a Global Perspective*, edited by Amrita Basu, 110–130. New York: Routledge, 2018.

Schroter, Susanne. "Islamic Feminism: National and Transnational Dimensions." In *Islam, Gender, and Democracy in Comparative Perspective*, edited by Jocelyne Cesari and Jose Casanova, 114–137. Oxford: Oxford University Press, 2017.

Sen, Debarati. *Everyday Sustainability: Gender Justice and Fair Trade Tea in Darjeeling.* Albany: State University of New York Press, 2017.

Shariatmadari, David. "Chimamanda Ngozi Adichie: Religious Leaders Must Help End Nigeria Violence." *Guardian*, January 13, 2012. Accessed July 7,

2019. https://www.theguardian.com/world/2012/jan/13/chimamanda-ngozi-adichie-nigeria-leaders

Shoneyin, Lola. *The Secret Lives of Baba Segi's Wives*. Lagos: Profile, 2010.

Shryock, Andrew. "Introduction: Islam as an Object of Fear and Affection." In *Islamophobia/Islamophilia: Beyond the Politics of Enemy and Friend*, edited by Andrew Shryock, 128. Bloomington: Indiana University Press, 2010.

Sontag, Susan. *On Photography*. New York: Picador, 1973.

Spivak, Gayatri Chakravarthy. *A Critique of Postcolonial Reason: Toward a History of the Vanishing Present*. Cambridge, MA: Harvard University Press, 1999.

Steiner, Tina. "Strategic Nostalgia, Islam and Cultural Translation in Leila Aboulela's *The Translator* and *Coloured Lights*." *Current Writing: Text and Reception in Southern Africa* 20, no. 2 (2008): 7–25.

Sudarkasa, Niara. "Conceptions of Motherhood in Nuclear and Extended Families, with Special Reference to Comparative Studies Involving African Societies." *JENdA: A Journal of Culture and African Women Studies* 5, no. 1 (2004). https://www.africaknowledgeproject.org/index.php/jenda/article/view/94. Accessed May 1, 2019.

Sule, E. E. *Sterile Sky*. Kano: Pearson PTR Interactive, 2013.

Swarr, Amanda Lock, and Richa Nagar. "Introduction: Theorizing Transnational Feminist Praxis." In *Critical Transnational Feminist Praxis*, edited by Amanda Lock Swarr and Richa Nagar, 1–22. Albany: State University of New York Press, 2010.

Tickamyer, Ann, and Siti Kusurjiati, *Power, Change, and Gender Relations in Rural Java: A Tale of Two Villages*. Athens: Ohio University Press, 2012.

Tripp, Aili Mari. "Challenges in Transnational Feminist Mobilization." In *Global Feminism: Transnational Women's Activism, Organizing and Human Rights*, edited by Myra Marx Ferree and Aili Mari Tripp, 296–312. New York: New York University Press, 2006.

Tunca, Daria, "The Confessions of a "Buddhist Catholic": Religion in the Works of Chimamanda Ngozi Adichie." *Research in African Literatures* 44, no. 3 (2013): 51–71.

Vadde, Aarthi. *Chimeras of Form: Modernist Internationalism beyond Europe, 1914–2016*. New York: Columbia University Press, 2016.

Vatuk, Sylvia. "Islamic Feminism in India: Indian Muslim Women Activists and the Reform of Muslim Personal Law." *Modern Asian Studies* 40, nos. 2–3 (2008): 489–518.

Vera, Yvonne. *Butterfly Burning*. New York: Farrar, Straus and Giroux, 2000.

Villareal, Gilbert G. Jr. "Operation Exodus: The Massacre of 44 Philippine Police Commandos in Mamasapano Clash." Master's thesis, Naval Postgraduate School, 2016. https://apps.dtic.mil/dtic/tr/fulltext/u2/1030109.pdf Accessed June 30, 2019.

Wadud, Amina. *Qur'an and Woman: Rereading the Sacred Text from a Woman's Perspective*. Kuala Lumpur: Penerbit Fajar Bakti Sdn. Bhd., 1992.
Watt, W. Montgomery. *Muhammad at Medina*. Oxford: Oxford University Press, 1956.
Werbner, Pnina. "Global Pathways: Working-Class Cosmopolitans and the Creation of Transnational Ethnic Worlds," *Social Anthropology* 7, no. 1 (1999): 19–20.
Yakubu, Balaraba Ramat. *Sin is a Puppy that Follows you Home*. Translated by Aliyu Kamal. Chennai: Blaft, 2012.
Zaman, Dina. *Holy Men, Holy Women: A Journey into the Faiths of Malaysians and Other Essays*. Selangor: Strategic Information and Research Development Center, 2018.
———. *I am Muslim*. Kuala Lumpur: Silverfish, 2007.
Zanchettin, Lindsey. "Articulations of Home & Muslim Identity in the Short Stories of Leila Aboulela." In *ALT 31 Writing Africa in the Short Story: African Literature Today*, edited by Ernest Emenyonu, 40–51. London: James Currey, 2013.

Index

Abbas, Sadia, 41–42, 65, 139–51, 199n3, 207n15
Abdulai, Jemila, 6, 188–90. *See also* "#Yennenga"
Aboulela, Leila, 6, 45, 127, 131–44, 149–51; criticism of, 138–44; depictions of Muslim women, 134–35. *See also individual works by name*
Abu Lughod, Lila, 107–108
Abubakar, Pearlsha, 6, 17, 126, 156–65, 181–83, 211n13. *See also individual works by name*
Achebe, Chinua, 39, 208n3. See also *Things Fall Apart*
activism, 9, 26–30, 83–85, 183–84, 186–88. *See also* everyday; non-governmental organizations; piety activism; women's studies
Adichie, Chimamanda Ngozie, 6, 36, 91, 93, 96–114, 120–21, 154–56, 208n3, 209n13; on Africa, 93; indictment of institutionalized religion, 111; and revision, 109–112. *See also individual works by name*
Afghanistan, 61
Africa: fiction, 208n2; novel and transnationalism, 91–92; place in the world, 93–95; shadow relationship, 92–94; spread of Christianity and Islam, 19. *See also* Afro-pessimism; countries by name
Afro-optimism. *See* Afro-pessimism
Afro-pessimism (Afro-optimism), 94
Afshar, Haleh, 173–74
Ahmed, Leila, 64
Ahmed, Sara, 30
al-Ahsan, Abdullah, 200n7, 204n41
al-Faruqi, Ismail Raji, 49–50, 68–69, 207n13
Alexander, Jacqui, 20–22
Alfassa, Mirra, 43–44
Alhaki Kuykeyo Ne... (Yakubu), 35, 40
Ali, Monica, 45
Alidou, Ousseina, 35
Aljunied, Khairudin, 46, 55, 80–82, 98. *See also* cosmopolitanism
Alkali, Zaynab, 144
Americanah (Adichie), 93
"Amirah" (Jamil), 177
Anandmath (Chatterje), 213n3
Anderson, Benedict, 46. *See also* imagined community
Andrews, C. F., 43–44
Appadurai, Arjun, 12–13, 24, 200n10. *See also* deterritorialization
Apter, Emily, 39–40. *See also* translation

archipelago, 129
Aslam, Nadeem, 45, 149–51. See also *Maps for Lost Lovers*
Aurobindo, Sri, 43–44
"Ayesha's Pretty Hate Machine" (Abubakar), 181–183

Ba, Mariama, 6, 21, 31, 36, 114–18, 120–21. See also *So Long a Letter*
Baba Segi's Wives (Shoneyin), 172
Badran, Margot, 64
Bahasa Indonesia, 30, 183. See also Indonesia
Bangladesh, 211n15
Barry, Coeli, 7, 157–58
Basu, Amrita, 28, 58–61, 84–85, 185, 206n8
biology. See gender; motherhood; sterility
Bhabha, Homi, 23, 200n12, 204n36
Boehmer, Elleke, 31, 172–73, 201n14
Boko Haram, 99–101. See also Nigeria
bride price. See dowry
Bugul, Ken, 21, 144, 149
Butterfly Burning (Vera), 172

capitalism: consumer, 152–53; fragmentation, 24–26; global, 202n23, 204n37. See also globalization; marketplace; shop
center. See periphery
Chatterjee (Chattopadhyay), Bankim Chandra, 128, 213n3. See also *Anandmath*
Chowdhury, Elora, 20–21, 74–75, 83–84. See also dependency chain
citizenship, 8–9. See also gender; nation
Clifford, James, 201n16
community. See *ummah*
Conference in Beijing (UN, 1995), 56
Conference in Kenya (UN, 1985), 57

Constitution of Medina (Madinah), 12, 26, 49, 129, 137, 158–59, 196–8, 200n7, 204n39, 204n41, 213n1. See also Islam; *ummah*
constructed opposition, 205n1
contact zone, 19, 46, 79–80, 82–83, 123–28, 196. See also marriage; mosque; Mary Louise Pratt
conversion, 182–83
cosmopolitanism: aesthetic, 55–56; and localism, 80; Muslim, 46, 80–83, 195–96; working-class, 23. See also everyday; Islam; transnational; *ummah*
counterpublic, 7
cross-national feminism. See transnational feminism

Dangarembga, Tsitsi, 21
Dao, Anna, 6, 178–81. See also "A Perfect Wife"
dawa (piety) movement, 71–78
decolonialism, 13–14
Deleuze, Gilles. See *Kafka: Toward a Minor Literature*
Denkyi-Manieson, Gladys, 102–103
dependency chain, 74–75. See also Elora Chowdhury
Desai, Manisha, 199n2
deterritorialization, 12–13, 24, 200n10. See also Arjun Appadurai
Dimock, Wai Chee, 89
Dirlik, Arif, 24–25
disjuncture, 9
dissident: friendships, 83, 113; relationality, 43–44, 89, 123–28, 179. See also Leela Gandhi; marriage
distant presence, 27, 44–46, 105–106, 109, 152, 160–61
domestic violence, 183–88. See also gender

dowry (bride price, gift giving, *mahr*), 18, 38–41, 203n34
DuBois, W. E. B., 21

education, 36, 99, 187–88, 195–96, 211n9. *See also* Boko Haram; Madarasah; vernacular
El Salvador, 24
Elmadmad, Khadija, 70, 207n14
Emecheta, Buchi, 172. See also *The Joys of Motherhood*
everyday, 6, 23, 30, 46, 50, 52, 81, 148, 151, 189–91, 195–96. *See also* activism; cosmopolitanism, Muslim; *ummah*; unmappability

family, as metonymy for society, 179–181. *See also* gender, and nation-state; marriage; motherhood; sterility
Fanon, Franz, 203n35
feminism: asymmetry of, 205n4; and community-based activism, 27–29; democratization of, 57; inaccessibility of, 8; knowledge production and flows of theory, 15, 78–79, 83–85; and Islam, 4; and literature, 202n29; perception of audiences for, 78–79; and political self-determination of Muslim women, 4; relationship of subordination and agency, 3, 76–77; reproducing inequality, 4; women's liberation, 31–32. *See also* family; gender; Islam; knowledge production; literature; marriage; motherhood; nation; sterility; solidarity; transnational feminism
Ferguson, James, 92–94
fertility. *See* sterility
Forna, Aminata, 171. See also *The Hired Man*

fragmentation. *See* capitalism
Friedman, Susan Stanford, 37–38, 41

Gandhi, Leela, 43–44, 83, 204n36. *See also* dissident, friendships
Gandhi, M. K., 43–44
Garcia Peña, Lorgia, 21
gender: absence and voicelessness, 169–70; agency, 2–4, 75–78, 209n10; and biology, 172–74, 176–83, 197; citizenship and, 8–9; domestic violence, 183–88; justice and media, 188–90; and nation-state, 11–12, 30–31, 75–76, 167–74, 177–181, 189–90, 193, 197; subordination, 76–78. *See also* feminism; Islam; marriage; motherhood; nation; solidarity; sterility; transnational feminism
Geni Jora (el-Khalieqy), 38
geography, 2–4; as hierarchy, 9; and human category of identities, 14; of place or territory, 12–13. *See also* transgeography
Ghana, 188–90
Ghose, Manmohan, 43–44
gift giving. *See* dowry; Nigeria
Gikandi, Simon, 41–42, 169–70
Gilroy, Paul, 13. *See also* planetary consciousness
Gimba, Abubakar, 6, 36, 118–21. See also *Sacred Apples*
Gitanjali (Tagore), 17
Glissant, Edouard, 13–14, 200n12
global, 10, 23–25. *See also* transgeography; transnationalism
Global English, 194, 201n15. *See also* Aamir Mufti
global feminism, 205n5. *See also* transnational feminism
Global North. *See* Global South

Global South, 4–5, 9, 26–28, 39, 42–43, 56, 65, 83–85, 128–32, 199n2, 206n8. See also periphery; transnationalism
globalectics. See transnationalism, minor
globalization, 29, 200n10
Guattari, Félix. See *Kafka: Toward a Minor Literature*

hadith (Muhammad's teachings on ideal speech and behavior). See Islam
hajj (pilgrimage to Mecca). See Islam
Hajjah Fatimah Mosque. See Singapore
Hassan, Waïl, 132–33
Hausa (ethnicity and language), 30, 35–36, 39–40, 96–99, 102–106, 109–110, 202n29, 203n30. See also Chimamanda Ngozie Adichie; Nigeria
heteronormativity, 3, 31
Hired Man, The (Forna), 171
Holy Men, Holy Women (Zaman), 82–83
Hosseini, Khaled, 45
Hosseini, Ziba Mir, 64
Hussain, Rokhaya Sakhwat, 34. See also *Sultana's Dream*

I Am Muslim (Zaman), 82–83
imagined community, 46
India: Hindu nationalism, 32–33; minority groups and patriarchal dominance, 33–34; and *sati*, 33
Indonesia, 75, 77, 183–88; Bahasa language, 30, 183; interfaith marriages, 1; and Islamic education, 187. See also Madarasah
informal community, 8
interfaith community, 119. See also marriage, interfaith; *ummah*

International Conference on Religion and Peace, 1
international feminism, 205n5. See also feminism; transnational feminism
intersectionality, 201n13
Islam: in academic circles, 144–151; in Africa, 17–20; diversity in, 18; feminism, 4, 63–66, 71, 74; *hadith* (Muhammad's teachings on ideal speech and behavior), 10–11, 48–49, 142, 150, 188; *hajj* (pilgrimage to Mecca), 37–38, 49; interactions with non-Muslims, 2; *jihad*, 145–49, 210n8; marriage, 209n2; as minority position, 193; *nafaqah* (financial maintenance of a wife), 18; *pesantren* (rural) culture and Madarasah, 187–88; post-9/11, 97; recuperation of female voices in, 200n9; relationship to Christianity, 96–97; Salafism, 138–51; scarf (*hijab*), 72–74, 111–12; in Southeast Asia, 17–20; story of Isra and Miraj, 212n16; Sufism, 143–51; tropes of contact, 20; *umra* (lesser pilgrimage to Mecca), 37; *wali* (male guardianship), 18; in West Africa, 211n10; women, 70, 75, 206n12, 206n14; *zakat* (obligatory act of charity), 48–49. See also Constitution of Medina; cosmopolitanism, Muslim; gender; Islamophobia; Madarasah; transnational feminism; *ummah*; women's studies
Islamophobia, 4, 45, 97, 209n11. See also Islam

Jacobs, Rayda, 169. See also *My Father's Orchid*
Jaji, Tsitsi, 152–53

Jalal, Ayesha, 145–46
Jamil, Arifa Macaqua, 6, 174–78. See also "Amirah"; "Sakeenah"
jihad. See Islam
Joys of Motherhood, The (Emecheta), 172

Kafka: Toward a Minor Literature (Deleuze and Guattari), 124–26, 158, 196, 210n3. See also literature; minor literature
Kalliney, Peter, 91–92
Kane, Cheikh Hamidou, 144
Kane, Ousmane, 146, 195–96, 211n9
Kaplan, Caren, 90. See also simultaneous worlds
Karim, Jamillah, 66–68, 70
Khalieqy, Abidah el-, 6, 17, 38, 183–88, 213n8. See also Geni Jora; "Road to Heaven"
knowledge production, 8, 15, 27–28. See also feminism; translation; transnational feminism
Kureishi, Hanif, 45
Kusurjiati, Siti, 185–86

language. See translation
Lecker, Michael, 213n1
Lionnet, Françoise, 41–42
literature: and feminist experience, 5–7; knowledge production and, 15; and transnationalism, 21. See also minor literature; short story; soyayya; translation; transnational feminism; women's studies
Littatfan Soyayya (books of love), 202n29. See also feminism, and literature; soyayya; Balaraba Ramat Yakubu
local. See global
locational feminism, 38–39, 44. See also transnational feminism

Loimeier, Roman, 99–101
Lughod, Lila Abu, 64–65

Madarasah, 187–88. See also education; Islam
"Maghrib" (Abubakar), 126, 156–63
Mahmood, Saba, 64, 66, 71–78, 147–48, 207n15
mahr. See dowry
"Majed" (Aboulela), 127, 131–38, 142
major literature. See minor literature
Malay (ethnicity and language). See Malaysia
Malaysia: and English, 35, 37; and Islam, 19–20; Malay (ethnicity and language), 19–20, 30, 35–38; and nationalist propaganda, 36
Mali, 178–81
Mandaville, Peter, 13
Mangasakan, Gutierriez, II, 174
Mani, Lata, 33
Maps for Lost Lovers (Aslam), 149–51
marketplace (space): and cosmopolitanism, 208n17; and encounter, 46, 98–101. See also capitalism; shop
marriage (trope): and dissident relationality, 123–28; interfaith, 154–55; and transnationalism, 115–18. See also contact zones; dissident relationality; gender; transgeography
Martin, Dahlia, 36–37
Marxism, limits of critique, 26
Mbembe, Achille, 94, 202n25
McCain, Carmen, 102–103, 209n9
McClintock, Anne, 9, 31–32, 125–26, 172, 197
McKenna, Thomas, 128–30
Menon, Jisha, 95
migration, 207n16

minor, minority, 41–43, 202n21, 203n35. *See also* transnationalism
minor literature, 124–26, 158, 196, 210n3. See also *Kafka: Toward a Minor Literature*
models of community, 46. *See also* Mary Louise Pratt
Morey, Peter, 45
Moro people. *See* Philippines
mosque, 56, 80–83. *See also* contact zone
motherhood, 167–172; in African societies, 212n1; and nationalism, 167, 172–74, 178–81. *See also* gender; nation; sterility
Mufti, Aamir, 22–23, 144–47, 194, 201n15, 202n21. *See also* Global English
Muhammad, 11–12, 49–50, 214n2-3. *See also* Islam
Muslim cosmopolitanism. *See* cosmopolitanism
My Father's Orchid (Jacobs), 169

nafaqah (financial maintenance of a wife). *See* Islam
Nancy, Jean-Luc, 200n12
Nasr, Seyyed Hosein, 69
nation, nationalism: and bourgeois family structure, 31–32; as contested, 193; and gender, 172–174, 197; as plural versus unitary, 31–34; and transnational imaginary, 5. *See also* cosmopolitanism; gender; motherhood; transnationalism
"Naunu Na Kaun Yan?" (Abubakar, What's Happening to You?), 126, 156, 163–65
Ng, Andrew Hock Soon, 35
NGO. *See* non-governmental organization

Ngugi, Mukoma wa, 42, 79, 171, 203n33
Nigeria, 151–54; and class, 102–105; colonial administration of, 96–97; Hausa (ethnicity and language), 30, 35–36, 39–40, 96–99, 102–106, 109–110, 202n29, 203n30; interfaith and interethnic relations in, 96–97, 110–11, 119; indirect rule, 208n6; *soyayya* fiction, 35. *See also* Boko Haram; Chimamanda Ngozie Adichie
non-governmental organization (NGO), 70, 127–28, 183–84, 199n2, 202n26, 206n10-11
nostalgia, 132–33

Omar, Noritah, 37
"Ostrich, The" (Aboulela), 137

Padilla, Yajaira, 24
"Perfect Wife, A" (Dao), 178–81
periphery (center), 5, 12–13, 41, 44–45, 60–63, 80, 83, 92–94, 103, 205n1, 206n8. *See also* Global South; minor; transgeography
pesantren (rural). *See* Islam
Philipose, Liz, 83
Philippines: Bangsamoro Basic Law, 174–75, 213n5; interfaith relationships, 156–65; and Islam, 19–20, 126–30, 156–65, 174–75; Mamasapanao incident (2015), 213n5; Moro people, 126–27, 174–75, 212n17, 213n5
photography, 182
piety. *See dawa* movement
piety activism, 71–72, 75–77. *See also* activism
planetary consciousness, 13
pluralism, 197
politics of location, 44–45
polygamy, 118, 181–83

postcolonialism, 16, 29, 36, 41–42, 60, 85, 135, 148–49, 194–95, 200n12, 211n12
postsecularism. *See* secularism
Pratt, Mary Louise, 19, 46, 80, 196. *See also* contact zone
prayer, 106–109. *See also* religion
"Private Experience, A" (Adichie), 36, 91, 96–114, 120–21, 154–56

Quayson, Ato, 170–71

Rajan, Rajeswari Sunder, 7. *See also* women's writing
Ray, Sangeeta, 32–34, 128
religion, 106–109
respatialization, 26–27. *See also* deterritorialization
Rinaldo, Rachel, 75, 77, 185–86
"Road to Heaven" (el-Khalieqy), 183–88
rooted transnationalism. *See* transnationalism
Rosa, Helvy Tiana, 188
Roy, Arundathi, 21

Sacred Apples (Gimba), 36, 118–21
Said, Edward, 204n36
"Sakeenah" (Jamil), 174–78
Sarkar, Sumit, 33
sati. *See* India
"Scarf, The" (Adichie), 91, 109–112
secularism, 75–76, 211n11, 147, 211n11; postsecularism, 143–45
Senegal, 114–18, 195
Senghor, Leopold Sedar, 21
sexuality, 177–78, 183–84
shadow (trope), 92–95
Shamsie, Kamila, 45
Shih, Shu Mei, 41–42
Shoneyin, Lola, 172. *See also Baba Segi's Wives*

shop (trope), 96–97. *See also* capitalism; marketplace
short story (genre), 6, 91, 168. *See also* individual stories by name; literature
Shryock, Andrew, 113
simultaneous worlds, 90
Singapore, 55–56, 82–83
So Long a Letter (Ba), 114–18, 120–21
social sciences. *See* women's studies
solidarity, 17, 155; and feminism, 15, 34–35, 57–58, 112–14; limits of, 40, 62. *See also* feminism; gender; transnational feminism
Sontag, Susan, 182
soyayya (genre). *See* literature; Nigeria; Balaraba Ramat Yakubu
space, 200n12. *See also* marketplace; transgeography; window
Spivak, Gayatri, 199n3
Steiner, Tina, 132–33
Sterile Sky (Sule), 126–27, 151–56
sterility (fertility), 167–72, 175–83. *See also* gender; motherhood
subalterneity, 14
Sudarkasa, Niara, 168
Sule, E. E., 6, 44, 126–27, 151–56. See also *Sterile Sky*
Sultana's Dream (Hussain), 34

Tagalog (language), 30, 157
Tagore, Rabindranath, 17, 32–33, 44, 202n28. See also *Gitanjali*
Tahir, Ibrahim, 144, 149
theory. *See* feminism; women's studies
"Thing Around Your Neck, The" (Adichie), 91
Things Fall Apart (Achebe), 39
third discourse, 170–71, 179
Tickamyer, Ann, 185–86
transculturation, 46, 80. *See also* contact zone; Mary Louise Pratt

transgeography, 2–4, 11–12, 197–98; as incomplete, 22–26; and marriage, 123–28, 154–55; and mosque, 72; relationships, 82; and respatialization, 26–27; and transnationalism, 12–15; and *ummah*, 10–12, 15. *See also* transnational feminism; ummah

translation, 37–40, 194; illegibility, 16–17; knowledge production and flow of influences, 8, 79; unmappability, 37; subsumption of writing traditions, 16. *See also* Emily Apter; unmappability

Translator, The (Aboulela), 139–41

translocalism, 12–13

transnational, transnationalism: and Africa, 94–95; and class, 23; and interfaith marriages, 115–18; and literature, 5–6; and migration, 205n6; minor, 41–43, 130–31; beyond nationalism, 20–22, 201n14; obstacles to, 3; redefining, 193; reversing, 25–26; as transgeography, 13–15, 197–98; beyond Western concepts of, 195–96. *See also* marriage; minor; transgeography; transnational feminism

transnational feminism, 2, 9, 206n8; actors of, 59; advocacy, 59–60; boundaries of, 186–88; challenges to, 60–63; constructed opposition, 205n1; as cross-nationalism, 9, 20–21; homogenizing women's struggles, 127–28; impetus for, 57; and intersectionality, 201n13; and Islam, 5; knowledge production and flow of theory, 5, 27–28; and literature, 16, 30, 194; sites of, 59; and solidarity, 40–41, 57–58, 112–14; topoi of, 58–59; and translation, 16–17; and *ummah*, 10. *See also* feminism; gender; Islam; knowledge production; transgeography; transnational; *ummah*; unmappability; women's studies

ummah (community), 3, 5, 47, 196, 207n13, 210n6, 211n14; in America, 66–68; and belief, 89–90; and diversity, 10–12, 19, 48–49, 70; and the everyday, 3, 10, 12, 64, 195–96; and feminism, 62–63, 66; and forms of oppression, 67–68; and *hajj* (pilgrimage to Mecca), 38; as literary aesthetic, 10; as model of governance, 25–26; and Muslim cosmopolitanism, 81–82, 200n7; and nation-state, 22–23, 69–71, 195–96; overemphasis on global, 10; and race, 36, 48–49; and religious difference, 49–50; spatializing relationships, 3, 129–30, 160–62, 164–65; as transgeography, 6, 1–12, 15; translation of, 68–69. *See also* Constitution of Medina; everyday; Islam; transgeography; transnational feminism

umra (lesser pilgrimage to Mecca). *See* Islam

UN. *See* United Nations

United Nations (UN), 56–57

unmapped, unmappability, 2, 4, 7–8, 194; and activism, 9; and everyday, 3, 9–10, 30; of feminist expression, 7; and translation, 39–40. *See also* everyday; transnational feminism

Updike, John, 45

Vera, Yvonne, 21, 172. *See also Butterfly Burning*

vernacular, 36, 194

Waldman, Amy, 45
wali (male guardianship). *See* Islam
Werbner, Pninia, 23
West Africa, 195, 211n10
Wilde, Oscar, 43–44
window (trope), 89–92, 94–99, 101–104. *See also* Africa, shadow relationship; space
women. *See* feminism; gender; motherhood; sterility; women's studies
women's studies: and activism, 9; and authority of social sciences, 29–30; and literature, 6, 8, 29, 199n4; and Muslim women, 71, 74–75; and national borders, 2. *See also* activism; Islam; literature; transnational feminism
women's writing, 7. *See also* Rajeswari Sunder Rajan
world literature, 207n16

Yakubu, Balaraba Ramat, 17, 35, 38–40, 202n29, 203n31. See also *Alhaki Kuykeyo Ne...*
"#Yennenga" (Abdulai), 188–90

zakat (obligatory act of charity). *See* Islam
Zaman, Dina, 82–83. See also *Holy Men, Holy Women; I Am Muslim*

www.ingramcontent.com/pod-product-compliance
Lightning Source LLC
Chambersburg PA
CBHW030540230426
43665CB00010B/972